The
Resident Retention
Revolution

Editorial Consultants

Natalie D. Brecher, CPM®

James H. Cantrell, CPM®

Lynn J. Shore, CPM®

Joseph T. Lannon

Publishing and Curriculum Development Manager

Caroline Scoulas

Senior Editor

The
Resident Retention
Revolution

Laurence C. Harmon, CPM®
Kathleen M. McKenna-Harmon, CPM®

Institute of Real Estate Management
of the NATIONAL ASSOCIATION OF REALTORS®
430 NORTH MICHIGAN AVENUE • CHICAGO, ILLINOIS 60611

© 1994 by the Institute of Real Estate Management
of the NATIONAL ASSOCIATION OF REALTORS ®

Library of Congress Cataloging-in-Publication Data

Harmon, Laurence C., 1943-
    The resident retention revolution / Laurence C. Harmon, Kathleen
  M. McKenna-Harmon
       p.   cm.
    Includes bibliographical references and index
    ISBN 0-944298-97-4 :
    1. Real estate management.   2. Apartment houses--Management.
  3. Rental housing--Resident satisfaction.   4. Customer service.
  I. McKenna-Harmon, Kathleen M., 1946-   II. Title.
  HD1394.H358   1994
  333.33′8--dc20   94-8856
                                                                   CIP

Printed in the United States of America

1 2 3 4 5 6 7 8 9 10 Printing / Year 03 02 01 00 99 98 97 96 95 94

The Resident Retention Revolution is dedicated
to the frontline servers in American apartment properties,
whose devotion to their customers provides so much of the value
of the product they market.

Preface

Several years ago, we began reading books about customer service. The more we read, the more we became convinced that the fundamental approaches that had proven to be productive in the retail environment could be applied in real estate management as well. In our book, *Contemporary Apartment Marketing,* which was published by IREM in 1992, we introduced the idea that a customer service approach could provide a means of differentiating similar apartment product and might enhance its profitability. There we discussed the interactions between apartment management personnel and individual residents as a series of finite, brief, and often intensive incidents, each of which is an opportunity to create an impression of management in the mind of the resident—what Jan Carlzon, the godfather of the retailing service revolution, called "moments of truth."

Having now read more than 50 books on different aspects of service, in *The Resident Retention Revolution,* we present a comprehensive overview of the many strategies we think are particularly relevant for apartment marketing and management. Specific strategies are described in general terms, then focused more precisely using the original authors' own words, after which their implications for and possible applications in the apartment industry are detailed. In addition to "moments of truth," you will find discussions of "benchmarking," "empowerment," and "service recovery." We even bring in a couple of Japanese concepts—"KAIZEN" and "shared fate"—and suggest how these can be applied in apartment management.

Because the service strategies are interrelated—indeed, many of them are outgrowths of earlier ideas that have evolved through years of application in the retailing and consumer services industries—we chose not to simply identify strategies and discuss them at length in separate chapters. Rather, it seemed more important to view them as a whole, like a tapestry comprised of various threads that, as they are interwoven, emerge into specific patterns.

How the Service Patterns Emerge

The Prologue establishes the context for the chapters that follow. Here we introduce some of the specific authors whose books launched the revolution in retailing customer service. Chapter 1 describes the revolution itself and suggests its implications for the apartment industry. Many of the specific threads of the tapestry introduced here will be picked up and elaborated in more detail in later chapters. Chapter 2 outlines a number of service strategies that have specific applications in apartment management. In particular, we address the significance of critical incidents (moments of truth), the importance of hiring nice people to serve at the front lines, and the need to create positive word of mouth. Chapter 3 looks more closely at the hiring issue. We point out how your employees are really your *internal customers* and how their job satisfaction is linked to retention of your *external customers*—your residents.

Chapter 4 differentiates prior marketing efforts aimed at acquiring customers (so-called conquest marketing) from newer strategies directed to retaining customers (retention marketing). In this chapter, we examine the costs of resident "churn," poor service, and negative word of mouth. Because poor service and resident dissatisfaction will remain undiscovered unless residents actually complain, chapter 5 presents strategies for surfacing residents' complaints. Chapter 6 carries this theme forward with a discussion of what constitutes customer satisfaction. Here we explore strategies for overcoming resident dissatisfaction—the notion of service recovery.

Chapter 7 examines service in the context of company leadership. Here we present ways to develop a customer-focused business, working from the top down, with an emphasis on strategic planning. Often the best sources for innovative approaches to problem-solving are to be found externally—beyond the particular property or management company and sometimes even outside the apartment industry. Benchmarking—seeking the best of the best—is discussed in chapter 8. In particular, we look at the marketing grid analysis exercise and suggest alternative approaches that can be used to define the advantages of your apartment product over that of your competition.

Finally, chapter 9 synthesizes the various strategic threads into a comprehensive tapestry that offers a revolutionary approach to resident retention. In addition to suggesting specific strategies and applications, we include real world examples of incidents and programs that are already contributing to resident retention for some management companies.

The Prologue and individual chapters open with one or more related quotations focused on the topics covered. Within the text, quotations longer than a single sentence are generally set off as indented blocks of copy. Whenever possible, the author whose words are used is named beforehand. These quotes are indicated with an arrowhead, and the sources are identified sequentially in Endnotes at the back of the book. Note, however, that we also set off examples related to the apartment industry; these do not include the arrowhead indicator. In addition to Endnotes, there is a Bibliography that lists the service books we have cited as well as those we did not quote from but used as background reading. The various service-related terms are defined in place or elaborated in their immediate context, obviating the need for a formal glossary. (We have assumed our readers are generally familiar with real estate terms.)

Other Considerations for Readers

While many of the innovative ideas described in this book have been tested by ourselves and others, we would caution against adopting some of them without first considering their consequences. Sometimes there are potential legal ramifications, especially in today's litigious society. In most situations, residents will participate willingly in on-site activities and appreciate what is being offered. If you suspect that your residents might respond otherwise, you can seek their approval beforehand—in writing, if necessary. We would suggest, however, that the outcomes in terms of long-term resident retention will make any efforts to improve your services worthwhile.

In chapter 3, we discuss certain lease clauses and house "rules" as potentially onerous from the resident's perspective. Recognizing that the safeguards provided in a written lease are important protections for the owner and the manager alike, we do not recommend abandoning them outright; instead, what we are suggesting is that you consider finding ways to modify the lease language—with the advice of legal counsel, of course—to state the requirements in a more positive way. Note in particular that fair housing laws govern apartment managers' activities related to apartment marketing and leasing. Under the Fair Housing Amendments Act of 1988, for example, you should be aware that "reasonable accommodation" of residents with disabilities may mean changing a no-pets policy to allow for the keeping of guide animals.

There are legal implications related to hiring practices, too. The value—and possible problems—of pre-employment psychological testing is addressed in chapter 3. We also suggest the use of group interviews to help determine a candidate's "fit" with your organization. It is important to remind all personnel involved in the interview process of the need to maintain confidentiality regarding conversations with job applicants.

Finally, *The Resident Retention Revolution* is, by definition, about residents as customers. As a consequence, we mention at several points that your owner-clients are important customers, too, but we have not concentrated on owners' specific requirements such as budgeting, reporting, and forecasting, within the text. The importance of these tasks in the broader context of real estate management has been addressed extensively in other IREM publications. It is vital to note that, while the subject of resident retention is somewhat unfamiliar to many owners and asset managers, we have found that our own owner-clients are increasingly supportive of efforts to improve resident relations and reduce resident churn, especially because success in these areas is economically beneficial to their properties, in terms of both improving their short-term performance and enhancing their value for eventual sale.

As owners increasingly become sensitized to the importance of resident relations, it will be interesting to see whether they will be willing to fully embrace the practical consequences of this fresh outlook toward their customers. We believe, for example, that retention efforts merit budgetary considerations and dollar allocations separate from, and in addition to, those accorded to advertising—which, after all, is simply business acquisition. Advertising, of course, has very little to do with nourishing long-term customer relations; it allows them to become a possibility. Moreover, it is our opinion that the success of retention efforts will be determined in major part by the friendliness and overall people skills of the site staff, rather than by their dexterity in handling paperwork. It has been our experience that, with rare exceptions, site personnel excel at either administrative tasks or selling and other interpersonal skills; clearly, resident retention spotlights the latter competence. Whether asset managers will defer to the revamped priorities that are required to excel at retention marketing remains to be seen. At the very least, it is likely that *Managing the Future*'s admonition to property managers to reduce resident "churn," if it is to become a true marketing strategy, will require behavioral changes in both property managers and real estate owners. (Economic issues are addressed specifically at several points in the text—including budgeting for resident retention [chapter 4] and the implications of "free rent" in a context of employee empowerment [chapter 7].)

Some Notes About Style

The Resident Retention Revolution is written from a very personal perspective—we manage a number of apartment properties, and many of the incidents, stories, and apartment-specific strategies presented in this book are from our own experience. Our descriptions of managing properties in receivership are an example of how our experience may differ from that of other managers in other areas. While many properties in our portfolio are what might be considered "upscale"—a point that is apparent when we discuss rental rates and amenities—most of the strategies we are describing are inexpensive, and usually they are readily adaptable to other situations by taking into consideration the size of a property, the types of apartments and amenities available there and among its competitors, and the profile of the current occupants.

To make the text more reader-friendly, the word "we" is used throughout in referring to our experiences and opinions, and the reader is addressed as "you." Except for some brief examples of lease language, we generally refer to apartment tenants as "residents." On the other hand, "landlord" is sometimes used to include the property owner, the apartment manager, and the management company when these entities can be presumed to be interchangeable, especially in regard to decision-making.

A number of terms used throughout the text have been borrowed—an example of benchmarking for more precise language. For example, we borrowed the term "churn" from the stock market: The way stock brokers move investors into and out of different stock investments primarily to gain additional commissions has been referred to as "churning" sales. While resident turnover is a reality at apartment properties, the seemingly unavoidable defections—whether of employees or residents—tend to sustain an atmosphere of constant turmoil at a property. Repeatedly acquiring new occupants for vacated apartments or replacing people in key staff positions is costly and similarly suggestive of a churning activity—thus the references to employee and resident "churn."

Although we manage apartments in several different locations, our business is headquartered in a market area that is unique. While the twin cities of Minneapolis and St. Paul, Minnesota, are separated from each other only by a line on a map, the division is often indistinguishable on the ground. Yet the two cities are distinctly different from each other in the makeup of their business districts, their residential neighborhoods, and their surrounding suburbs. The fact of their being separate cities means we have had opportunities to manage a variety of interesting and unique apartment properties within a rather limited geographic area.

ACKNOWLEDGMENTS

In the prologue, we mentioned the concept of *partnering*. We will have much more to say about this powerful concept in Chapters 4 and 9. After reading the voluminous literature on customer service and related subjects, it seems to us entirely sensible for companies to work aggressively to forge alliances with both their internal customers—their own employees—and their external ones—suppliers and purchasers of product. The realization that both types of customers are invested in a company's success presents impressive possibilities for its future prosperity. Our own partners, and our "internal" and "external" customers have contributed to making this book possible. We are pleased to acknowledge their various contributions.

People and institutions whom we consider to be our "partners" include those who have been particularly meaningful in our personal and professional lives. Members of this group are the following:

Barbara L. Holland, CPM®, of Las Vegas, Nevada, who initially challenged us to become authors, and who has since encouraged us to preserve our vision of what our books should be.

Petra A. Marquart of Hennepin Technical College in Eden Prairie, Minnesota, whose pioneering work on the frontiers of customer service, personnel management and organizational theory is a source of particular inspiration to us.

Jim Collins, CPM, President of Leasing Legends in Davidson, North Carolina, a good friend and stimulating colleague, who has exciting plans for his own notable contribution to the literature of apartment marketing.

Three members of our extended family, Catherine L. Antil and Carolee L. Harmon, who have consistently loved and supported us in all of our endeavors, and Robert H. Harmon, who not only encouraged this particular book but who made valuable contributions to its content.

Mark W. Reiling, President of Towle Real Estate in Minneapolis, and CEO of the Towle McKenna Company, a partner in the more traditional sense, who is also working to improve his company's customer focus.

Arnie J. Gregory, President of TRIAD Development, Inc., of Minneapolis, and Betty L. O'Shaughnessy, President of O'Shaughnessy Corporation of Chaska, Minnesota, our partners in developing the first— the first of many, we hope—apartment property that we will own in the Twin Cities.

Mary Rippe, Executive Vice President of the Minnesota MultiHousing Association, who recently assumed her leadership role in our state's apartment association and who has consistently impressed her internal and external customers with her enthusiastic professionalism.

Howard K. Lundeen, CPM, of Dallas, Texas, who has graciously agreed to become a partner with us on an IREM-approved commercial tenant retention book that is scheduled for publication next Spring.

Bill Deters, founder of Great Places, Inc., in Bloomington, Minnesota, whose enlightened understanding of the customer service revolution that is underway in the retail trades has not only transformed his own company but has provided intriguing wisdom for the multifamily industry as well.

Norman P. Bjornnes, Esq., of the Minneapolis law firm of Mulligan & Bjornnes, who, in his unique role as apartment owner, attorney, accountant and friend, has enriched our lives and insulated us from many of its most unpleasant aspects.

We wish to recognize several friends and associates among the Institute of Real Estate Management professional staff, most especially Joseph T. Lannon, who made substantial recommendations to sharpen and improve this book; Sander J. Smiles, who has consistently stimulated our thinking about residential property management, which has in turn helped our writing and teaching; and Caroline Scoulas, Senior Editor, who has spent much of three years of her professional career helping to focus and enrich this book and its predecessor, *Contemporary Apartment Marketing*. Because *The Resident Retention Revolution* benchmarks recent customer-service and related literature, as well as developments in resident relations from within our industry, Caroline's editorial burden has been considerable. We are enormously indebted to her for her sunny virtuosity and absolute commitment to excellence.

Thanks also to Natalie D. Brecher, CPM, of Forest City Management, Inc., in Los Angeles; James H. Cantrell, CPM, of Cantrell, Harris Associates in San Francisco; and Lynn J. Shore, CPM, of Battlement Mesa Management Company in Parachute, Colorado, practicing real estate managers who read and reviewed drafts of this text, and whose experience-based insights improved our thinking and benefitted our book. Their contributions to the sections focusing on empowerment and company mission statements are especially valuable.

Lorelei L. Koester, Chief Operating Officer of McKenna Management, our trusted partner, internal customer and ally, whose passionate professionalism and dedication have literally transformed our company and established its exciting future direction.

We wish to acknowledge other internal customers of McKenna Management: Linda F. Fieldman, Elaine S. Abramson, Maureen Herzog, Kathy Ruesink, Julie Sothman, and Rita Freer-Ahrens. Their devotion to superiority in the profession of property management and loyalty to us have provided us with the opportunity not only to research and write *The Resident Retention Revolution* but also to become involved in so many fascinating collateral pursuits.

We are blessed with other "internal customers" who are exceptional frontline servers as well. They are a constant reminder that the business of real estate management is inescapably a people-driven enterprise as well.

They have helped our company to become and remain resident-passionate. They are Barbara Mack; Diane Peterson; Kari Raasch; Christie Jones; George Lahr; Steven Hanson; Pamela A. Stine, ARM®; Susan Picotte; Nancy Trout; Ken Callihan; and Jayne Hayes.

Finally, our "external customers" have entrusted their real estate investments to our care, which, among other benefits, has provided our company with a laboratory to demonstrate the validity of the principles that are described in this book. We wish to express our appreciation to Terry Sullivan and Allan Olans of Boston Bay Capital, Inc.; David Young and Daniel W. Davitt of Merrill Lynch, Hubbard in New York City; John Brandstatter, CPM, of Mellon Bank, Pittsburgh; and Darleen Derma, Michael Schack, and Katherine McCarthy of MetLife in St. Louis.

Special thanks to Cynthiann King of WilsonSchanzer Real Estate Services in San Antonio; Jim Cantrell, CPM, of Cantrell, Harris & Associates in San Francisco; Mitzi West of Dominion Management of Atlanta; Paula Wagner, CPM, of Compass Alliance Real Estate Services in San Antonio; Jill Mosko of the Ryan Companies, a Minneapolis-based construction and property management firm; and Patricia Hartman, CPM, Director of Housing Management and Services for the Columbus (Ohio) Metropolitan Housing Authority, who contributed many of the examples incorporated into chapter 9.

We also extend our thanks to the various authors and publishers who granted us permission to excerpt from their books. Specific acknowledgments are indicated in the Bibliography and incorporated on exhibits, as appropriate.

Laurence C. Harmon, CPM®
Kathleen M. McKenna-Harmon, CPM®

About the Authors

Laurence C. Harmon, CPM®, is Chief Executive Officer of McKenna Management Associates, Inc., AMO®, and President of GreaterData, Inc., both in Minneapolis. His real estate experience includes eight years at McKenna Management, initially as a property manager and marketing director. His current responsibilities include business acquisition, teaching and consulting, and property management for institutional investors. GreaterData conducts marketing research and market research related to residential property management. In addition to his marketing experience and expertise, Mr. Harmon has a law degree from Stanford University and is admitted to practice law in California, Oregon, and Minnesota.

Mr. Harmon achieved the CPM designation in 1990 and is an active member of the Institute of Real Estate Management, where he serves on the Publishing, Management Plan, and Ethics Committees at the national level. He is currently chairman of the Ethics Appeal Board. He has served as Executive Councillor and Chairman of the Candidate Guidance Committee of the Minnesota Chapter of IREM; he founded the Minnesota "Buddy-Up!" system that links CPM members and Candidates for the purpose of helping Candidates with the preparation of their management plans. "Buddy-Up!" and similar programs have been widely adopted in several states. In addition, Mr. Harmon teaches apartment marketing courses at Hennepin Technical College in Minneapolis.

Kathleen M. McKenna-Harmon, CPM®, is President of McKenna Management Associates, Inc., AMO®, and the Towle McKenna Company also in Minneapolis. These management firms have a combined portfolio of approximately 3,500 apartment, condominium, and townhouse residential units in 20 properties, as well as some 500,000 square feet of commercial space. Ms. McKenna-Harmon has more than 22 years experience in managing and marketing residential properties. She has also taught real estate courses at Saint Cloud State University (Minnesota), University of Wisconsin (Stout), and the University of Minnesota.

Ms. McKenna-Harmon achieved the CPM designation in 1980 and is an active member of the Institute of Real Estate Management at both the chapter and national levels. Currently, she is a member of IREM's Executive Committee and serves on the IREM National Faculty. She is a Vice Division Director and a member of several national committees. She has served on the Membership Standards Committee and the Advanced Membership Standards Committee for six years; she chaired these two committees in 1989–1990 and again in 1990–1991. A former IREM Regional Vice President, Ms. McKenna-Harmon was president of the Minnesota chapter of IREM in 1984 and its CPM of the Year in 1992. She has chaired every chapter committee and served in all councillor and officer positions in that organization. In addition, Ms. McKenna-Harmon is an active member of the Minnesota MultiHousing Association. She has held each executive office and served as MHA president in 1990–1991.

The Harmons are co-authors of *Contemporary Apartment Marketing: Strategies and Applications,* which was published by IREM in 1992. They are working with Howard K. Lundeen, CPM®, on a companion volume to *The Resident Retention Revolution.* This third book—on the subject of tenant retention in commercial properties—is scheduled for publication in 1995.

The Harmons lecture and consult extensively on the subjects of market research, property management and marketing, and resident retention.

About the Institute of Real Estate Management

The Institute of Real Estate Management (IREM) was founded in 1933 with the goals of establishing a Code of Ethics and standards of practice in real estate management as well as fostering knowledge, integrity, and efficiency among its practitioners. The Institute confers the CERTIFIED PROPERTY MANAGER® (CPM®) designation on individuals who meet specified criteria of education and experience in real estate management and subscribe to an established Code of Ethics. Real estate management firms that meet specific organizational and professional criteria are granted the status of ACCREDITED MANAGEMENT ORGANIZATION® (AMO®). Individuals who meet specified educational and professional requirements in residential site management and subscribe to a Code of Ethics are granted the status of ACCREDITED RESIDENTIAL MANAGER (ARM®).

The Institute's membership includes more than 9,350 CPM members, nearly 3,300 ARM participants, and approximately 650 AMO firms. CPM members manage nearly 25% of U.S. multifamily rental housing properties and approximately 32% of condominium and cooperative ownership properties; CPM members also manage 63% of U.S. subsidized housing. In addition, they manage nearly 44% of the office space and roughly 10% of the shopping center and retail space in the United States.

For more than sixty years, IREM has been enhancing the prestige of property management through its activities and publications. The Institute offers a wide selection of courses, seminars, periodicals, books, and other materials about real estate management and related topics. To obtain a current catalog, write to the Institute of Real Estate Management, 430 North Michigan Avenue, P.O. Box 109025, Chicago, Illinois 60610-9025, or telephone (312) 661-1953.

Contents

The
Resident Retention
Revolution

Prologue

Psychologists say that any one or a combination of three things is needed to overcome resistance to change: (1) a cataclysmic event, (2) a clear vision of where the change will lead, and (3) the experience of taking the first step in a new direction.

For many American businesses, the first condition—a cataclysmic event—is already a reality or is lurking just beneath the surface, like an incipient earthquake. . . . Whatever the case, the cataclysm will either force the company to change for the better or will drive it out of business.

The second condition for change—a clear vision of where you want to go—is one that tests the leadership qualities of any management group. [That] vision is indelibly clear. American companies *must* set their sights on improving service delivery, product quality, and customer satisfaction.

As for the third condition, taking those first steps can be scary, but you'll never get anywhere if you don't start. Some companies have already started, and we can learn from them.

—Laura A. Liswood

Beginning in 1985 with the publication of *Service America!* (Ron Zemke and Karl Albrecht's manifesto to American businesses on behalf of American consumers), there has been a cascade of self-help books—and a host of reform movements—designed to improve the quality of sellers' economic relationships with buyers. The stimuli have been numerous, organic, and complementary: The upsurge in competition from Japan and other Pacific Rim countries; consumers' heightened awareness of value and its relationship to price, and their jealousy of their dwindling leisure time; and the disturbing tailspin in the quality of customer service are only three among those most obvious and notable.

Two years after the publication of *Service America,* the godfather of the service-regeneration movement, Scandinavian Airlines' president Jan Carlzon, added his articulate voice to the reform effort. In his semi-autobiographical treatise, *Moments of Truth,* Carlzon recorded his experiences in revitalizing SAS, which he accomplished in a remarkably short time: In 1981, the year he was appointed president, SAS lost $8 million; two years later, it posted a hefty $71 million profit while the airline industry overall was losing $2 billion annually.

Carlzon and later commentators have much to teach American companies about improving the way they do business. Carlzon, for example, was one of the first to recognize not only the singular importance of frontline employees to business success, but also the need to revamp the corporate hierarchy in order to enable the front line to flourish. Indeed, the definition of the roles, rights, and responsibilities of company leadership and frontline servers can be traced directly to Carlzon and his contemporaries. Such potent concepts as "partnering"—that is, nontraditional yet powerful alliances between a firm and its own staff and customers—and "benchmarking"—identification and importation of the "best practice" of industry leaders into a company's own operations—are two recent outgrowths of Carlzon's insights into enhancing a firm's operations.

Running parallel to the self-help concepts pioneered by Carlzon and his followers—this school embraced, explored, and applied such notions as "customer service," "satisfaction," and "value"—is the "quality" movement launched by Joseph Juran and W. Edwards Deming. Deming, a statistician, was one of the founders of quality control in the United States and is considered the catalyst behind the success of Japanese industry.

Change agents in a particular business may consider themselves to be proponents of one or more of the "customer service," "satisfaction," or "total quality management" philosophies. Fortunately, there is a rich and varied literature to guide the journey to service excellence. Many of the publications are cited at length in this book. (See also the Bibliography.)

The Incipient Resident Retention Revolution

Whether the goal is described as cementing relations between a company and its customers, improving the volume and quality of repeat business the firm does with its customers, or helping to deliver better value to clients, the overriding purpose of any company's self-help efforts is to enable it to stay in business and, perhaps, also to prosper. For a company to become customer-focused, which is an essential prerequisite to achieving this purpose, it needs to undergo a radical transformation—from compulsively inward-looking to resolutely outward-looking. The companies of the future will increasingly and aggressively strategize ways to prune the bureaucratic shrubbery that interferes with providing intensive kid-glove treatment for their customers.

Unfortunately, most businesses need substantial prodding to be roused from their self-satisfied, bureaucracy-buttressing slumber. The quote at the beginning of this prologue sets out the three prerequisites, any one (or a combination) of which can trigger awakening: First, a cataclysmic event; second, a good idea of what the post-revolution finished product will look like; and third, the first step along the revolutionary freeway.

There have been several national-scope cataclysmic events in the multi-family housing industry that have affected its economic viability during the past decade. Arguably, the most ruinous are the drastic tax reforms of 1986, which gutted most of the after-tax yields to real estate investors and owners, and the consequent collapse of the savings and loans a few years later. A variety of other national calamities—overbuilding, spiraling property taxes and energy costs, environmental concerns, and low-interest mortgage rates that stimulate single-family homeownership—have contributed their share to the decline of the apartment industry. At the local level, other debacles may actually overwhelm the national issues. In any event, there has been a surplus of situations and circumstances in the apartment industry that may be accurately characterized as "cataclysmic." Liswood's first requisite to over-coming resistance to change is clearly met.

The second stage—the image of the eventual, post-enhancement condi-tion—is difficult to visualize. Indeed, the transformation of a company from resident-tolerant to resident-passionate, from self-centered to client-driven, and from conquest marketer to aftermarketer, is probably the most profound metamorphosis that a firm can experience. A central purpose of this book is to provide an outline—a roadmap—for the journey.

The final condition, of course, is to take the first step in the direction of the finish line. As the Chinese proverb instructs us: "A journey of a thousand miles begins with but a single step." This statement, of course, is beyond dispute; what is less clear in the business context is *who* is responsible for taking it. We argue that company leadership needs to initiate the expedition. We suggest an itinerary in this book; equally important, we recommend that the trip be undertaken in a spirit of *KAIZEN*—that is, a step at a time, bit-by-bit, rather than in the tumultuous way that typifies most revolutions.

1

The Customer Service Revolution

People can have the Model T in any color—so long as it's black.
—HENRY FORD

Everybody in the company has to understand that the total existence of a company depends upon the customer, so if the customer is not satisfied, he is not going to be a customer tomorrow, and if he is not a customer tomorrow, we don't have a business tomorrow.
—HARVEY LAMM, President of Subaru of America

When you hear hoofbeats, expect horses.
—DONALD R. LIBEY, *Libey on Customers*

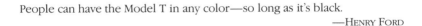

Henry Ford never heard the "hoofbeats" that are ringing in the ears of Harvey Lamm—and of everyone who markets goods and services to the finicky, value-conscious consumers of the 1990s. In 1910, Ford produced and sold 19,000 "Tin Lizzies," enjoying a virtual monopoly in the new car business; but 80 years later, when annual production had reached 1,380,000—a nearly 75-fold increase over 1910 figures—the Ford Motor Company's market share of new car and truck sales in the United States had dropped to less than 15 percent. (Its market share continued to slide, falling nearly one percent the next year).

Those "hoofbeats," after all, are the sounds of the competition, thundering after capricious consumers. Whether you are selling thoroughbreds, Thunderbirds, or three-bedroom apartments, your potential customers can select from a marvelous cornucopia of options undreamed-of in Ford's day. Once you have captured them, your customers are, as Richard Schonberger vividly remarked, "poised to fly, like a nervous flock of geese in a grain field."

Faced with the test of trying to compete with one of the Big Three automakers, what options are available to a Harvey Lamm whose market share for the sporty Subaru Justy, Imprezza, and their brethren is less than one percent of the U.S. car market? If Lamm is anything like other Davids who grapple with such Goliaths as Nordstrom, Federal Express, L. L. Bean, Domino's Pizza, Marriott, SAS (Scandinavian Airlines System), Xerox, IBM, and Disney World, his challenge is especially daunting. Each of these institutions has spent tens of millions—and sometimes *billions*—of dollars in an effort to transform their companies into customer-aware, customer-attentive, customer-focused, or *customer-driven* firms. Based on the quotation that opened this chapter, it is reasonable to assume that Lamm opted for a customer-centered orientation. In doing so, however, he was committing himself, his company, his employees, and Subaru stockholders to a lengthy, dreary, and generally thankless process that was very likely to fail. As Karl Albrecht and Ron Zemke describe the transformation required, Subaru's task would be akin to "trying to teach an elephant to dance."

The Revolution in Retailing

The commercial revolution that burst forth in the mid-1980s, spearheaded by a marketing wizard who had recently been promoted to head a sinking Swedish airline, is fundamentally about customers—current customers, former customers, potential customers. The foundation of this revolution is that producers of goods and services must ascertain what people want to buy before trying to sell to them; thereafter, the bundle of characteristics and components of the purchase—all of its nonphysical attributes—are designed according to consumer preferences as well. Taken to its extreme, this focus on—even obsession with—customers absolutely transforms the corporation: For example, customers of the so-called 360-degree company decide who is hired, promoted, bonused, and fired. In these and other firms, owners and managers abandon their corner offices to work on the front lines where they can listen to and talk with their customers directly. A variety of approaches have sprung up in an effort to win customer allegiance—the "total quality management," "customer service," "total customer satisfaction," "value," "customer-driven/learning organization" and "defection management" movements, as well as a host of others. This retailing revolution involves a paradigm shift about the way companies do business. It is a movement from one way of seeing the world to another—the "Aha!" phenomenon that transforms how people think and act—and has the potential to transform the very *nature* of retailers' businesses.

Implications of the Revolution
for Apartment Management

What are the implications of this retailing revolution for the real estate industry and, in particular, for the multifamily housing business?

First, the underlying principles of *conquest marketing* (predominant in the 1970s and early 1980s)—that prospective customers are readily accessible in unending supply; that the essence of marketing is to attract new customers; that retention of loyal customers is irrelevant—applies equally in the apartment rental industry and the retail trades. The flip side of conquest marketing, so-called *retention marketing* in which customers are considered to be *stakeholders* in the enterprise, is equally available to apartment managers. (Retention marketing is considered in chapter 4.)

Second, apartment properties traditionally have been operated in the same manner as fast-food restaurants, drycleaners, and tanning booths—the longer a company is in business, the less attention it pays to its customers. The natural propensity of any company engaged in any enterprise is to turn inward and, in its introspection, to isolate itself from its clients. Imperceptibly, its operations are arranged to cater to the owners, managers, and employees—its so-called internal customers—at the expense of its external patrons, the people who buy the products and thereby pay the staff's salaries and keep the companies afloat. As a result, the customer relations process becomes impersonal, aloof, and mechanized. Rules and regulations, policies and procedures, standards and forms are prepared, interpreted, and revised so that the company comes first, the customer last. From signs in convenience stores blaring "No Shoes, No Shirt, No Service!" to lease provisions that proscribe, prohibit, and punish, companies establish—and then nourish—adversarial, potentially confrontational, and probably unpleasant relationships with their customers. Fortunately, as is the case with conquest marketing, retailers have developed a collection of customer-friendly approaches that can be productively transported to the apartment management business.

Third, the stimulus to emigrate from an inward to an outward focus—that is, from serving themselves to delighting their customers—is almost invariably the result of some calamity. For American retailers, the crisis has grown out of market conditions that force them to devise a means of differentiating their products from those of their competitors. Often the competition includes foreign firms that turn out mass-produced goods of comparable quality at substantially lower prices.

As a flood of lower-priced, look-alike products saturates U.S. markets, the quality of customer service in that competitive environment has likewise deteriorated. There is a crisis in selling that mirrors the downturn in sales. Shoddy selling practices have fueled customer cynicism to the point that consumers have become conditioned to negative outcomes from the products they buy and the services they receive, both at the point of sale and thereafter.

Customer service is appallingly bad at the front lines and no better at the middle or the rear, where the managers and owners can be found.

Recognizing that there are only two primary ways to attain competitive advantage—either by doing things better than others, or by doing them differently—retailers have overwhelmingly opted for the former. Market leaders are breaking away from the pack by bundling one or more "intangible perquisites" together with their goods, thereby leaping ahead of their rivals. The adjunct may consist of various service elements (implementing complaint practices or offering guarantees), satisfaction gauges (testing to ensure that customers are happy postpurchase), or quality measures (instituting "total quality management" or aiming for "zero defects")—all designed to provide greater (perceived) value for the price paid.

This newfound devotion to customers is based on a blinding flash of the obvious: *Satisfied customers are a company's most precious resource*. Retailers have discovered, albeit belatedly, that the essence of their business—whatever their business—is to "manufacture" satisfied customers, and then to look for ways to improve their customers' satisfaction. Satisfied customers are the source of the company's profits and referrals to potential customers. They are, in fact, *partners* of the firm whose repeat purchases will help grow the business in the future and serve as a barricade against the insidious infiltration of competition. The myriad techniques that retailers have discovered, then tested and refined, are illustrative for apartment managers and marketers, and we will consider them in detail in subsequent chapters.

As you can see, two complementary calamities—increasing competition and decreasing quality of customer service—spurred a commercial revolution that has resulted in the evolution and appreciation of the art of creating and retaining retail customers. Two parallel predicaments of equal seriousness are transforming the rental housing industry.

First, there has been explosive growth in the number of apartment units brought to market, especially during the last decade—an increase that has outstripped population growth and demographic demand. In 1990, there were 32,922,000 renter-occupied housing units in the United States, an increase of 4,328,000 units (approximately 15 percent) during the decade of the 1980s. By contrast, the population only grew approximately 10 percent (from 227 million to 250 million) during this period. Worse yet, the numbers of people in the 15–34 age groups—the typical-renter cohorts—grew by only 8 percent. There are, in short, too many apartments searching frantically for renters. A complicating factor is that much of this product was designed without adequate consideration being given to the preferences of apartment prospects. As a result, vacancy rates have escalated, and owners and managers have resorted to widespread price-cutting in an effort to reduce their losses. This approach invariably leads to a diminution in the *value* of apartment properties, as well as a camouflaging of actual economic occupancy of the buildings beneath physical occupancy figures and an undercutting of the *pro*

The Value-Price Relationship

In the 5,000 or so years it has taken human beings to evolve from cave-dwelling to highrise-living, what might be called their "customer quotient" has changed radically. Whereas survival once required people to devote no less than 80 percent of their time to production (participating as consumers perhaps 20 percent of the time), they now devote nearly full time—and at least as much effort and attention—to being customers.

In a pure purchase environment constructed on a multilayered, multinational, competitive infrastructure, individuals develop a singular skill and talent for consumption. Americans are especially sophisticated and masterful customers because of the extent, variety, and intensity of their experiences. If there is any one characteristic that can be used to describe us in the waning moments of the twentieth century, it is our single-minded devotion to consumption.

It has become commonplace for retailers to include "value" and other attributes—"quality" and "service" are noteworthy examples—together with their basic product offering. This technique, known as "bundling," enables sellers to compete on a basis other than, or in addition to, mere price. Product attributes such as value, quality, and service, which have nothing to do with price competition and little to do with the underlying product, are calculated to *overwhelm* price as a purchase motivator. Consequently, in almost every type of marketplace, price as the sole determining sales message no longer has anything like its previous vitality.

---

forma rent projections for future years' operations. The result is that the properties do not deliver economic performance consistent with the estimates at the time they were financed initially. Despite the best intentions of these owners and managers, appalling numbers of apartment properties have failed, and the receivership business of many real estate management companies has soared. Receiverships, however, are exceedingly labor intensive, especially at start-up. Because its longevity is unpredictable, receivership work is often unprofitable for the manager. In addition, there is little challenge or satisfaction in it. Even worse, because managers are admonished only to prevent waste during the period of receivership, the properties themselves are held in suspended animation, waiting patiently for someone to reclaim them and finally address the problems that caused their financial predicament in the first place. [NOTE: This reflects our experience, which may differ from other managers' situations.]

The failure of the thrifts, which is the second calamity to befall the real estate industry during the last decade, has resulted in the sale of $330 billion

The Value-Price Relationship (*continued*)

Those in the apartment marketing and management business are in a unique position: Many of the marketing concepts that have revolutionized retailing, "bundling" among them, have yet to impact the multihousing industry greatly. It is striking to note, however, that the people who work and/or live in properties owned or managed by others—the industry's customers—are themselves pioneers and practitioners of these very concepts.

Customers recognize that the *value-to-price relationship* determines their satisfaction with their purchases. If the value of the product exceeds its price, whether the price is low or high, customers are satisfied. Indeed, customers will *always* be willing to pay for what they get. The most savvy customers inevitably are willing to pay a high price to obtain high value: This is how they define a "bargain."

From a seller's point of view, a price supported by a high margin of profit is always the most satisfactory price. From a customer's perspective, high value is the prerequisite to satisfaction. The most mutually satisfying consumer relationships combine high value and high price. Thus, the "win-win" situation for both customer and vendor is *always value and never price.*

In the housing industry, value will be sought—regardless of price—because where people live involves a continuing "purchase," twenty-four hours a day, seven days a week, and year after year of paying rent or a mortgage. Regardless of the dollar amount, renters perceive their particular rent as "high"—often it is the most they can afford. Because of this perception, the expectation of value will be high as well. It is expectations, perceptions, and actual experiences with the product that define value, especially in the area of rental housing.

in securities, properties, and loans to date, with another estimated $100 billion yet to come. The Resolution Trust Corporation (RTC), the disposition agent created by federal legislation—the Financial Institutions Reform, Recovery and Enforcement Act of 1989 (FIRREA)—reported sales of affordable housing as of November 30, 1992, including 25,000 multifamily units in 295 properties which sold for $288 million, with an additional 28,000 units in 272 properties under contract. A total of 736 properties of this type have been conveyed, with 90 still available.

In this disheartening environment characterized by too much of the wrong product, much of which has failed or is failing in the market, resourceful apartment marketers have begun to experiment with techniques to differentiate apartment communities. They know that the financial fortunes of apartment properties depend to a great extent on marketing skills—tactics that will attract prospective residents to a particular property instead of its competition. Many of them, either out of desperation or following the example of successful retail marketers, have seized on various "intangible per-quisites"—especially those having a service component—as means of positioning their buildings ahead of their competition.

At about the time that the faint outlines of the looming savings and loan (S&L) disaster could be discerned, the Institute of Real Estate Management (IREM) Foundation commissioned Arthur Andersen and Company to conduct a survey of the real estate industry. The results were published in 1991 as *Managing the Future: Real Estate in the 1990s.* In addition to cataloging the nation's real estate and identifying its owners, the goals of the survey were to discover what major players in the investment real estate field considered to be the most critical issues facing the industry, as well as significant short-term trends and important factors in managing their inventory.

The authors of *Managing the Future* found that all U.S. real estate, including single-family homes, is worth nearly $9 trillion, slightly more than $6 trillion of which is residential property. Of that, approximately $5.5 trillion comprises single-family homes, with the remainder—some $550 billion—representing multifamily housing. Moving to survey results, the authors discovered, not surprisingly, that the chief concern of major owners is the "space glut and what it means for the future." The owners consider the most likely solution to this immense problem to be tenant retention:

▶ Almost every interviewee said the most important tasks involve serving tenants. . . . Retaining tenants is more important than obtaining them. . . . [They] regard retention as more efficient and less disruptive than continual, successful re-leasing. . . . In the interviews, it was heard repeatedly that real estate is revenue-driven, and that without good tenant retention there are no other problems to solve.

This report constitutes an especially thorough job description for the property manager of the future. In ranking the importance of property management tasks, tenant retention, lease negotiation, obtaining tenants, and handling tenant relations are at the very top of the list. The findings in the 1991 IREM Foundation report are echoed in the more recent *Emerging Trends in Real Estate: 1994,* which states: "Strong tenant relations are a must for stemming tenant turnover, which can lead to re-leasing costs averaging $1,000 to $1,500 per unit." (We will present more specifics related to these costs in chapter 4.)

A Basis for Revolution.   How do you go about launching a campaign to retain residents (rather than churning them through your properties)? When the history of the apartment business has been conquest marketing—treating residents as though they are just rent checks—is there a good starting point for instituting retention marketing?

It may be best to turn for guidance to the godfather of relationship selling—Jan Carlzon, the president of Scandinavian Airlines System (SAS). Carlzon took the reins at SAS in 1981, when the company had lost $8 million the previous year. Within two years, the airline turned a $71 million profit while the airline industry remained in a deep recession, losing $2 billion annually.

Carlzon realized that the future of his company was being decided in the routine contacts between his customers and his frontline employees. Whether SAS succeeded or failed, then, depended more on people than on airplanes. He described the situation in this way:

▶ Last year, each of our 10 million customers came in contact with approximately five SAS employees, and this contact lasted an average of 15 seconds each time. Thus, SAS is "created" in the minds of our customers 50 million times a year, 15 seconds at a time. These 50 million "moments of truth" are the moments that ultimately determine whether SAS will succeed or fail as a company. They are the moments when we must prove to our customers that SAS is their best alternative.

Moments of Truth. This sensational thought—that the fortune of any company is being decided, right now, on the spot, out on the front lines where the least-experienced, presumably lowest-paid, and least-motivated employees are deciding the fate of the company—is the foundation for the drastic changes in customer relations that followed. The revolution in service, satisfaction, quality, and value is founded on Carlzon's "moments of truth."

Because moments of truth provide the vibrant intellectual foundation for the customer service revolution, it is important to understand what they are and why they are central to the success of every business. Karl Albrecht defined the moment of truth as "any episode in which the customer comes into contact with any aspect of the organization and gets an impression of the quality of its service." A moment of truth, then, is the basic atom of a firm's service orientation, the indivisible building-block upon which its wares— goods, services, whatever—are presented to the public. The totality of a company's moments of truth constitute its image, its reputation, its good name.

Moments of truth in the apartment business come in endless variety. Many of them involve direct interaction between apartment employees and residents. Others, the ones that might be characterized as "impersonal" moments of truth, nonetheless create impressions. Your advertising, for example, is a moment of truth. Another is the "curb appeal" of your building—entering a parking lot, dialing a leasing agent on an intercom, walking through an elevator lobby, being greeted by a resident manager—these are all powerful, indelible moments of truth that occur within a span of minutes. A conversation with the accounts receivable clerk in a company's main office, calling in a service request, picking up a package in the management office—the bouillabaisse of potential moments of truth is boundless.

Carlzon's genius lay not only in recognizing (and christening) moments of truth, but also in conceding that he was powerless to supervise their transmission—by his own estimate, 50 million of them, every year! Instead, he realized that the only way to improve his company's chances to deliver quality moments was to transform SAS into a truly customer-focused company. This required, in his view, several basic, yet drastic, steps. The first was to refashion the airline:

▶ In a customer-driven company, the distribution of roles is radically different. The organization is decentralized, with responsibility delegated to those who until now have comprised the order-obeying bottom of the pyramid. The traditional, hierarchical corporate structure, in other words, is beginning to give way to a flattened, more horizontal, structure. This is particularly true in service businesses that begin not with the product but with the customer.

The frontline employee, according to the Carlzon model, became the nucleus of the company:

▶ [Their] efforts were suddenly imbued with greater value within the company. All the employees received special training on providing service and, to many of them, the content of these courses was secondary to the fact that the company was investing time and resources in them. They had frequently gone unappreciated. Now they were in the limelight.

The stimulus for this transformation was, of course, the company leadership, the people who, ironically, stood to lose the most because of the change, at least in terms of traditional measures of status:

▶ The initiative for [change] must originate in the executive suite. It is up to the top executive to become a true leader, devoted to creating an environment in which employees can accept and execute their responsibilities with confidence and finesse. . . . To succeed he can no longer be an isolated and autocratic decision-maker. Instead, he must be a visionary, a strategist, an informer, a teacher, and an inspirer.

According to Carlzon, being customer-focused requires vigilant attention to the interests of a company's clients, beginning with a redefining of the nature of the business from the customer's perspective:

▶ Given today's increased competitiveness and emphasis on service, the first step must be to acquire a customer orientation. To a certain extent, this means looking at your company and deciding, from the customer's point of view, what business you're really in. For example, is SAS in the airline business? Or is it really in the business of transporting people from one place to another in the safest and most efficient way possible? I think it's obvious that the answer is the latter.

The next step is to isolate, and then eradicate, potential impediments to a customer's access to the company's services. As Carlzon soon realized, many of these obstacles—what might be called "negative" moments of truth—have been erected over time by the company itself:

▶ As I learned more about SAS, I was amazed at how many of its policies and procedures catered to the equipment or the employees, even if they inconvenienced the passengers. Equally amazing was how easy these practices were to spot—and to rectify—by looking at them from the point of view of our target customer, the frequent business traveler.

As you can see, the notion of "moments of truth" and the implications of this illuminating concept suggest that traditional ways of organizing and operating corporations are fundamentally flawed. Indeed, the numerous Fortune 500 companies and others who took Carlzon's message to heart followed his lead and "flattened" the organization of their companies. This model literally places frontline employees toward the top of the organization chart; middle managers, "bosses," and all other employees are clearly subordinate. The message? *"If you're not serving the customer, you'd better be serving someone who is."* This principle, in turn, became the foundation for what has come to be known as *empowerment*. As Carlzon explained it:

▶ If we are truly dedicated to orienting our company toward each customer's individual needs, then we cannot rely on rule books and instructions from distant corporate offices. We have to place responsibility for ideas, decisions, and actions with the people who *are* SAS during those 15 seconds: ticket agents, flight attendants, baggage handlers, and all the other frontline employees. If they have to go up the organizational chain of command for a decision on an individual problem, then those 15 golden seconds will elapse without a response, and we will have lost an opportunity to earn a loyal customer.

Customer Focus.   Becoming customer-focused means regenerating the corporation, redefining its leadership, empowering its employees. Heady thoughts, and ones that have not been much in evidence in real estate management. The potential for improving apartment operations is huge, and potentially overwhelming. Before we begin to consider the implications of Carlzon's thinking for the apartment business, we need to maintain our perspective:

▶ The story is told of the sultan who awoke in the middle of the night and summoned his wizard. "Wizard," he said, "my sleep is troubled. Tell me: What is holding up the earth?"

"Majesty," replied the wizard, "the earth rests on the back of a giant elephant."

The sultan was satisfied and went back to sleep. He then awoke in a cold sweat and summoned the wizard. "Wizard," he said, "what's holding up the elephant?"

The wizard looked at him and said, "The elephant stands on the back of a giant turtle. And you can stop right there, Majesty. *It's turtles all the way down.*"

We include this story as an admonition. While it is absolutely essential to begin to restructure your companies with a view to improving service to your residents, the restructuring process is potentially overwhelming. You need to remember that you can institute this process by adopting a rather minimalist approach: It is possible to begin the task by making small improvements in the daily delivery of value to your customers; apartment managers can, as Jan Carlzon himself suggests, decide to be "one percent better at 100 things instead of being 100 percent better at one thing."

It is well to remember that the Japanese, who have perfected in practice the abstruse theories of total quality management, zero defects, and all the rest, have a word—*KAIZEN*—that means ongoing, daily enhancement in the performance of a company, undertaken by everyone in the organization. In contrast to the Western style, which tends to adopt drastic overhauls—usually fueled by huge infusions of capital—as a means to achieving its goals, KAIZEN would have managers realize small improvements in the status quo as a result of ongoing efforts. The Japanese can appreciate the simplicity of turtles.

2

The Roads to Revolution

If you don't know where you are going, THE SCARECROW SAID TO DOROTHY, it doesn't matter which road you take.

—The Wizard of Oz

When the goal is to develop a service orientation, there are three roads apartment managers may choose. One road leads to control of your customers' experiences. Another road guides the hiring of service personnel. The third leads to a pot of gold—word-of-mouth advertising.

Road One: Managing Your Customers' Experiences

Apartment managers know from their own backgrounds as consumers that customers decide whether to be patrons of a company (or to continue their patronage) primarily on the basis of their contacts with its frontline employees. Whether these episodes are characterized as "moments of truth" (per Jan Carlzon), or as "guest contact points," "critical incidents," or "points of encounter" (according to later commentators), the quality of customers' interactions with a company's frontline servers—its clerks, receptionists, waiters, etc.—are instrumental in its success.

Carlzon teaches that these interactions between customer and company are inherently random, subjective, and unpredictable. Moments of truth are frequently unsupervised as well—because of their nature, *they are not susceptible to being supervised.* While moments of truth may or may not involve direct human contact, those incidents of human association—the so-called high-touch connections that occur in such places as apartment hallways and leasing offices—are especially vivid and memorable to the customer. These contacts might be characterized as customer-initiated interviews with the products and services the company offers to the market. Such interviews are a test of the value of the goods; the results provide a perception of the quality of the company's customer service. Only if they are satisfied with how the company defines the service component of the product will prospects become customers and current customers be transformed into long-term clients.

Once apartment managers understand the fluky nature of moments of truth and recognize their significance in initiating and maintaining long-lasting customer relationships with the organization, they can manage these moments in two complementary ways: first, by trying to control moments of truth whenever possible and, second, by attempting to influence moments when they cannot be controlled.

Retailing versus Apartment "Moments of Truth."   The challenge of managing moments of truth in the multifamily housing industry is probably more demanding than it is elsewhere. The difficulty is that the most significant moments of truth in apartment management—the interactions between staff members and customers and potential customers—are *continuous*. Unlike the situation in the retail trades, where the workday ends when the store closes, apartment managers and their staffs are *never* off duty. For those who live in the buildings where they work, the encounters with their customers are inescapable. Working at an apartment property is akin to working at a hospital or hotel—commercial businesses in which the moments of truth are high touch, occasionally unpleasant, and perpetual.

Although moments of truth in the apartment business are potentially incessant, it is prudent to attempt to catalog and control them. Managing customers' experiences—the *outcomes* that your clients have with your company—is the goal. If you assume that your customers are continually assessing and then banking the positive and negative outcomes they have with you, then their decisions whether to continue doing business with you are always at risk. If you inventory the most likely interactions your residents can have with your products and your personnel, and if you strategize ways to improve the quality of those interactions, then you can boost the number of *beneficial outcomes* your customers experience.

Cataloging "Moments of Truth."   It is possible to chart the most prevalent moments of truth that residents and prospective residents have with apartment buildings and their staffs. This process, called critical incident analysis or service blueprinting, is the first step in building a service-oriented culture in your company. Blueprinting maps the critical contacts between your customers and your products to help you devise ways to add value to these contacts. Here's an example.

Because apartments are "wasting" assets—i.e., they break down, gradually deteriorate, and become obsolete over time—preventive maintenance and repair are exceedingly important. They delay the aging process and preserve value for the owners. Consequently, repair and maintenance is a significant part of the site staff's responsibility and comprises a major portion of the property's annual budget. It is also a critical incident in the relationship between apartment property and apartment resident. Typically called a work order as directed to your internal customers (i.e., staff), it is actually a service request from an external customer (i.e., a resident).

When you endeavor to map this particular critical incident, you might find that its component elements are the following:

1. A maintenance need is discovered by an apartment resident;

2. The maintenance request is transmitted to a member of the apartment site staff, who prepares a written order that describes the problem;

3. The written request is directed to a maintenance employee;

4. The employee proceeds to the apartment and effects the repair; and

5. Some follow-up is done to ensure resident satisfaction.

This sounds simple and fairly routine. Yet if apartment managers wish to *add value* to the service-delivery process, there are several ways to do so. First, they might consider encouraging residents to contact a particular maintenance person *directly* by circulating the worker's digital or voice pager number to them. Before implementing this innovative method of processing service requests, you would, of course, need to do some fairly extensive advance planning. This might include developing relevant hiring and training procedures for maintenance workers, providing appropriate supervision and feedback, and establishing rewards for successful performance. Once in place, however, this enhancement to traditional practice would reduce, and perhaps eliminate, the paper-processing and possible misinterpretation or mishandling of service requests that can occur when someone who answers a call is unfamiliar with maintenance problems—or, just as likely, busy with other responsibilities.

Second, whether or not you adopt such a revolutionary way of handling service requests, you might revamp your maintenance schedule—in particular, the hours that maintenance personnel are on duty. Service delivery generally conforms to a certain *demand rhythm*. For example, because patrons of fast-food establishments and banks tend to frequent those establishments at certain hours, line personnel are scheduled to accommodate the periods of greatest demand, and additional resources are made available when they are required. We believe that service rhythms can be detected in the apartment business as well, and that it is worthwhile to make plans to accommodate them.

There is a likelihood that most renters are typically "at home" both before and after the shifts when maintenance people are normally at work. Apartment residents are therefore more likely to discover maintenance needs when help is *not* immediately available. If you were to schedule maintenance personnel in shifts corresponding to residents' needs, you might have staff on duty, say, between six and nine o'clock in the mornings, from 3:30 in the afternoon until shortly after dinner, and on weekends. The work could be done while residents were present to watch its progress—and to ask personally for additional service if they needed it. The fact that work is *visible*—that is, that the consumers of the service are allowed to see the work being done, as well as its results—tends to make the work *more valuable* to the customer as well.

We would offer this caution, however: These innovative approaches to provision of maintenance services require careful planning and much forethought because of the potential for loss of control, especially at large properties.

Visibility Adds Value.   Have you ever gone to a restaurant where a salad, the main course, or dessert was prepared by the chef right at your table? It is certainly a unique experience because you can judge first-hand the excellence of the food, appreciate the skills—and personality—of the chef, and savor the sights and smells while the food is being prepared. Perhaps best of all, the experience can be quite entertaining. Restaurants that do this have made the visibility of work-in-progress their distinguishing feature. Apartment managers can follow their lead by letting residents see what is being done for them as well. For example, you can schedule your housekeeping functions so that a staff member is cleaning the mailbox area when residents are coming home from work, or a caretaker is sweeping the sidewalks as they leave for work at 7:30 A.M.

Third, even if you do not put any of the suggested work order refinements in place, you might consider a variety of ways to follow up with residents to ensure their satisfaction with work that has been done for them. Typically, the resident manager, or someone acting on behalf of the management office, telephones a resident after the work has been completed to determine whether it was acceptable. A better way to measure residents' satisfaction with the results of a service request is to invite them to complete a simple questionnaire that asks whether the maintenance personnel were pleasant, whether the work was timely and appropriate, and whether there is additional work that could be done. While a questionnaire is less personal than face to face contact, it is more likely to foster candor.

A basic characteristic of service-oriented organizations is that customers

Service Visibility and "Getting Your Hands Dirty"

Although value and its allied attributes—service and quality—are intangible and invisible, they are nonetheless measurable. Consumers routinely focus their five senses, along with intuition, judgment, and other skills to decide, for example, whether goods appear to be worth their selling price, whether a store employee has served them capably, or whether to return unsatisfactory purchases for a refund—and, indeed, whether they wish to continue patronizing the particular store at all.

People's talent for gauging the merit of goods and services is probably a consequence of living in a pure, multilayered, global consumer environment. By habit, inclination, and education, consumers make these determinations almost instinctively. However, as impersonal as much of consumers' behavior is, they are regularly and rudely made aware of the deplorable state of customer service—despite its scarcity, consumers nonetheless value the human touch. As Zemke and Schaaf have observed:

► Service in America today is terrible. Everybody says so, right? If true, that's ironic, because today's consumers are willing to pay a premium to have their basic needs met in a timely and efficient manner, and they'll be pleasantly surprised if they're treated with a little dignity and respect in the bargain. In principle they're not asking for much. In practice it seems that today's consumers—be they wholesale, retail, commercial, or trade—might as well ask for the moon as for a modicum of responsive, respectful treatment.

In this environment in which customers yearn for personal attention, care, and concern, yet almost invariably expect and receive the opposite, savvy marketers can deliver products "bundled" with additional desirable characteristics—intangible perquisites, if you will—and will make their customers aware that the "bundle" contains these additional features. Ron McCann made this recommendation:

► Let people know what they are receiving. This can be done in many ways. You will find ways to suit your situation. Banks could advertise their commitment to get statements out on time. Repair companies could inform customers of special warranties. How can *you* let people know they just received extraordinary service? Answer that question and you'll fulfill the last of the three steps to becoming extraordinary.

are encouraged to complain and to register needs for additional service. When these needs are discovered and met, customer loyalty usually follows. The problem, of course, is that apartment managers have to know about a deficiency before they can remedy it. The example follow-up form in exhibit 2.1 accomplishes this purpose and, equally important, provides a

Service Visibility (*continued*)

Michael LeBoeuf admonished businesses to keep in touch with their customers:

▶ If you fail to stay in touch with your customers, they won't be aware of the good service you're giving them until something goes wrong and they don't get it. But by staying in touch after the sale or between sales, you can remind them of the fine service you give, make them aware of new products and services, and offer information to help them get more for their money. Periodic telephone calls, personal letters, newsletters, and occasional social calls are all good vehicles for staying in touch. But by all means, stay in touch and let them know that their satisfaction is priority number 1 with both word and deed.

Making service *visible* is nearly as important as providing it at all. Consider the array of ethnic restaurants that perform the entire food preparation and cooking procedure at the diner's table—and then charge a premium price for the experience—or expensive car wash operations that allow the patron to see the entire process, from high-powered washing through sudsing and, finally, waxing. How about bakeries that publicly feature their employees' cake-decorating skills? The examples are numerous, and the lesson is clear: Visible service is valuable service. Visibility becomes part of the product "bundle" and thereby is entitled to pricing consideration in addition to—and separate from—the goods themselves.

Apartment managers have a host of opportunities to let their residents know they are being served. For instance, grounds cleaning, lawn mowing, and window washing can be scheduled at times when residents are leaving for or returning home from work. Straightening the mailbox area at the end of the day also makes it apparent that this work is being done. Even though these tasks are ordinary, people generally are not aware that they are being handled until, for some reason, they are not done. The wise property manager will strategize ways to make even routine tasks visible to residents.

A related, and equally important, service principle is the admonition to "get your hands dirty!" This means that service is more meaningful if the service provider becomes *personally involved* in its delivery. Here is an example:

The site manager at Martinique Apartments scheduled parking lot maintenance and sweeping of the underground garage. She provided notice to her residents in advance of the work telling them that their cars should be moved and that these areas would not be available again for parking until the jobs were completed.

Despite this notice, a few residents either failed to move their vehicles or returned them to the lot before the work was done. As a result, four cars were splattered with mud and covered with dirt.

Service Visibility (*concluded*)

Although these residents technically were at fault, the manager decided to have their cars washed and waxed. Instead of delivering coupons to the residents or arranging to have the work done by professionals either on or off the site, the manager and her staff held an impromptu car wash in the parking lot. Because they volunteered to do the work themselves—even though it would have been much easier to hire professionals—the surprised residents showered the staff with praise. One of the delighted residents reciprocated by baking a cake and serving it at the monthly staff meeting. Thereafter, the "Great Annual Martinique Car Wash and Barbecue," in which the staff washed residents' cars, sponsored a picnic for residents, and played volleyball and softball with them, became the centerpiece of the property's resident retention program.

Davidow and Uttal believe leaders should take an active role in service-delivery:

▶ Getting their hands dirty keeps top managers in touch with the problems of customers and the experience of the front line, and it shows everybody that serving customers is important. Never getting down into the trenches is dangerous.

Finally, Soichiro Honda, the founder of one of the most successful multinational companies (Honda Motors), recounted his personal, "hands-dirty" formula for success as follows:

▶ The man at the top of an organization must personally do things that others would hate to do most.

---

nominal paper backup that can be used for record-keeping purposes on site or in the central office. Such a service questionnaire can become a self-perpetuating opportunity to provide service to your residents upon their continuing request. (See pages 22 and 23.)

Blueprinting and Mapping Critical Incidents. These suggested refinements to the traditional work order processing systems in place at apartment communities illustrate how "blueprinting"—the process of identifying and characterizing customer-contact opportunities—can improve service delivery processes. The key to these improvements is mapping the contacts between your residents, your property, and your site staff in order to see how these contacts occur; writing them down in sequential order; and then deciding how you can intervene to improve their quality for your clients. The blueprinting process is vastly improved when as many participants as possible are involved, either formally or informally. Seen in this way, the methodology is akin to brainstorming sessions where people spontaneously con-

Exhibit 2.1
Example Service Follow-Up Questionnaire

_____

Hi!

*Someone
was in your
apartment
today—*

it was: _____

To: _____

_____

_____

tribute all kinds of ideas, primarily solutions to particular problems. The site staff—most especially including representatives from management and marketing, maintenance and housekeeping—play a part, as do central office personnel and the residents themselves. The involvement of the residents may range from sitting in during staff meetings to one-on-one interviews where you ask them such questions as, "What would you think if we did . . . this way?" or "We've been thinking of trying something a different way. How would you like it if we did . . . ?" Such questions ask for a reaction or response to your proposals. If you want the residents to make suggestions, you might ask, "How do you think we should do . . . ?" or "How can we make . . . better for you?"

Exhibit 2.1 *(continued)*

LET US KNOW HOW YOUR SERVICE WAS.

PLEASE FILL THIS OUT AND DROP IN THE COMMENT BOX.

	YES	NO
WERE WE PROMPT?	☐	☐
WERE WE FRIENDLY?	☐	☐
WAS THE REPAIR ADEQUATE?	☐	☐
IS THERE ANYTHING ELSE WE CAN DO?	☐	☐

COMMENTS: _____

_____

_____

_____

_____

_____

_____

_____

We have these follow-up questionnaires printed as a two-sided "notice" on brightly colored card stock (about 4″ wide x 5″ deep). The spaces on the face are for the apartment number, the name of the person who provided the service, and a description of the work done. Residents return the completed card to the "comment" box in the lobby.

Any requests for additional work produce more work orders which, in turn, yield more completed questionnaires.

Brainstorming "Failpoints" in Service Delivery. What are some other productive subjects for blueprinting? Remember, the goal is to improve the so-called critical incidents that contribute to customers' and potential customers' satisfaction—i.e., to resident satisfaction and retention. In addition to work order processing, critical incidents that spring to mind include curb appeal, billing and collections procedures, staff appearance (a dress code), advertising and marketing enhancements, techniques for dealing with overly demanding residents, handling after-hours emergencies, resident parties and other social events, and a host of others.

We recommend that you focus on a single critical incident in each staff meeting. In considering what items to include for discussion, try to determine those areas in your customer relations program where you are most likely to disappoint your residents. Some examples might be:

Tardy or incomplete maintenance
Inadequate housekeeping
Poor telephone techniques

Whatever the particulars, the purpose is to identify all of the failpoints that make your resident retention efforts chancy. *Failpoints* are critical incidents that demand the immediate and close attention of your entire staff.

Whether you call it blueprinting, mapping, critical incident analysis, or something else, this type of strategizing can be extraordinarily productive, not only because collaborative thinking tends to bring particularly valuable insights to the surface, but also because the results are collectively "owned" by all of the participants—those whose enthusiasm to implement their solutions is correspondingly higher. ("Outer-circle" thinking, an elegant form of brainstorming, will be discussed later in this chapter.)

Employee Failpoints and Burnout.   Thus far we have considered planning for predictable moments of truth from the perspective of your customers. It is also worthwhile to consider the benefits that blueprinting can provide to your employees.

We believe that one of the negative features of apartment management is that frontline employees are inordinately subject to burnout. The intense, nonstop, and sometimes negative moments of truth that occur between site personnel and residents are emotionally laborious and result in employee dissatisfaction and turnover. This is particularly true for staff members who live on site—they never leave their worksite. As Petra Marquart, a former property manager who teaches customer service techniques, put it, our business is "hard on the spirit." We agree.

For employees, strategizing moments of truth is also a means of combatting the draining effects of the emotional labor that characterizes many aspects of the apartment business. Blueprinting, as we have described it in this chapter, enables them to plan in advance how to handle a variety of critical incidents, some of which involve high-touch contacts with residents. Having collectively considered alternative possibilities and arrived at a preferred approach, frontline personnel will comprehend both that there is a satisfactory way to respond to these situations—they have, in a sense, been *empowered to act*—and that their fellow employees (including their supervisors and the

---

Positive and Negative Moments of Truth

It is imperative to acknowledge—and accept—that there are two possible outcomes from every incident. *Positive* moments of truth—those contacts that have been handled successfully—prove that a strategy works. *Negative* moments of truth, on the other hand, are particular failpoints. While they do not necessarily disprove a strategy, they do indicate that the individual involved in the interaction somehow did not connect.

While it is possible to establish strategies for the ordinary moments of truth (the routine service request, for example), it is even more important to have procedures in place for handling the *extra*-ordinary contacts—the so-called failpoints (e.g., emergencies or personal crises).

---

company executives) understand the realities of the intensely human interactions that occur at the front line.

Jeffrey Disend described the importance of support for frontline personnel this way:

▶ Frontline people need to know that the rest of the organization is there to support and assist them in serving customers. When people know they can depend on the systems, equipment, procedures, and people behind the scenes to deliver, keep commitments, and handle problems, they can act more confidently and with less stress.

Employee satisfaction will be revisited in chapter 3, where we will consider empowerment and its benefits in greater detail. To continue this discussion, we need to look more closely at the importance of frontline servers and the difficulty of their task. Rick Johnson, manager of business seminars for Walt Disney World, one of the premier customer-driven companies, had this to say on the subject:

▶ How many times will your people on the front lines be tested today? And how many times will they succeed in earning or renewing the respect and loyalty of another customer or client? Your organization's reputation, its investment in facilities, products, services, and staff, even its prospects for the future, are all on the line every time your people deal with your customers.

Obviously people are the key to enriching customer contacts with your company. According to Donald Porter, director of customer service quality assurance for British Airways, the server *is* the company for the customer:

▶ If you're a service person, and you get it wrong at your point in the customer's chain of experience, you are very likely erasing from the customer's mind all the memories of the good treatment he or she may have had up until you. But if you get it right, you have a chance to undo all the wrongs that may have happened before the customer got to you. *You* really are the moment of truth.

Road Two: Hiring Nice People to Serve Your Customers

Hal Rosenbluth is the owner of Rosenbluth Travel, a Philadelphia-based travel agency that experienced a 7,500 percent growth in revenue—from $20 million to $1.5 billion—in about twenty years. His strategy for success—which is embodied in the title of the book he co-wrote with Diane McFerrin Peters, *The Customer Comes Second, and Other Secrets of Exceptional Service,*—is that employee quality is *the* single most significant "moment of truth" for his firm's customers.

▶ At its most basic common denominator, the formula for our company's success is that we have more nice people than [our competitors] do. Niceness is among our highest priorities because nice people do better work.

Rosenbluth reasoned that if he had nice people serving clients, and if he took personal responsibility for ensuring his employees' own on-the-job satisfaction, his customers would be the beneficiaries:

▶ Companies are only fooling themselves when they believe that "The Customer Comes First." People do not inherently put the customer first, and they certainly don't do it because their employer expects it. Only when people know what it feels like to be first in someone else's eyes can they sincerely share that feeling with others.

Hiring As an Exercise in KAIZEN. The example from Hal Rosenbluth can be used to recall one important point and make another. First, as we noted in chapter 1, the Japanese theory of steady, gradual, continuous progress as a means to excellence—called KAIZEN—is a revolutionary departure from the American approach which assumes that improvement is accomplished only by means of fundamental, thorough, radical change. KAIZEN enables you to seek ways to leverage the greatest possible benefits for your company and yourself by looking for incremental improvements achieved daily over the life of your business. These points of leverage can become what some commentators term "lighthouses for change"—that is, specific initiatives undertaken companywide for the customer's benefit that will have the greatest positive and visible impact in focusing attention on the company's capacity to deliver quality at the lowest feasible cost. We think apartment managers can follow the Japanese example and begin to reinvent their companies by taking the first step outlined here—i.e., concentrating on the quality of the company's employees and their job satisfaction.

Benchmarking Rosenbluth Travel.   Second, Rosenbluth's teachings can be coupled with another approach called *benchmarking*. This approach is based on the theory that the best practices in place at one company or in an industry may be imported by another business, even if the two firms are not engaged in the same enterprise. For example, in an effort to improve the "welcome packets" they provide to new residents, apartment managers might look at how a particular hotel chain handles guest gifts. Or they might seek guidance from certain retailers in the areas of signage, customer newsletters, or collections practices. Although benchmarking has evolved into a rather sophisticated technique for effecting improvements in business practices, at its heart lies the old admonition to avoid reinventing the wheel wherever possible. (Using marketing grids as a benchmarking tool will be discussed in chapter 8.) A closer examination of the experiences of Rosenbluth Travel reveals some benchmarks that can be helpful to apartment managers.

First, you need to keep constantly in mind the importance and the contentment of your employees as the foundation for improving the performance of your business. As Rosenbluth put it:

▶ Every company operates on a hierarchy of concerns. Ours is: people, service, profits. In that order. The company's focus is on its people. Our people then focus on serving our clients. Profits are the end result.

Hal Rosenbluth believes that the successful economic performance of a company is driven by the happiness of its employees, rather than the reverse, and that contented employees are less likely to seek out other employment in an attempt to find satisfaction.

Second, as apartment managers direct attention to their "internal" customers—that is, their employees—they need to begin by hiring nice people, as Hal Rosenbluth did:

▶ Tenet number one is, *look for nice people*. The rest will fall into place. Too often, a person's job history carries more weight than his or her human values. What's in someone's heart can't be discovered in a resume.

The truth is, in apartment management, energy, enthusiasm, and attitude are often more important than specific experience.

Employees as Business Partners.   "Hiring nice" requires both common sense and a willingness to change the way you do business. No longer can you hire only on the basis of a prospective employee's prior job experience and skills: You are looking for "people" people—those who derive their satisfaction mostly from interacting with others. When you adopt as a company credo "people, service, profits," you redirect—and sharpen—your focus. If colleagues come first, customers second, and profits third, your employees become your business partners—i.e., your associates, colleagues, and friends. When apartment managers hire service personnel, they are not only hiring for their customers, they are implicitly asking the question, "Is this prospect a person I want to trust with the future of my company?"

One way to "hire nice" is to go about the process as Rosenbluth Travel does—by seeking the participation of other nice people (i.e., current employees) in your hiring and promoting decisions:

▶   It's important to get as many people as possible involved in the selection process, because we need to bring into the company only those who can work well with the team we have in place. For that reason, candidates for senior leadership positions spend time with our current senior leaders, and their input is crucial. To round out the process, prospective leaders are often interviewed by those they will lead as well. We're seeking people who will inspire their teams. Who better to make that judgment than the team itself?

"Shared Fate."   Rosenbluth's skepticism of resumes and his firm's reliance on its employees (its internal customers) in arriving at hiring and promoting decisions is an extension of another Japanese concept—shared fate. "Mike" Morita, head of Sony Corporation's Rancho Bernardo manufacturing facility in California, described it this way:

▶   In the Japanese business culture, we think of our jobs in terms of *shared fate.* That means that all employees in the company share the same fate. The success—or failure—of the company affects all of us the same. The only way we can make our lives secure as individuals . is to make sure the company remains competitive. We have to work together to make the best products we possibly can. So it is extremely important that each person understands the needs of the company, and each is willing to contribute his or her best efforts to make it successful. . . . Each person's contribution goes together with the contribution of every other person for the best result.

Once the principle of shared fate is understood, digested, and practiced in the company, the ability of the firm to focus its attention on achieving good results for its external client—the customer—is enhanced. According to William Ouchi, author of *Theory Z: How American Business Can Meet the Japanese Challenge:*

▶   The successful delivery of service requires people to perform an unnatural act: to work at an extraordinarily high level of interdependence, working not only for their own ends but toward a successful outcome for the customer.

The subject of hiring will be augmented in the next chapter with a discussion of empowering and compensating employees. The road to a service orientation turns now to customer referrals.

Road Three: Compelling Customers to Tell Others About You

A look at another company provides an opportunity to benchmark techniques for "wowing" your customers. T. Scott Gross has brought a unique brand of showmanship and salesmanship to an otherwise ordinary business—a drive-through fried chicken restaurant in San Antonio, Texas. He has been so successful that he has written a book, *Positively Outrageous Service: New and Easy Ways to Win Customers for Life,* and has constructed a successful consulting practice based on his experiences. According to Gross, "Positively Outrageous Service is the story you can't wait to tell."

The idea that it makes sense to try to "wow" a customer is probably based on the common-sense notion that much of what one vendor is trying to sell—or rent—is pretty much the same as what is generally available in the market, and sometimes the competition is even priced lower. In a competitive environment filled with products that are essentially equivalent, attempting to *delight* potential customers, as well as current customers, makes good marketing sense. If you are successful, you set your product ahead of the competition and add lasting value to it.

"Positively Outrageous Service"—Gross uses the acronym POS—has five elements.

1. It is *random and unexpected*—that is, it contains an element of surprise and novelty that jolts the customer because it is so unexpected.

2. It is *out of proportion to the circumstance.* This characteristic solidifies the unexpected nature of the service activity—because it is disproportionate, it is also extraordinary.

3. It invites the customer *to play, or be highly involved* in the activity. This quality requires that the service incident be fun for the customer—if it is, it solidifies the impression that the company itself is user-friendly.

4. It generates *compelling word of mouth.* The "Wow!" experience is so stunning that the customer simply cannot wait to tell others about it.

5. It creates *lifetime buying decisions* and fosters customer retention.

What Is Service?

Karl Albrecht and Ron Zemke are the pioneers who first identified the importance of service and attempted to characterize it. Their books have been widely read for almost a decade, and they have had tremendous influence on American and international businesses, especially those whose operations include a specific service component (e.g., retail sales) or consist primarily of a rendered service (e.g., a beauty salon). In *Service America! Doing Business in the New Economy,* they defined ten characteristics of service. We think these can be expressed as seven general attributes of service that are directly applicable to real estate management and resident retention.

1. Unlike manufacturing, which requires a defined location, service is *decentralized*—it is rendered where the customer receives it. Apartment renters receive your services where they live, which can bring additional factors such as emotions into play.
2. Service is *time-bounded;* it is created at the instant of delivery. In apartment management, the instants of delivery are not only the fulfillment of specific service requests, but also the points of contact when requests or complaints are received—e.g., the moment the telephone is answered.
3. While the experience of a rendered service is *personal,* someone has to deliver it. This is the defining role for apartment management personnel.
4. The service experience is unique to the recipient, but the requirement for delivery makes it *interactive.* It is important for the customer to connect with the right person to solve a problem quickly.
5. Service is *nonreproducible;* proper delivery of service the first time is critical because opportunities to do it again are rare. If service cannot be delivered properly, the only recourse is to make reparations or apologize. Because of this, you must have in place strategies for service recovery.
6. Because service is *experience-specific,* customer satisfaction is usually greatest when service can be rendered one-on-one. Having to deal with many different people to make a purchase or file a complaint—to get any kind of action—reduces customer satisfaction.
7. The quality of a service is *expectation-related.* Customer satisfaction depends on the recipient's subjective perception of the service, which is based on his or her expectations.

When the service encounter is unexpected, disproportionate, fun, and compelling, customers are disinclined to shop elsewhere because they are convinced they will be disappointed if they do.

One of the reasons apartment managers should strive to provide their residents with an unexpected service experience is precisely because so

---

What Is Service? (*continued*)

A commitment to service delivery is critical to assuring the quality or value of a service. Planning and training—and staff buy-in to your service program—are key steps along the path to success. Ron Zemke and Dick Schaaf distinguished between products and services this way:

▶ To begin with, a product is a tangible, a service an intangible. A product takes up shelf space, has a shelf life, can be inventoried, depreciated, and taxed. A service doesn't exist until it is called for by the recipient. It needs no shelf space, has no shelf life, and most certainly is not an asset that can be easily inventoried.

Because service is intangible, it does not exist until it is requested. Its existence depends on the recipient not only wanting and needing it, but also taking an active role in its production as well as its consumption. Involving residents in the service process will add to their satisfaction overall. Even more important, it will reduce the cost to the provider. Heskett et al. elaborated on this point:

▶ Self-service concepts employ customers as part of the service delivery system. The most effective insure that customers are trained, through clear instructions, in how to be good "helpers." The range of activities in which customers are willing to engage is rather remarkable. Whether they pump their own gas, as a majority of U.S. consumers do; bus their own dishes; or haul their own furniture purchases, customers enable service providers to reduce demand on the delivery system during peak periods, thereby providing incentives in the form of lower prices to encourage customers to increase their participation further.

---

much of the service people receive is so shoddy. Indeed, as Davidow and Uttal have described the situation:

▶ "Crisis" is a strong word but no exaggeration. Most customer service is poor, much of it is awful, and service quality generally appears to be falling. At the same time, the penalty is growing for companies that render inferior service. Customers . . . are getting smarter about the value of service. They're increasingly frustrated and more willing than ever to take their business elsewhere.

The other reason apartment managers should strive to improve their level of service delivery is that it pays to do so. Good service organizations strive to meet their customers' expectations; outstanding service companies endeavor to dazzle their customers in unforgettable ways. If they are successful, these firms achieve a marketing advantage that can be detected at the bottom line. In the words of Dunckel and Taylor:

▶   If you are selling the same product as your competitor, the difference in success will be measured by how the customer is treated,
both during and after the sale. Initially, you and your competitor start
evenly matched. But it is the intangible, cosseting and concern, the
customer service, that adds value and makes the buyer return again
and again. Then you have a very measurable assessment of service:
the bottom line—the repeat customer—money—greater profits.

In an attempt to create a "Wow!" experience for your customers, whether it
is designed to meet Scott Gross's requirements or to pass other tests that are
more or less rigorous, you need to keep two disclaimers in mind: First, it is
fruitless to capture the attention of your customers in order to direct it to an
inferior product. To make this point more colloquially, if you put lipstick on
a pig, what you have is a pig with red lips. Second, as soon as customers
begin to anticipate the little extras you provide, those extras become part of
the "bundle," the package of value that you are selling. That is why it is vital
to keep in mind Gross's admonition that the "Wow!" experience must be
random and unexpected.

How do you go about creating "Wow!" experiences for your residents?
One place to start is to find out how "Wow!" differs from merely "okay" or
"pretty good." Fortunately, Theodore Levitt, a professor of marketing at
Harvard (and a true marketing genius) has provided a model. In *The Marketing Imagination,* Levitt describes four levels of attributes that customers expect every product or service to have: generic, expected, augmented, and
potential.

The *generic* product, according to Levitt, is the package containing the
fundamental attributes of the goods—the rudimentary, substantive "thing"
that people require the product to have. For the steel producer, as Levitt says,
the generic product is the steel itself; for a bank, it would be money to loan.
The generic product, then, is the "table stakes" necessary to be minimally in
business. In the apartment business, the generic product would be the physical apartment that the prospect rents—the four white walls and a rug, together with certain working appliances and fixtures, and a landlord or a contact person who acts on the landlord's behalf.

As businesses move outward beyond the so-called generic product, they
bundle additional levels of support and service with their goods, thereby
increasing the customer's perception of their value. This naturally results in
a higher price for the improved goods, as well as greater customer satisfaction, product loyalty, and splendid word-of-mouth. The *expected* product
might be termed support because it includes whatever the organization does
to make the basic product more reliable, accessible, usable, enjoyable, convenient, dependable, accurate, or useful. In the apartment business, the expected product, in addition to the "four white walls and a rug," might be
contemporary amenities that are characteristic of other comparable properties in its market. Depending on the market and the resident profile, the

so-called amenities might range from an on-site laundry room with coin-operated equipment or availability of parking to a swimming pool or recreation room. The expected apartment property most likely would also have friendly, helpful on-site personnel who handle the general caretaking and are readily available at all times to assist with maintenance needs, and service is prompt, competent, friendly.

The *augmented* product goes beyond what customers expect, by bundling additional benefits with the expected product, offering more than customers believe they need or have come to expect. The augmented product becomes "aspirational"—what buyers would really prefer among the competition, assuming that real or anticipated impediments (for example, high price or limited availability) could be overcome. Certain automobiles, vacation locales, and brands of jewelry—how about Lexus, Gstaad, Rolex?—are readily identifiable as leaders among augmented products. They are presumed to be peerless, supreme, incomparable. Whether or not they are the most expensive—and some augmented products are not—prospective customers consider them to be the *ultimate* acquisition of their type; their proud owners believe that they enjoy a *relationship* with such products and the people who sold them. In the apartment business, the augmented product, in addition to offering the qualities and characteristics of expected apartments, probably has the traits of the finest hotels and resorts. Their in-unit and common-area amenities would be unique in their markets—e.g., maid services, a concierge, so-called valet services (dry cleaning, laundry, shoe-shining), a well-equipped fitness center (including a personal trainer). More important, their site staffs would be matchless in their responsiveness, friendliness, and helpfulness. It is significant to note that the augmented services tend to be more people-intensive. Every feasible means would be employed to determine resident satisfaction. No resident need or preference that was uncovered would go unmet. Apartment residents would describe their living experience as delightful or perfect, and they would boast to others about their pleasure.

Interestingly, the enhancements to expected products that result in augmented goods usually entail small dollar investments that yield enormous payoffs. Typically, enrichment by means of meaningful human touches is involved—warmth, attention, intuitive gestures that make having the item absolutely exceptional in every respect. Of course, the challenge to those who wish to distinguish their products from others—i.e., to market augmented goods—is to motivate the frontline performers in their companies to deliver moments of truth that are consistent with this enhanced concept of the product. As Jan Carlzon knew, employees at the front lines of companies—often the most junior, lowest paid, and presumably least motivated—do business in the third ring (the outer circle of the defined components of a product). That is where they get their job satisfaction. The third ring is their territory.

Too often, however, the augmented product becomes the expected product, and customers can easily be seduced by a competitor offering a lower price or a new or different service. The *potential* product, then, relates to customer satisfaction based on perceptions—service is perceived as "good" when expectations are exceeded and "poor" when expectations are not met. According to Levitt, "'Augmented' is everything that has been done or is being done to attract or keep the customer, while 'potential' is anything that could be done but isn't being done yet." (The Levitt paradigm will be revisited in chapter 8.)

Outer-Circle Thinking.   Using the Levitt paradigm, the goal should be to market an augmented apartment property to your customers, current and future. You need to plan a strategy for reaching—and surpassing—that goal for defining the potential product. One way to achieve this is to use a form of old-fashioned brainstorming—called outer-circle thinking—among the site staff. While brainstorming is often used to focus on solutions to a single problem, the goal here is to explore possibilities without limitations. Exhibit 2.2 is a representation of the Levitt paradigm as it might be applied to apartments.

Outer-circle thinking is a creative, unrestrained process for bringing ideas and suggestions, especially nontraditional ones, to the surface among members of a group. The first rule is that the participants cannot be judgmental about any thought that surfaces. Indeed, group members should be encouraged by the leader to propose, at least initially, the most unlikely and even outlandish and extravagant ideas.

The leader begins the session by summarizing the purpose of the meeting. The statement might be something like this: "We need to think about improving our apartments. We'd like our residents and prospective residents to have a once-in-a-lifetime experience, one they can't wait to tell their friends about. What could we do—or what could we provide them—that they would consider absolutely incredible? Don't worry about what it might cost: Let's talk about what it would take to make them say 'WOW!' "

Each member of the group is asked to contribute one idea which the leader records on a flip chart. If the group is large, perhaps it can be divided into sections, with each section reporting a thought until every contribution has been listed.

We have led or participated in several "outer-circle" brainstorming sessions. Here is what the results of one such session looked like:

> Manager prepares a birthday cake and delivers it to the residents on their birthday. *Whole staff* goes to the door and sings "Happy Birthday."

> Hold a garage sale in the courtyard. Schedule all-day Saturday, early in Spring. Publicize it in the newsletter. Call all of the residents 10 days in advance to remind/encourage participation.

Exhibit 2.2
The Levitt Paradigm Applied to Apartments

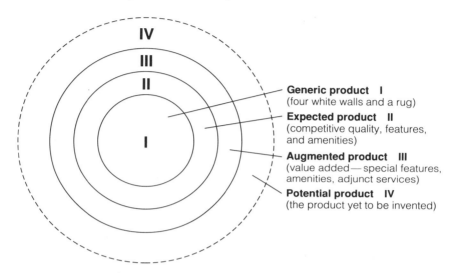

Generic product   I
(four white walls and a rug)

Expected product   II
(competitive quality, features, and amenities)

Augmented product   III
(value added—special features, amenities, adjunct services)

Potential product   IV
(the product yet to be invented)

In the marketplace, the generic product is what it is; in general, it is sold on the basis of price. The expected product includes features and amenities equivalent to comparable properties; it is sold on the basis of quality. The augmented product, on the other hand, encompasses features and amenities that exceed the competition; because a major component is personal service, its selling point is a relationship. The potential product requires constantly changing definition.

Deliver a personalized welcome mat to residents on the day of move-in. Could have property logo, too. Or have inscribed name plate for front door.

Send out "anytime" card to residents—not only on holidays—thanking them for their business.

Have a car wash in the parking lot. *Whole staff participates.* Maybe schedule barbecue/potluck dinner or ice cream social at end of day.

Provide toys for residents'/prospects' kids in management/leasing office. Coloring books, too, and crayons. Tape the pictures up on the office walls.

Staff-sponsored babysitting from time to time (one night/month maximum). Different nights of week/weekend nights. Make it a surprise.

Have a monthly party for all residents whose birthdays fall during that month. Staff bakes cake. Should be angel food, in case there are diabetics.

Buy ice chests with the building logo. Fill them with soft drinks and sandwiches. Have someone from maintenance deliver them to new residents on move-in day. See if there are any problems that maintenance can fix *right away!*

The possibilities are almost endless. What is surprising is that many of the ideas involve very little or no expense. Almost all of them require the sort of high-touch, personal contact between frontline employee and resident that has the potential to *delight.*

The following quote from David Freemantle, an English expert on the subject of customer service, effectively summarizes the purpose of outer-circle thinking:

▶ One of the most exciting aspects of customer service . . . is to discover innovative little ways of pleasing the customer even more. This can be a real test for any progressive customer caring company. The provision of unsolicited little extras is a creative and challenging opportunity all staff can enthusiastically respond to. It enables people to be themselves, to give of themselves, to express themselves in a way that is pleasing to the customer. It enables staff to put themselves out for the customer.

3

Revolutionary Hiring and "Zapping"

Managers have to select their people well, provide them with a strong foundational culture in which to work, offer them strategic direction, and equip them with the company-specific skills and knowledge they need to perform their roles. *And then the managers need to get out of the way, so the people can get the job done.*

—Valarie A. Zeithaml, A. Parasuraman, and Leonard L. Berry

In truly customer-driven companies—the firms of the future—the aim is to *delight* customers, to serve them in increasingly imaginative and memorable ways, to forge ongoing bonds with them, and to smash barriers that impede these relationships with customers or make them unpleasant in any way.

The firms of the future are beginning to acknowledge that their customers include not only patrons who purchase their goods and services (external customers), but also clients who work within the organization (internal customers—their fellow employees), and even suppliers whose products are transformed by the company for sale. Cultivating affiliations between these various customers and the company is the essence of what is known as "relationship marketing," or "partnering," where buyer and seller acknowledge their common interests and consider themselves to be invested in each other's continued success. Terry Vavra put it this way:

▶ Marketing has, over the years, shifted in its orientation from *tricking* customers to *blaming* customers to *satisfying* customers. Its future success depends upon its skill to integrate customers systematically into the conduct of business. Whether this is an accurate character-ization or not, marketing's posture to date has caused an escalating confidence gap between marketers and consumers. Today, consum-ers cynically anticipate marketers making a profit by exploiting them rather than by satisfying their wants and needs.

The goal of having satisfied customers is a revolutionary—and highly pleas-urable—concept, and one we believe is at least as achievable in the multi-family housing industry as in retail enterprises. Our goal as apartment man-agers should be to create contented residents who believe they are partners in their landlords' success. Realizing this ideal begins with attending to our employees. That is the approach advocated by Whiteley:

▶ You create service quality by hiring externally focused people—people who like people—then giving them a vision of service, a knowledge of what the customer needs, and support that lets them do their job.

Strategizing Ways to Hire Customer Service Superstars

Begin the hiring process by carefully designing a composite *abilities and attitudes profile* of the employee you are seeking. It will be clear from a review of the job description for the position what technical skills are re-quired; that is the easy part. The challenge is to include in the list the *person-ality traits* that would make a candidate a winner in your organization. To get started, ask yourself: "Who among my current employees has a history of *delighting* residents and supporting his or her fellow employees?" Try to isolate the characteristics of these people; write them down—and then ag-gressively pursue them as you interview applicants. Zemke and Bell offered this additional counsel on the process:

▶ The quest for the potential service star begins with a clear view of the service role you are seeking to fill. Treat the vacancy as an open-ing in a play. If you select an ideal (the applicant who comes closest to embodying the qualities best suited for the service role) rather than choosing someone "just like me," you may skirt the lure of choice that results in an unfair personnel practice.

Some companies, recognizing that their own best employees may be an ex-cellent source for finding others, initiate the employment process internally. That is what T. Scott Gross has advocated:

▶ Find one knock-down, drag-out winner and you're hot on the trail of a whole flock of them! Start with your own employees. Which one is a [winner]? Next ask her [or him] to help you recruit a friend.

Don't worry. They won't just drag in a warm body. Winners like to work with other winners, and that's exactly whom a winner will recommend.

Carl Sewell, a Dallas automobile dealer who now owns ten Cadillac dealerships—having expanded his business from $10 million in the late 1960s to $250 million in 1990—uses this technique as the centerpiece of an aggressive hiring program.

▶   We almost never advertise. The people we really want—the best people—already have jobs. They're not searching the help wanted ads or updating their resumes. In fact, most of the successful people we've hired have never had a resume. We sought *them* out, because we had heard about the job they were doing somewhere else, or, as happens most often, they were referred by a friend. *As a rule, people who are exceptional performers are friends with people who are exceptional performers, so we pay a lot of attention when one of our people recommends a friend.*

Other firms, recognizing that service winners are in short supply, hire such people even when they have no jobs available. As Scott Gross has said, "The problem with winners is that, like cops, they never seem to be around when you need one. If you are serious about hiring winners, you must be prepared to hire one anytime you find one."

Marketing for Human Resources.   One reason why customer service is so poor is that companies recruit job candidates based on their technical skills, rather than on the basis of their history of delivering service at the front lines. We believe that the hiring decision should be based in part on an assessment of the candidate's ability to relate to customers, to respond appropriately to their needs, to take initiatives on their behalf, to be an advocate for their interests (to the company). Recruiters fail to look for these qualities because customer service is not a priority within the company, because they do not aim high enough when they set minimum qualifications for new hires, and because they are not very creative in their recruiting efforts. Berry and Parasuraman addressed these same issues:

▶   Why do so many executives permit the wrong people to carry the company flag in front of customers? Part of the answer is the failure to think and act like a marketer when it comes to human resource issues. Marketing is used by most firms to compete for *sales* market share but not *talent* market share. Read the look-alike employment ads in the fine print in a local newspaper. Is this an effective way to compete for talent? The same firms that compete intensely and imaginatively for customers compete meekly and mundanely for employees.

Jim Clemmer, an advocate of service quality, decried the shortsightedness that he found in both hiring and training:

▶ Take a look at your *internal* education and awareness. It is amazing how many organizations will spend megabucks and megahours planning and executing powerful, slick campaigns aimed at their external customers. Many will then turn around and spend 10 bucks and two hours bringing the people on board who ultimately decide whether those external advertising messages are fact or fiction.

In other words, employees are an investment, and recruiting and hiring should be considered in those terms. The need to fill a vacant position—and the effort to do so quickly—can lead to hiring the wrong candidate. Ultimately, the time and cost to correct the error—i.e., to terminate and replace the inappropriate (ineffectual) employee—will exceed the expense of hiring the right person in the first place.

Searching for Company Ambassadors and Business Partners.   Because your objective should be to employ people who will be ambassadors for your company as well your own professional colleagues—i.e., your *business partners*—the first hiring rule for the firm of the future is: *Look for nice people.* Apartment managers need to employ people who naturally care about others, who *thrive* on personal (customer) contact and believe it to be a vital component of their business lives. Isolating people-oriented applicants from others is a difficult task—because job applicants so often claim that they "love people," resumes and past job references are unreliable predictors of this skill. As Rosenbluth and Peters warned, "Too often, a person's job history carries more weight than his or her human values. What's in someone's heart can't be discovered in a resume."

You know from your own experiences that some people prefer to work with things—they are project-driven—while others truly gravitate to situations in which human contacts, and sometimes unpleasant or challenging ones, predominate.

Hiring in the real estate management business is complicated by the fact that apartment management is increasingly the province of a performance appraisal format that prefers computerized reporting to personal narrative. The apartment business naturally lends itself to computer applications—rent rolls, financial analyses and forecasting, and year-to-date comparisons of a host of subjects are all number-based—and people who are good at working with machines frequently prefer programs over people. Of course, there is nothing wrong with this preference; the problem is that such people should not be at or near the front line where customer contact is inescapable. The reason, as you will see later in this chapter, is that the firms of the future will be horizontally structured rather than hierarchically organized. Thus, *all* employees—not just those who answer telephones, respond to service requests, or staff the leasing office—will be customer service personnel who work at the front line.

As apartment managers, when you go about the hiring process, you are really performing two complementary—and momentous—tasks: First, you are recruiting for your residents; and by doing so, you are in fact searching for that unique person in whom you are willing to entrust the future of your company. You should begin by looking for *customer-friendly* employees who have outgoing personalities, enthusiasm, and an honest desire to serve. The firms of the future—companies that succeed in creating superior value for their customers—are, as William Band observed, "nearly fanatical in their desire to recruit good 'human raw material' into their organizations. They spend inordinate amounts of time and energy getting it right the first time in their hiring decisions." Part of "getting it right" means searching until you find a candidate who *thrives* on customer contact.

Team Interviewing. One way to set about the hiring task is to involve as many people as possible, not only in job interviews, but also in the eventual hiring decision. After all, part of the "fit" you should be looking for is between the new employee and your current team. For this reason, the entire organization should be given the opportunity to evaluate the candidate's suitability for the job, as well as explore his or her match with the company culture. Tom Peters gave similar advice:

▶ The task of transforming raw recruits into committed stars, able to cope with the pace of change that is becoming normal, begins with the recruiting process per se. The best [companies] follow three tenets, unfortunately ignored by most: (1) spend time, lots of it; (2) insist that line people dominate the process; and (3) don't waffle about the qualities you are looking for in candidates.

Here's an example of what we mean: The personnel department at Disney—known as "central casting"—places the ability to get along with others at the top of the list of job specifications for new "cast members" (prospective Disney employees). On the theory that the personal dynamics occurring during the interview process can provide useful clues about candidates' friendliness and attentiveness to others, Disney relies on group interviews of job candidates.

We recommend that interviews for apartment management jobs include an opportunity for applicants to recount stories that reveal their attitudes toward residents. For example, you might say, "Tell me about a time when you encountered a particularly irate resident and how you resolved the problem." A variation on this approach goes like this: "It's understandable that sometimes we get really upset with our residents. Everybody does once in a while, but there's a big difference between an angry confrontation with a resident and reminding someone about the rules. Tell me about one time during the last six months when you had to get tough with a resident and how you handled it."

So-called open-ended questions are designed to reveal a prospect's attitudes, although they probably do so less effectively than the "story-telling" technique suggested in the preceding paragraph. Examples of open-ended questions that are designed to display a candidate's service values, are: "What does customer service mean to you?" Or, "Have you ever encountered what you would consider to be *world-class* customer service? Describe the situation for me."

Other strategies that reveal a candidate's attitudes toward customer service include role-playing techniques. For example, the interviewer might play the part of an irate resident who has waited an inordinate amount of time to have an appliance serviced, while the candidate acts as the recipient of the after-hours telephone call.

In these situations, whether a candidate's answers are "correct" is less important than the quality of the process that he or she uses to answer your questions. Remember, interviews are inherently artificial and false. Freemantle has characterized them as "a process of mutual seduction . . . based on illusion, pose, facade and front." Accepting this reality as a caution, we would commend the group interview as a potential way to expose deception and phoniness in a candidate's responses.

Furthermore, as we noted earlier in this chapter, intensive group interviewing gives the team the opportunity to gauge an applicant's "fit" with the company culture. Equally important, because group interviewing communicates the firm's mission to all participants, this type of employee selection process allows an applicant to evaluate whether he or she shares the firm's values. The procedure is thus a *dual-purpose* selection strategy: In effect, you are *selecting-in* employees who meet your exacting employment standards and, in addition, helping candidates *select-out* for themselves if they feel this "fit" is missing for them. Part of the interview process should therefore be devoted to letting candidates know the team's expectations and vision for their performance, as well as what they should anticipate—good and bad—in their daily work. Most important, prospective employees need to understand that serving residents is what keeps the company in business. Considered in this way, the interview process is a *training opportunity* that should not be missed.

Now, assume that you have completed the interviews, and that several of your employees have been involved in the screening effort. How should you proceed? One way is to ask the participants the "feel good" questions:

How did you feel when you were talking with this person?

After you filter-out the applicant's natural nervousness in the interview situation, do you feel good about the applicant?

Pre-Employment Psychological Testing

Yet another potentially fruitful employee screening technique, though also a legal minefield, is pre-employment psychological testing. The use of certain types of aptitude, intelligence, and personality tests is designed to assist employers in determining the fit between a candidate's attitudes and personality and an available job. These tests can be used to measure specific personality traits in order to avoid hiring individuals who are likely to commit illegal acts for which an owner or manager may be liable, as well as to help in the determination of an employee's aptitude for assignments requiring certain personality traits.

While the use of these types of tests generally appears to be allowed by the law, there are significant legal risks for the employer who implements such testing indiscriminately as an employment screening device. One potential restriction on the use of psychological testing for this purpose is the Americans with Disabilities Act (ADA). In addition, a case decided by the California First District Court of Appeal in 1991 *(Soroka v. Dayton Hudson Corporation)*, has sharply limited the use of pre-employment psychological testing in California. The ADA and *Soroka* may be construed in the future to preclude employers from asking questions in pre-employment psychological tests which probe into areas now covered by civil rights laws. Nonetheless, it appears that current law in most states allows an employer to use a standardized psychological test so long as it has been screened by an expert in the field to remove questions that carry a potential of revealing the prospective employee's religion, gender preference, mental disability, or other factors identifiable as relating to classes protected by federal or state civil rights law.

NOTE: It is imperative for the employer who wishes to utilize psychological techniques for screening prospective or current employees to *seek advice of legal counsel before proceeding, minimally to avoid claims of discriminatory practices.*

Do you think this person will help or hurt the performance of your team? Is this a person who will fit in?

Scott Gross has recommended:

▶ Spend a few minutes in casual conversation. If you wind up feeling good (and you don't have to quantify this scientifically), chances are you've got a winner on your hands. It shouldn't take you long to decide. In fact, if after more than a minute or two you don't have a strong, positive intuitive message, call in the next applicant. *After all, most service jobs—and nearly every job is a service job—rely heavily on first impressions.*

Intuition-Based Selection.   Although you will need to evaluate candidates based on objective criteria that can be documented, the use of intuition to *assist* in making a hiring decision seems entirely appropriate. Assessing a candidate's communication skills, friendliness, compatibility, and service orientation, among other qualities, is inherently subjective. Part of what you will be looking for in the new hire is itself intuitive and instinctive—how well will the candidate respond under pressure when there are no guidelines and no supervisors around to help? Consider this example:

> Halloween 1992, more than three feet of snow fell in the Twin Cities area—the earliest and heaviest snowfall in history. Apartment managers and owners, unprepared for a storm of such magnitude, scrambled to find individuals and companies who could plow-out their sites. At one sprawling suburban townhouse property, however, the best efforts of the owner couldn't accomplish snow removal. Several days dragged by. Residents attempted to dig their cars out of the parking lots, producing banged fenders and fiery tempers, the latter vented upon the innocent staff, one of whom was an unfortunate part-time leasing agent named Sharon. Bombarded by angry residents, yet unable on her own to get the plowing done, Sharon decided to try to make amends. Donning boots, goose-down coat, and mittens, she slogged off for downtown. Nearly an hour later, she entered a flower shop and purchased every single red rose in its stock. Sharon returned to her property and delivered one rose to each apartment, apologizing to the residents for their inconvenience. The response was instantaneous: Their venom immediately disappeared, and the irate telephone calls evaporated.

We include this story of "The Rose in the Snow" to illustrate an important point: The hiring process should be designed so that the participants in the job interview can evaluate candidates' ability to be resourceful, to "think on their feet." Intuition is a trait that is, unfortunately, in short supply—in apartment management as it is in other types of business. When we hire on the basis of technical skills alone, we risk screening-out people like Sharon, and that is a mistake. (Some other, similar, stories will be included in chapter 9.) Shannon Johnston of Kaset, Inc., a customer consulting company in Tampa, Florida, said the same thing:

> ▶   [There] are two parts to every customer interaction—the business side and the human side. Both are there, and they exert themselves more or less at the same time. Most people want to—at least try to—ignore the human side. My rule of thumb is that if you teach people to handle the human side first, the business side goes much quicker.

One way to ascertain a candidate's potential resourcefulness is to ask, "What would you change—what innovations would you implement—in your current job to become more people-responsive?"

Company Acculturation and Skills Training

A major part of the training task is successfully completed when the recruiting and hiring processes have been handled competently. We believe that service winners need less training, at least at the outset of their employment, than do nonservice winners who may have abundant technical skills but lack a service orientation. Davidow and Uttal drew the distinction between these abilities as follows:

▶ Service leaders seem to have found a working balance between technical training, which covers the details of performing a job correctly, and social training, which focuses on the interpersonal values, attitudes, and techniques needed to render good service. And they understand that customer service training fails unless it includes lessons in how to treat internal customers, the people inside the company whose ability to serve outside customers depends on their getting service from colleagues.

The goal of the hiring process, then, is to employ people who will bring to the job those interpersonal traits that the organization believes to be essential. Social skills are therefore a hiring issue rather than a subject for training. We believe that training programs designed to improve employees' attitudes—whether the employees are new hires or already in place—are inappropriate and ineffective. Moreover, they indicate a sense of desperation that the company's own employees are quick to detect. People do not respond to lectures that teach such platitudes as "the customer is always right." Indeed, although the bulk of in-service instruction is devoted either to improving skills or improving attitudes, most of the latter is really so-called smile training. Karl Albrecht, who coined the phrase "smile training," characterized it this way:

▶ Smile training is another popular fix with executives who want to do something quick and noticeable [to improve employee performance]. I use the term *smile training* to denote the style and intent of such training, not to disparage the general idea of training frontline people in service skills. Effective training almost always has a useful place in a major service initiative, but the key word is *effective*.

In effect, frontline employees *are* the company. Meaningful investments in their learning and development are really product development. Attention to employees' information needs, therefore, assures that the company is marketing the best product it is capable of producing. Smile training, by contrast, is condescending—it insults employees' intelligence by implying that smiles (or other "cosmetic" approaches) are an acceptable substitute for sincere attention and caring.

Having distinguished social instruction and so-called smile training from skills education, we turn to what we believe is an appropriate curriculum for new hires in apartment management positions. First, new employees need to know how they fit with the organization. They also need to understand the company's goals, strategies, objectives, and philosophy—the corporate vision. We call this phase of learning "acculturation." Jeffrey Disend described it this way:

▶ The first phase [of employee training] is a general orientation to the organization. This orientation covers who you are and what you do; your history, traditions, and values; how you're organized and where you're located; who your customers are; how you do business; your goals and mission; your products and services; and your industry and your competition.

In addition, the new employee needs basic administrative facts about the new company that will allow him or her to function properly—work schedules, pay dates, insurance information, etc.

We mentioned so-called smile training earlier and cautioned against its use, mostly because it is trivial: It frequently degenerates into attempts to teach employees literally how to smile at customers. The goal of such training—helping frontline employees deal effectively with customers—is not objectionable. The problem is that the methodology is too demeaning to accomplish the purpose. What is really needed is an ability to solve problems and delight the customer with the process.

On the other hand, no matter how personable new employees are, we believe that some instruction in how to achieve good resident relations is imperative, even if it is refresher work and even though the content may be "soft." In this phase of employee indoctrination, the new hire not only learns the skills that will facilitate productive resident relations, but also—and perhaps more important—discovers that the company places a premium on positive dealings with its clients. Here are some subjects we recommend be included:

- Telephone techniques

- Listening and responsive communications skills

- Handling upset residents

- Ways to establish credibility and trust in interactions

- Determining resident expectations

Notice that nowhere in this curriculum for the first stage of employee training is job-specific instruction mentioned. We believe that skills training should be reserved for a later phase. At the beginning, the organization needs to concentrate on impressing upon the new hire the fundamental importance of the customer to the business. According to Donald Libey:

► [The new employee needs to learn] the company's culture about customers and the importance of thinking of them as the [company's] primary asset. . . . Your objective for this portion of the training process should be the creation of a fully furnished customer advocate and customer ambassador for your company.

Libey admonishes companies to:

► Begin looking at your training program from The Customer's point of view. Focus all of your training from the outside in, not from the inside out. And, most important, make sure that the people who are responsible for training at your company are the people who have spent the most time in direct customer contact.

The next phase of new-hire training orients the employee to a specific work unit, which is the site of the property or the management company's central office. This instruction includes how communications flow within the unit and between the unit and the central office or site, how problems are resolved, how decisions are made, what behavior is rewarded and what behavior is punished.

Finally, in the last phase of employee training, job-specific instruction is highlighted. The new employee receives instruction in his or her position, including a review of job descriptions, standards, and responsibilities. The employee is taught how the job meshes with the mission of the organization, why it is important, and how its outputs (and errors) affect others. It is only during this phase that specific job skill training begins.

Empowering Your Company's "Quality Strategists" to Let the Resident Win

Quality hiring and training is designed to prepare new employees to represent you to the market, in effect to *be* your company for your residents. You want new employees to be effective in their work, but what does it mean to "be effective?" We believe that, for the firms of the future, employees' effectiveness will increasingly be measured by whether they serve as "quality strategists" for the companies that hire them. All of the hands-on attention during the hiring and training process—as we described it here—creates employees who are *empowered* to devise ways of delighting your internal and external clients, to take risks on behalf of your customers—the residents of your properties. In short, the future rallying cry in apartment management will be, "Let the Resident Win!"

"Let the Resident Win!" is the contemporary version of "user-friendly," a term that was used extensively to gauge the ease of using computers and other consumer products. (The discipline of *ergonomics* was an outgrowth of that concept; we will discuss "customer ergonomics" in chapter 9.) What we are talking about is devising strategies to make apartment management companies and apartment properties user-friendly. One such strategy is to empower frontline personnel to act independently as all-around, autonomous, customer-pleasing company ambassadors.

Empowering Employees to Be "Boss Surrogates." What does it mean to say that an employee is "empowered?" Why should you go through an exhaustive recruiting and training process for the purpose of producing "empowered" employees? Employees are "empowered" when they are boss-surrogates—people who act as though they own the business—they take responsibility; they have the authority to make on-the-spot decisions. The empowerment process visibly removes any shackles, real or imagined, that an employee might have felt impeded the fulfillment of a customer's needs or wishes. Zeithaml and co-workers described the hiring-training-empowerment loop this way:

> ▶   Managers have to give back to service providers the freedom to serve that they have unnecessarily and unproductively taken away from them. Managers have to select their people well, provide them with a strong foundational culture in which to work, offer them strategic direction, and equip them with the company-specific skills and knowledge they need to perform their roles. *And then the managers need to get out of the way, so the people can get the job done*. Managers cannot make the transition to leadership as long as employees are so bundled in red tape that they cannot follow the lead.

According to Disend, the message from managers to employees who have been empowered is essentially this:

> ▶   You can only control what *you* do, so you must act at all times as if you are the *only one* in the organization who can help customers. In everything you do, especially when dealing with customers, assume that no one else in the organization is available at that moment to help the customer. You have to do what is right for the customer and what is best for the company. You're *it*. It's your responsibility.

Empowering Employees to Deliver Matchless "Moments of Truth." Companies empower employees for several reasons. The main reason is that *empowerment is unavoidable:* The owner cannot be everywhere at once. In the apartment management business, it is physically impossible for an owner—or a management company, for that matter—to be present simultaneously at all of the points of contact between the resident, the property, and the staff. There may be a housekeeper busily vacuuming hallways and chatting with residents' children about an upcoming Little League championship, while other staff members are helping an elderly resident carry groceries in from her daughter's car, talking with a resident on the telephone to reserve the party room, showing the common areas of the property to a prospect, installing a set of draperies at a resident's direction. All of this, in a thousand variations and permutations, is part of the everyday, day-after-day business of apartment management and maintenance. The common characteristics of this work are that it is conducted simultaneously, it requires resident contact, and, while it can be supervised, all of it cannot be supervised on-the-spot by a single person.

Jan Carlzon recognized the challenges and importance of these customer-contact interludes. In his opinion, moments of truth determine whether a company will succeed or fail. Moments of truth between employees and customers are the line of scrimmage for amusement parks as well as airlines—and apartment buildings. Rick Johnson, manager of business seminars for Walt Disney World, believes that every aspect of an organization is on the line whenever frontline people deal with customers. However, it was Carlzon who proposed the solution to the puzzle of how to ensure that SAS' "moments of truth" could be instilled with quality, even though he could not be physically present at each point of delivery. His approach? Place responsibility for ideas, decisions, and actions with the frontline employees.

"Zapping" Your Employees. Jan Carlzon's legacy to business management is enormous. The core of it, in addition to the "moments of truth" nomenclature already noted, is that the inspiration for empowering employees—which, as we have noted, is inescapable—lies in the leadership of the company, specifically leadership that is ready to embrace change and take risks. As Carlzon described the situation:

▶   The top executive . . . must communicate with his employees, imparting the company's vision and listening to what they need to make that vision a reality.

Empowerment, then, is born of necessity and imparted by visionaries. Yet, while delegation of authority is fated, it is also desirable. The second reason for empowering employees is that their job satisfaction and productivity soar, and the company reaps the benefits, not just in improved employee morale and performance, but in reduced resident defections caused by poor service and mechanical reliance on rule books and company policy for decisions.

One of the most popular, albeit improbable, nonfiction best-sellers in recent years is a slim paperback book titled, *Zapp! The Lightning of Empow-*

erment: How to Improve Quality, Productivity, and Employee Satisfaction. Written in the form of a fable, *Zapp!* recounts the adventures of one Joe Mode, a supervisor in a fictional business whose department is being beset by escalating demands on the part of his boss, his owners, and his customers, while the company itself is trying to fend off increasingly effective competition. The solution to all of these problems—not surprisingly, in light of the book's title—is employee empowerment, the state of being *Zapped.*

Prior to initiating the empowerment effort, Joe Mode's company has experimented with pep talks, quality circles, higher pay, participative management, job enrichment, quality of work life, work teams, suggestion systems, and a host of other approaches, all to little effect. Joe listed what was wrong with his company as follows:

▶ • Hardly anybody gets excited about anything that has to do with work.

  • The things [employees] do get excited about are outside of work.

  • My people care about their paychecks, their vacations, and their pensions. Beyond that, forget it.

  • The general attitude is: Don't do anything you don't have to do. Then do as little as possible.

  • All day, it's like everybody is in slow motion—until it's time to go home. Then it's like watching a videotape in fast forward.

  • I talk about doing a better job and what happens? Lots of blank looks.

  • Nobody takes any more responsibility than they have to. If the jobs don't get done, it's my problem, not theirs.

  • Everybody just does enough to get by so they won't get yelled at or get fired.

  • Nobody cares about improvements; they're all afraid of change. (Me, too, if I'm honest about it.)

  • I say, "If you don't shape up you won't have jobs." But all that does is demoralize them, which makes it worse.

  • Whenever I try to motivate people, the results (if any) are short-lived.

We have described Joe Mode's predicament in such detail not only because it typifies the state of much of apartment management—and American business generally—but also because the post-empowerment situation is such an improvement.

Job Satisfaction and Reducing Employee—and Resident—Churn.

The satisfaction of frontline employees is at least as important in the apartment business as in traditional retailing. We believe that "burnout"—the state of emotional fatigue caused by repetitive job tasks and incessant customer contact—leads to dissatisfaction and resignations and is a direct cause of employee (internal customer) "churn."

The latter component of burnout—what psychologists have identified as the "contact-overload syndrome" and what service commentators describe as "emotional labor"—can contaminate the quality of the moments of truth that employees have with residents. Employees who are angry, apathetic, or withdrawn transfer these feelings to residents and create a negative impression of themselves, their apartment product, and their companies—a direct and avoidable cause of resident (external customer) "churn."

Dealing with "Contact Overload."   What are the antidotes, if any, to contact overload? We believe there are several. One, of course, is initial instruction in such "soft" subjects as listening (skill development), telephone techniques, handling upset customers, and the like. Zeithaml et al. described the significance of this component of training this way:

▶   Companies can engender confidence in employees by training them in the skills needed to satisfy customers. Training that relates to the specific services offered by the firm helps the contact person be and feel capable when dealing with customers. Training in communication skills, especially in listening to customers and understanding what customers expect, gives employees a sense of mastery over the inevitable problems that arise in service encounters.

Another technique, which we discussed in Chapter 2, is to ensure that frontline employees have the resources of the company, whether financial, personnel or administrative, available when needed. We might describe these as internal employee support systems. As Jeffrey Disend has characterized the situation, when frontline people know they have support within the organization, they can act with confidence and will be less stressed. Clearly, the essential vaccine against contact overload is employee empowerment. According to Disend:

▶   Employees are superstars whose talent is waiting to be unleashed. They can do anything and everything—set standards, check quality, manage budgets, train. Employees can be trusted if they feel important and responsible. The people closest to the customer—the front line—can and should have the freedom to make decisions on the spot about how to satisfy customers. Their decisions are supported by management. Rules and practices that demean people or hinder their ability to serve the customer are eliminated.

Employee Empowerment in the Apartment Business.   How do apartment managers go about the process of empowering their employees? One starting point is to consider techniques for empowering both "internal"

"Firing" Customers: The Pareto Principle

An early twentieth-century Italian economist, one Vilfredo Pareto, formulated what is known as the "80–20 rule" or the "law of maldistribution." The Pareto Principle hypothesizes that as much as 80 percent of the effort expended in a process is caused by as little as 20 percent of the input. Pareto's insight has led others to extrapolate from the principle, concluding, for instance, that 80 percent of a result—a firm's sales, for example—are produced by 20 percent of another driving force—in this situation, a particular segment of the company's products.

The Pareto Principle has significant potential for American businesses in general. An analyst might observe that a particular one-fifth of a firm's goods draws four-fifths of company resources, and this knowledge leads the business to revamp its product line. Marketing personnel might note that approximately 80 percent of purchases in any one year are made by fewer than 20 percent of customers. As a consequence, they could recommend that the bulk of the firm's customer relations campaign be redirected to those few clients who are vital to success, with less attention paid to their many other clients, each of whom has only a modest impact on the company's profitability.

This principle clearly has less significance for the rental housing business than it does for other industries. The provisions contained in federal and state laws and municipal ordinances aimed at ensuring even-handed treatment in rental housing and related matters rightly discourage landlords from selecting residents for preferential treatment or treating residents differentially based on perceptions of their economic value to the property owner.

Nonetheless, we believe that a slightly modified Pareto Principle has an important application in the apartment industry. Stated succinctly, we believe that a very few residents—probably no more than 3 percent—consume perhaps as much as 95 percent of the "emotional labor" that an apartment community has available. By emotional labor, we mean the effort expended by front-line personnel to meet the service expectations of residents. Because this work has a significant emotional—as well as physical—component, those who perform it are subject to a substantial amount of stress. Berry and Parasuraman described the problem this way:

▶ The morale, job satisfaction, and job commitment of front-line service employees are inversely related to the frustration levels of customers they deal with day after day. Interacting with frustrated customers demanding explanations and restitution for defective services can demoralize employees, deflate their enthusiasm for their jobs, and decrease their commitment to their companies.

Psychologists have characterized this reaction as the "contact-overload syndrome"—akin to job "burnout"—which, in turn, is

---

"Firing" Customers (*continued*)

responsible for so much obnoxious behavior that frontline personnel display to their customers. As Karl Albrecht put it:

▶ The person we're tempted to describe as lazy, indifferent, uncaring, and not qualified for a service job may actually be in the advanced stages of burnout because of contact overload. In other words, a great deal of negative behavior on the part of frontline service people is *normal behavior.* That doesn't mean we have to approve of it or consider it acceptable, but it does mean we need to understand it and deal with it in human and humane terms.

Company management's ability to recognize this syndrome, together with its willingness to take effective action to remedy the problem, demonstrates the firm's support for its own internal customers. In their book, Berry and Parasuraman observed that:

▶ Companies should make a concerted effort to explore ways for assisting their service-recovery staff to relieve tension. Courses on coping with stress, group meeting with peers to discuss job-related pressures, and facilities for physical exercise are some of the possibilities. Providing customer service personnel with a pleasant and soothing work environment also will be helpful.

We believe that frontline apartment management personnel are especially prone to contact overload. Their business day, unlike those of retailers and other service providers, does not end at 5:00 P.M. indeed, the business "day" may be only *starting* for the site staff *precisely because* it is the end of the workday for others. Contacts with residents are potentially infinite in number and indefinite in duration.

Because contact overload is commonplace in the apartment business, and because we agree with Albrecht that it is appropriate for owners and managers to take action to reduce its impact on their personnel, we recommend that an owner or property manager consider "firing" those few residents whose demands are so overwhelming as to cause burnout among members of the site staff. "Firing" in this instance, of course, involves notifying the resident of the decision not to renew his or her lease, in accordance with the notice provisions of the lease document (and applicable law).

This is a risky concept, yet one that, in our opinion, deserves consideration. We have found that some apartment residents are so demanding that they make it exceedingly difficult for apartment managers not only to satisfy their needs, but also to provide an acceptable level of service to other residents. In effect, the toxins that are accumulated when servers try unsuccessfully to meet the exorbitant requirements of a handful of demanding residents spill over and contaminate dealings with the vast majority of reasonable ones. This is, perhaps, the clearest application of the Pareto Principle in the apartment business.

"Firing" Customers (*concluded*)

Most often, some few residents have expectations that are impossible in a practical sense to satisfy. Here are some examples from our experience.

A resident who telephoned the site manager at 2:30 A.M., demanding that he rush to her apartment to change the light bulb above her electric range.

A resident who approached a maintenance worker who was working on an emergency involving the fire alarm system, insisting that he install her living room drapes immediately.

A resident who, without notice, demanded that the site manager reschedule her appointments to provide him with transportation to the airport.

Each of these situations was merely the culminating event in a sequence of similar episodes. They were typified by the resident-imposed requirement of immediacy, false emergencies occurring either at the end of the day or at a time when the employee's other duties justifiably deserved priority. They caused an inordinate amount of stress. As Albrecht noted:

▶ A person can handle just so many of these miniature emotional events in a given period before he or she begins to feel tense, overloaded, tired, and jaded. . . . [The contact-overload syndrome] is unhealthy for the person having it. It can induce psychological stress that can carry over into his or her personal life as well as make work life unpleasant and unrewarding.

"Firing" residents is a last resort. It should never be employed as an excuse for poor performance by the staff; it ought to be undertaken only when other, less extreme measures (such as telephone calls and meetings with the property manager) have failed to produce results. The fact is, certain apartment residents have requirements that are so outlandish and unreasonable that reasonable people, even people accustomed to working in labor-intensive, high-stress environments, cannot satisfy them. In these circumstances, we believe that owners and property managers should consider the needs of their other customers—internal and external—and discontinue those unfortunate business relationships that are continually problematic.

NOTE: The decision to "fire" a resident should not be taken lightly. Although we know of no legal requirement to state a reason for not renewing a lease when the current term expires, advice of legal counsel should be sought if your intended actions could be interpreted as discriminatory or an infringement of a resident's rights under landlord-tenant law.

customers and "external" customers simultaneously. As we noted earlier in this chapter, "Let the Resident Win!" will increasingly be the motto of the apartment management firms of the future. One purpose of empowerment, therefore, should be to enable your internal customers to use their imaginations to solve the problems brought to them by your external customers. Here's an example: One constant in the business of apartment management is that coin-operated washers and dryers and vending machines are subject to breakdowns. Apartment managers learn about the failures of these machines only when residents, sometimes quite forcefully, let them know about problems. We'll return to the subject of *planning* for the inevitable equipment breakdown in Chapter 6. (Service "recovery" is a way of providing structure to employee empowerment.) For now, we will consider some alternatives that are available to the manager confronted by a frustrated resident who has fed a fistful of coins into the third-floor soft drink machine without success. Consider these responses:

> "I'm sorry. I know how you feel, but I'm afraid I can't help you. We've been having a lot of problems with that machine. You see, it's serviced by a vending company. It's their company policy to have you fill out this claim form and they'll reimburse you directly."

> "I'm really sorry; I hate it when that happens to me. And it always seems to happen on those really hot days, when you could really use a cold drink, doesn't it? Let me try to make it up to you: take these two dollars. You look pretty warm; would you like to sit down for a few minutes and cool off while I call the vending company? I need to get this problem taken care of right away."

> "I feel really badly that you lost your money; I'll give the vending company a call immediately. But what can I do to make up for your inconvenience?"

All of these vignettes indicated that the manager was sincerely apologetic about the resident's frustration; each wanted to do something to compensate for it. In the first instance, "company policy" prevented the manager from providing immediate satisfaction; and the "solution" that was offered instead—completing a claim form and trusting the vending company to provide compensation—would undoubtedly be unsatisfactory to the resident, escalating his or her dissatisfaction and possibly resulting in a truly unpleasant experience for both the resident and the manager. This would constitute both a negative "moment of truth" for the resident and an instance of "contact overload" for the manager. Both could easily have been circumvented by empowering the manager to act independently of the rulebook.

The second situation illustrates a manager who has the freedom to settle the problem on the spot. The disparity between the amount of the loss and the amount offered—probably at least a dollar—is an effort to account for the so-called "hassle factor" that the resident has experienced.

In the third situation, the manager is not only empowered to solve the problem immediately, but also to *involve the resident in the solution.* Hervey Feldman, president of Embassy Suites hotels, prefers resolutions of customer problems that involve the guests themselves:

▶   We let customers adjust their own grievances. We ask for their opinion of what it will take to make things right, and if they can't think of anything, we often refund the room charge. . . . Employees and hotel managers learn about the adjustments we've made after the fact, and that may irritate them, but I really don't care about who's right. The customer is *always* right. Explanations, excuses, and alibis don't cut it.

In their book, *Service Breakthroughs: Changing the Rules of the Game,* Professors James L. Heskett, W. Earl Sasser, Jr., and Christopher W. L. Hart reported the following from their own studies:

▶   More than half of all efforts to respond to customer complaints actually reinforce negative reactions to service. The surest way to recover from service mishaps is for workers on the front line to identify and solve the customer's problem. Doing so requires decision making and rule breaking—exactly what employees have been conditioned against. . . . Even if they'd like to help the customer, they are frustrated by the fact that they are not allowed to do it.

Most often, the company is the source of this frustration. Karl Albrecht said as much:

▶   Employees, for the most part, want to a do a good job; they want to give good service to their customers. If they're not doing it, more than likely something is standing in their way, and more than likely it's the organization. It's up to management to create the conditions that make service excellence possible and worthwhile. Employees will come through.

The Illusory Risk of Oversatisfying Customers.   The notion that employees should be empowered to use their imaginations rather than company guidelines to solve customers' problems, to make instantaneous decisions at the front lines without the benefit of supervision, is unsettling to some. One concern is that employees will go overboard on behalf of customers. However, Jan Carlzon has provided a common-sense answer to this:

▶   What's the danger of [employees'] giving away too much? Are you worried about having an oversatisfied customer? That's not much of a worry. You can forget about an oversatisfied customer, but an unsatisfied customer is one of the most expensive problems you can have. [The] danger is not that employees will give away too much. It's that they won't give away anything—because they don't dare.

Colorful Rules and Regulations.   Empowering employees to satisfy customers requires a company to be a "learning organization" in order to adjust to changing circumstances. Michael Beer, Russell Eisenstat, and Bert Spector, a group of organizational behavior and management professors, put it this way:

▶   Create an asset that did not exist before—a learning organization capable of adapting to a changing competitive environment. The organization has to know how to continually monitor its behavior—in effect, to learn how to learn.

This means the firms of the future will have to "get out of the way" and allow customers—both internal and external—to work cooperatively to resolve problems. These companies will have to strive as well to liberate their customers from unnecessary regimentation. Here's an example: Apartment leases, in addition to listing the names of the landlord and the tenant(s) and specifying the lease terms, typically contain a swarm of rules and regulations which are supposedly designed to protect the property and other residents from inappropriate conduct. For instance, the lease that is in force in our company includes these provisions:

> RENTAL APPLICATION. Owner has entered into this lease based on Tenant's written statements in the rental application. If Owner's Agent determines that Tenant has made any false statements in the rental application, this lease may be terminated immediately by Owner. Tenant may be evicted without prior notice and will be responsible for any damages and may lose all or part of the security deposit.

> DUTIES AND LIABILITIES OF TENANT. DISTURBANCES. Tenant's conduct and the conduct of Tenant's children or Tenant's guests shall not disturb or cause injury to other tenants or damage the reputation of the Owner or Owner's Agent.

> RE-RENT AND SUBLETTING. Tenant shall not re-rent, sublet or otherwise assign the apartment or garage, unless Owner signs a re-rent agreement. If Tenant requests Owner to prepare a re-rent agreement, it shall be according to such terms as Owner determines.

These types of lease clauses are fairly typical in the apartment business. The first is designed to allow the landlord to evict the tenant if the landlord discovers material misrepresentations in the prospect's rental application that would have led the landlord to decide not to enter into the lease. The second is meant to protect residents from aggravation caused by others. The last restricts a tenant's ability to sublet the apartment and thereby leave the owner with a potentially unsavory successor.

Just how likely is it that apartment managers will encounter instances of wrongdoing that these provisions are designed to prevent? Probably not very: In most situations, the incidence of falsifying applications, damage to the reputation of the Owner's Agent caused by tenant disturbances, and flagrant subletting is low, perhaps less than five percent overall. In effect, by promulgating and enforcing these lease clauses, apartment managers are treating the overwhelming majority of quality residents like potential offenders in order to catch the very small number who really *are* offenders. Worse, the impression conveyed to your customers by including this sort of language in your leases is unnecessarily harsh. In effect, you are telling your residents at the outset of your business relationship that you predict they will misbehave. You are letting them know beforehand that the punishment for doing so will be swift, sure, and painful. In our opinion, most residential leases are akin to antenuptial agreements—and just as offensive.

In fact, service commentators condemn this practice. For example, Peter Glen is striving to create a generation of service "guerrillas" who will demand to be served in accordance with their own unique preferences. (His motto is: Tell 'em what you want, and how you want it, and make 'em do it, just that way!) As he put it:

▶ Doesn't it lift your heart when you show up at the front door of the store and signs greet you saying, NO FOOD, NO DRINKS, NO TANK TOPS, NO EXCHANGES, NO RETURNS, NO STROLLERS, NO BARE FEET, NO SMOKING or NO SHIRT, NO SHOES, NO SERVICE? *Welcome to the store!*

Also according to Glen, "Bad signs are any signs that depress the customer. Bad signs are bad service."

Everyone would agree that some rules and regulations are essential tools for apartment managers. The rent-payment requirement, for example, is absolutely necessary—if apartment managers fail to enforce it, the property will be bankrupted. There are some other "requirements" as well.

* Rules preventing the storage of flammable materials in apartment buildings are necessary to ensure residents' safety.

* Regulations that deter residents from installing their own locks are indispensable because law enforcement and emergency services personnel may need access to their apartments.

* Restrictions on the use of barbecue grills on balconies and patios may be dictated by city fire-prevention ordinances.

These examples are representative of the handful of rules and regulations that are in place to prevent injury or damage to persons or property—most of them are prescribed by local fire codes or other laws. Such rules cannot be broken, and apartment managers would be considered negligent if they failed to enforce them. These types of rules might be referred to as "red" rules. Conversely, there are other rules that exist for the convenience of the landlord, the site employees, or the management company; these can be called "blue" rules. The following, another lease provision, is an example.

> PETS. Pets are not permitted UNLESS prior written authorization is received from the management office. Deposits are required with every pet. Violation will result in loss of damage deposit or eviction of owner and/or pet or both. Maximum number of pets per apartment is one dog OR two cats. All cats must be declawed on the front paws and spayed or neutered. All dogs must be under 10 pounds, spayed or neutered, and over one year of age. Puppies are not allowed. Veterinary papers verifying the above information are required to be included in the lease file. Violations of the above result in fines to the Tenant. The first fine is twenty-five dollars ($25.00), and the second fine is fifty dollars ($50.00). A third violation results in a seventy-five dollar ($75.00) fine and eviction of the pet. Any eviction of a pet does NOT release the Tenant from any of the terms of the lease.

While this provision is fairly punitive and certainly disagreeable, landlords include it in leases because it represents a desirable means of regulating pets living at an apartment property. From prospective residents' viewpoint, however, this proviso would seem to be designed to make pet ownership burdensome. To paraphrase Peter Glen, in this instance "bad lease clauses are bad service."

The question for the apartment manager is identical to the one to be considered by the retailer: Which rules are clearly "red" ones, and which are "blue?" Then, are the blue rules really necessary, or do they exist "because we've always done it this way?" Alternatively, can the same goals be achieved in ways that are more customer-friendly?

We recommend that you keep in mind certain complementary guidelines propounded by the service gurus as you cull the red rules from the blue and decide whether to keep the blue ones in place. Anderson and Zemke have cautioned against thoughtlessly discarding rules:

▶ Without formal and informal rules, service would become chaotic— and customers would never know what to expect. Just because you think that breaking or bending a rule won't cause the ceiling to fall down doesn't mean you should take it lightly. Know the nature of the rule in question, the reason for the rule, the consequences of not following it, then help your customer make the system work.

On the other hand, A. S. Neill has recommended activism in making these decisions:

▶ Think of your role as that of a release valve, not that of a restraining force. We need more green flags and less yellow; more rivers and less dams.

The goal of apartment managers, then, should not be to discard the rulebook or eliminate all policies and procedures but, rather, to thin the rulebook to its bare essentials in order to eliminate as much as possible the barriers between themselves and their customers. (This includes working with legal counsel to develop a more user-friendly, customer service-oriented—yet legally enforceable—lease.) *Empowering your people makes the necessary rules work for a company's external customers as well as its internal ones.*

4

The Retention Revolution

Customer Type	Marketing Effort	Value to Marketers	Cost of Programs
New customers (acquisition programs)	High	Low	High
Current customers (retention programs)	Moderate	High	Moderate
Current customers (expansion programs)	Low	Moderate	Low

—KEVIN J. CLANCY and ROBERT S. SHULMAN

Clancy and Shulman are former principals of Yankelovich Clancy Shulman, an international marketing research and consulting firm. They call these marketing alternatives the "Death Wish Paradox." It illustrates the point that the relentless pursuit of new customers is the most expensive and labor-intensive, yet least cost-effective, strategy a company can pursue. Conversely, the practice of marketing to a company's current customers, either in an effort to retain them or to induce them to expand the business they are currently doing, results in the greatest yield.

The Fallacy of Conquest Marketing

"Conquest" or "acquisition" marketing has been and continues to be a centerpiece of American business. Expansion of a company's client base by luring first-time customers or a competitor's clientele is both a staple of retailing and the overriding goal of traditional advertising and marketing. Consider these facts:

- During the period 1960 to 1990, U.S. advertising expenditures increased more than tenfold, from slightly less than $12 billion annually to nearly $130 billion.

- Between 1965 and 1991, the cost of a 30-second television spot rose from $19,700 to $106,000.

- In 1989, the top 100 advertisers spent a combined $34 billion on advertising—an average of $340 million each.

- From 1984 to 1991, the number of television advertising vehicles increased to an annual volume of more than 300,000 commercials.

There has been an explosion in the number and types of advertising media. During the last decade or so, consumers have witnessed the debut of cable TV and the proprietary television program (the "infomercial"); videocassette sponsorships; specialized television networks in schools, airports, restaurants, supermarkets and the like; sponsored sporting events and even sports arenas; as well as targeted direct mail, outward and inward telemarketing, and a swarm of others.

The temptations of this cornucopia of seductive media are almost irresistible, and no less so for the apartment marketer than for the retailer. Their applications for the multifamily environment are apparent and alluring; apartment marketers are constrained only by their budgets and their imaginations—and, hopefully, common sense.

The apartment environment—its ethos, its very *culture*—validates conquest marketing and all it entails. Advertising is one of the few discretionary expenditures that even the spendthrift owner or manager strives to protect or perhaps augment. When occupancies lag, apartment managers are pressured to root out new residents and to free up whatever funds are deemed necessary to launch new advertising adventures to entice them. Bonus structures and commission schedules are crafted specifically and exclusively to reward leasing velocity. Disagreements, disputes, and confrontations among leasing personnel over entitlements to bonuses are commonplace, and reporting formats that display "kill" ratios—conversion rates of advertising dollars to site visits and signed leases—distract attention from other, more valid, gauges of a property's success. Especially disturbing is the tendency to offer the best deals in their marketing arsenals to prospects: Newcomers get the benefit of a totally refurbished apartment—with new or freshly cleaned carpeting, just-painted walls and ceilings, sparkling appliances—while current residents are expected to pay top rates and swallow hefty annual rent increases in exchange for a touch-up paint job and perhaps a bit of carpet cleaning in the areas of heaviest traffic. Indeed, the main business—even the *exclusive* business—of the apartment business is to snare new customers. Clancy and Shulman put it this way:

▶ Surprisingly, there seems to be a sense in marketing that finding and closing new customers (acquisition programs) are more exciting than holding on to current customers (retention programs) or increasing business volume among current customers (expansion programs).

In this chapter, we will examine the conquest marketing mentality—to see how it holds up under scrutiny—and suggest some alternatives that might supplant it. We will begin with a discussion of the Tenant Churn Index shown in exhibit 4.1.

The Costs of Resident "Churn"

One of the principal complaints of property managers, ourselves included, is that there seems to be little opportunity to control—or even influence—the financial performance of the properties in our portfolios. So many of the major expenses—utilities, for instance, as well as property taxes, insurance, and mortgage payments—are for the most part beyond our control, surging upward to engulf whatever modest gains we may have realized by instituting rent increases or reining in maintenance costs or capital expenditures. The business of apartment management in these circumstances is mostly *reactive*—comparing the performances of our buildings to budgetary forecasts, responding to resident complaints, repairing outdated capital equipment. As we noted in chapter 1, the similarities of property management to mere caretaking are especially apparent in the *receivership* business, which has recently constituted a large portion of many managers' portfolios. Property management can be a lifeless business indeed when the imaginations of its practitioners are so confined.

Nonetheless, there are significant opportunities for an apartment manager to be *proactive*. An accurate "Churn Index" quantifies a number of costs whose magnitude you may not be aware of, yet ones that a skillful manager *can* affect. The data needed to construct the Index are easily captured from a monthly financial statement, although individual items may be concealed in various categories. A sound Index will illustrate, first, the cost in dollars of losing a typical resident and, second, a close estimate of the annual cost to the property of all the residents who are "churned" through it.

There are likely to be some surprises in store when your Index is completed. First, you will have a heightened appreciation of the economic value each of your residents adds to the properties you manage. Sharing this information with your site staff may prompt all of you to be more attentive to your residents, more responsive to their concerns, and even more creative in

Exhibit 4.1

The "Tenant Churn Index"

Data Needed for the Calculation:

Average Number of Units Vacated/Year:	_____ A
Average Vacancy Period:	_____ B
Average Monthly Rent:	_____ C

Average Turnover Cost:

Painting	_____
Cleaning	_____
Shampooing	_____
Maintenance	_____
Total	_____ D
Advertising and Marketing	_____ E

Calculation:

Total turnover cost (D)
+ Advertising and marketing cost ÷ Average number of vacancies/year (E ÷ A)
+ Average vacancy period × Average monthly rent (B × C)
= Cost of *one* churned resident
× Average number of vacancies/year (C)
= The cost of *ALL* "churn" to the property

NOTE: This does not account for leasing incentives (e.g., rent concessions), commissions, or administrative costs related to closing a resident's file and opening a new one. Nor does it account for in-unit
utilities (gas, electricity) which are typically the resident's responsibility. Amounts for the various components of the turnover cost will be affected by how these are typically accounted at the property (actual
costs versus weighted averages by unit type; whether labor costs are included or excluded). The figures are annualized, and the vacancy period is a decimal fraction (days vacant ÷ 30 days in a month).

dreaming up imaginative ways to delight them. Second, you will be able to
quantify—and properly categorize—the costs to the property of lost business
with current residents. This latter aspect may persuade you to create an aggressive resident retention program and then allocate to it the financial resources that your analysis has demonstrated it deserves. Exhibit 4.2 is an
example of what we learned from calculating a "Churn Index" as part of a
consulting assignment.

What are the lessons to be learned from this exercise? First of all, we
discovered that what appeared to be a healthy, 81-unit property was, in fact,
losing an exorbitant amount of money due to resident "churn." Despite an
annualized occupancy in excess of 94 percent, with residents paying rents in
amounts consistent with what the market indicated were appropriate, overall
operations that were generally sound, and an active, although inadequately
funded, resident retention program that had been in place for several years,
the property was turning over nearly half of its occupants in a year (34 vacancies ÷ 81 units = 0.42). While the costs attributable to this factor were
readily identifiable, their magnitude had been camouflaged because they

Exhibit 4.2
Example of a Churn Index

Property Name: **Steeplechase**   Date: **December 31, 1993**

Average Number of Units Vacated/Year:		34	A
Average Vacancy Period:		.7 month	B
Average Monthly Rent:		$585	C
Average Turnover Cost:			
Painting	$100		
Cleaning	$20		
Shampooing	$10		
Maintenance	$20		
Total		$150	D
Advertising and Marketing (per year)		$11,000	E

Calculation:

"D"	$150.00	
+ "E" divided by "A"	$323.53	
+ "B" multiplied by "C"	$409.50	
= Cost of *one* "churned" resident	$883.00	
× "A"	× 34	
= Cost of *all* "churn" to the property	$30,023.00	

were spread innocuously among various expense categories. We understand that in some areas of the United States—e.g., the Sunbelt and the West Coast—the churn rate can easily average 70 percent. That same percentage at Steeplechase would have yielded an even more disparate loss of income— 70 percent of 81 units = 57 vacancies; multiplying vacancies by the $883 cost per churned resident would increase the churn index to $50,331.00. (Later in this chapter we will illustrate the magnitude of *potential reduction in cash flow* to Steeplechase from income lost due to resident "churn," as well as *potential costs of negative word of mouth* to the property.)

Second, we learned that, in addition to his or her monthly rent payment, the average resident who was retained as a paying customer—by lease renewal or other means—was worth nearly $900.00 each year to the property. In other words, controlling "churn" at this particular building could produce, on average, the equivalent of an additional one and one-half months' rent for each apartment *not* vacated every year!

Shortly after we shared these results with the property manager for Steeplechase, an angry resident, dissatisfied with the response he had received from the site manager, telephoned to complain about a maintenance problem he had experienced. Here's a summary of the call:

Resident: Last Saturday, during that terrible thunderstorm we had, the roof must have leaked water into my apartment. I was out of town, and when I came back yesterday, my dining room table was ruined. I just bought it six weeks ago; it cost $475. I have the receipt right here. My table is ruined, and I think it's your fault. If you don't buy me a new table, I'm going to move out.

In the pre-Churn Index days, the response would have been roughly as follows:

> *Property Manager:* I'm sorry that happened. You're right: There was some wind and rain damage at Steeplechase, and I understand that some water infiltrated into your unit. But it's not our fault. And anyway, that's what your renters' insurance is supposed to cover. It's too bad we can't help you. I'm sure you understand our situation.

By contrast, armed with the cost data from the Index, the manager might respond in this way:

> *Property Manager:* I'm sorry that happened. We fixed the roof right after it dried out. You're right: It isn't fair that your renter's insurance should have to pay for something that wasn't your fault. The claim would raise your premium, and it might even affect your insurability. I'd appreciate it if you would make a copy of your receipt and send it to me. I'll messenger a check to you for the full amount the same day. How does that sound?

The question might arise whether everybody who makes a claim such as this is entitled to reimbursement. We think it is up to you: If your negligence causes loss, you can pay everyone who is injured—or only a few of them—the choice is yours.

The "Unavoidability" of Resident Churn.   Although there are a number of techniques that may be employed to defuse an angry resident and avert the consequent canceled lease, some would argue that resident "churn" is generally unavoidable: Temptingly low mortgage interest rates and involuntary business transfers, to cite just two examples, provide justification for residents to go elsewhere.

We agree with this, at least to a point. Nonetheless, we have frequently discovered, by means of follow-up telephone calls to former residents of apartment properties we managed, that they had concealed their real motivations for moving out. It is often easier for them to claim that single-family homeownership was the lure when, in fact, the underlying reason for leaving was dissatisfaction with the *quality* of the apartment product they were receiving. This gentle deception is particularly prevalent because most apartment residents prefer to fib about their real reasons for moving rather than risk hurting the manager's feelings by telling the truth.

It is interesting to compare our anecdotal experience with statistics on the reasons why customers stop doing business with retailers. One survey concluded that customers stop buying because:

1% *die*

3% move away

5% form other relationships

9% leave for "competitive" reasons (e.g., price)

14% leave due to dissatisfaction with product [and]

68% leave *because someone—some representative of the seller—was rude, indifferent, or discourteous to them.*

These statistics underscore one striking fact that is fundamental to understanding why some companies—and not others—are successful: Price, whether high, low, or middling, is *not* a pivotal ingredient in most business relationships, although it may have been instrumental in their formation. Instead, the critical factor is the way sellers treat their customers. This *attitudinal* component of commercial affiliations—the seller's friendliness, reliability, and honesty, among a host of companionable traits—drives commercial prosperity. Sellers' attitudes, then, clearly influence customers' assessments of whether they have received *value* from the product they purchased commensurate with the *price* they paid for it. Indeed, when a customer feels that a vendor—or more likely, an agent of the vendor, such as a salesclerk—has been "rude, indifferent, or discourteous" at some point, the buyer feels *poorly served.* Rudeness, indifference, and discourtesy are characteristic of the negative "moments of truth" that poison commercial dealings. In our opinion, attitude is one of the ways that buyers measure the quality of the service they receive, and it is a determinant of the value of the product itself. The same can be said of renters and apartments.

The Costs of Poor Service

Service researchers have discovered additional disturbing data that illustrate the instability of most buyer-seller relationships. Kristin Anderson and Ron Zemke described the phenomenon this way:

▶ As many as *one customer in four* is dissatisfied enough to start doing business with someone else—if he or she can find someone else who promises to do the same thing that you do but in a slightly more satisfying way.

In short, at any point along the consumption continuum, twenty-five percent of any business is undependable.

As if *that* bit of news is not frightening enough, pollsters have discovered that perhaps as few as *four percent* of those disenchanted customers bother

---

Exhibit 4.3

The Costs of Poor Service

Gross potential rent	$	_____	Line A
Total number of residents		_____	Line B
Percentage of dissatisfied residents	×	_____ .25	Line C
Number of dissatisfied residents (C × B)	=	_____	Line D
Percentage of dissatisfied residents apt to switch	×	_____ .70	Line E
Number of dissatisfied residents who are apt to switch	=	_____	Line F
Average annual revenue per resident (A ÷ B)	$	_____	Line G
Annual revenue at risk because of poor service (F × G)	$	_____	Line H

Adapted from *How to Provide Excellent Service in Any Organization: A Blueprint for Making All the Theories Work* by Jeffrey E. Disend (Radnor, Pennsylvania: Chilton Book Company, 1991), p. 74. Copyright 1991 by the author. Used with the permission of the publisher.

NOTE: Percentages are from the TARP report cited in the text (from Disend). This calculation is based on residents rather than apartments because it is individuals who become dissatisfied. The results of the analysis may be understated if the calculation is based on units.

---

to communicate their discontent to their business partners. Instead, most of them—seventy percent is a conservative estimate—simply pack up their checkbooks and credit cards and take their business elsewhere. (Because these dealings are potentially fragile, chapter 5 will address techniques for smoking out customer complaints and converting them into ties that will bind buyers and sellers.)

Calculating the Costs of Poor Service in Apartments. Assuming the same considerations that clinch success in other commercial enterprises operate in the multifamily housing business, the same percentages can be used to calculate an apartment property's lost revenue because of poor service to residents by means of the formula shown in exhibit 4.3. The results of applying this formula to Steeplechase Apartments are shown in exhibit 4.4.

You may recall from the Churn Index calculated in exhibit 4.2 that Steeplechase had lost approximately $30,000 during the previous year on account of resident "churn." Compare that to the calculation in exhibit 4.4, which illustrates the *potential* financial detriment to the owners of Steeplechase because of poor customer service. In this instance, nearly twenty percent of the property's gross potential rental income—nearly *three and one-half times* the actual dollar amount lost—is *at risk* if an effective resident retention program is not in place at Steeplechase. Equally important, these figures demonstrate the disastrous impact that a mistaken hiring decision—particularly one at the front line—can have on a property's bottom line. In a six-month period, for example, a surly resident manager at Steeplechase could cost the property $50,000 or more.

Exhibit 4.4
Example of The Costs of Poor Service

Property Name: **Steeplechase**

Gross Potential Rent	$593,620.00
Total number of residents	149
Percentage of dissatisfied residents	.25
Number of dissatisfied residents	37
Percentage of dissatisfied residents apt to switch	.70
Number of dissatisfied residents who are apt to switch	26
Average annual revenue per resident	$3,984.03
Annual revenue at risk because of poor service	$103,585.00

NOTE: This same calculation based on units (an assumption of single occupancy), would yield ±20 units with dissatisfied occupants, 14 of which would be vacated. The average annual revenue *per unit* would be $7,329 (gross potential rent ÷ 81 units), and the revenue at risk would be $102,606.00 ($7,329 × 14 move-outs).

The Costs of Negative "Word-of-Mouth"

A third set of data—what might be termed the "word-of-mouth" numbers— illustrates the power of negative personal recommendations and suggests how reputations are made—and lost. In a landmark study, the Technical Assistance Research Project (TARP) reported that, after customers stop doing business with a particular vendor—and as we have already shown, most do so because of one or more negative "moments of truth" that they have experienced—they eagerly share these episodes with others. According to the TARP report, the average dissatisfied customer tells eight to ten other people about his or her ordeal; fully *thirteen percent* of unhappy customers tell *twenty or more* people! Furthermore, even if they complain, and their complaint is resolved satisfactorily, it takes twelve *positive experiences* to correct for each bad one.

In addition to quantifying the costs of poor service (exhibits 4.3 and 4.4,) it is possible to measure the amount of revenue that is lost because of negative word of mouth by applying the lessons from the TARP study. Exhibit 4.5 constitutes an extension of the calculation in exhibit 4.3. Applying this same methodology to Steeplechase Apartments, exhibit 4.6 shows the number of potential residents whose impressions of Steeplechase are apt to be impacted by the negative word of mouth from former residents who may have been disenchanted with the property, as well as the *potential lost revenue opportunity*—the dollars at risk—because of the same phenomenon. What is most frightening about the negative-word-of-mouth numbers is that you will never have an opportunity to do business with these potential renters—they will

---

Exhibit 4.5
Costs of Negative Word of Mouth

Number of dissatisfied residents who will switch (Line F)   _____   Line I

Number of potential residents who rent elsewhere due to
negative word of mouth, assuming the average dissatisfied
resident told eight others about his or her negative
experience (Line I × 8)   _____   Line J

Potential lost revenue opportunity to the property caused
by negative word of mouth (Line J × Line G)   _____   Line K

References are to exhibit 4.3.
Line F is the number of dissatisfied residents apt to switch.
Line G is the average annual revenue per resident.

NOTE: Here, again, the calculation is based on individual residents rather than apartments, for the
same reason.

---

have rejected you outright *before* you could invite them to see your property
for themselves.

The Importance of Reducing Resident Churn.   Evidence that owners
of investment real estate are becoming aware of the exorbitant costs of tenant
"churn" through their properties can be found in *Managing the Future: Real
Estate in the 1990s,* a study commissioned by the Institute of Real Estate Management Foundation and conducted by the Arthur Andersen Real Estate Services Group. The study found that the chief concern of the major owners of
U.S. real estate—among both interviewees and survey respondents—is "the
space glut and what it means for the future. On a scale of one (high significance) to three (low significance), survey respondents scored vacancy at
1.24. . . . Tenant procurement, and especially tenant retention, are major concerns." The IREM Foundation report concluded that owners expect that the
property manager of the future will have demonstrated skills in controlling
tenant "churn":

▶   The dominant theme is tenant relations. Almost every interviewee
said the most important tasks involve serving tenants. Most interviewees said retaining tenants is more important than obtaining them.
While emphasizing that the entire real estate business is revenue-
driven, [owners] regard retention as more efficient and less disruptive than continual, successful re-leasing.

Asked to rank 36 management tasks on a five-point scale (5 = very important;
1 = not important), survey respondents replied similarly:

Exhibit 4.6

Example of the Costs of Negative Word of Mouth

Number of dissatisfied residents who will switch	26
Number of potential residents who rent elsewhere due to negative word of mouth	208
Potential lost revenue opportunity to Steeplechase—the dollars at risk because of negative word of mouth	$828,678.24

NOTE: On a unit basis (presumed single occupancy), the 14 residents who would move out of Steeple-chase would tell 112 other people (14 × 8), yielding a potential revenue opportunity loss of $820,848 (112 × $7,329 average annual revenue per unit).

▶   Tenant relations, with the greatest emphasis on tenant retention, takes top priority. In fact, the four top-rated tasks are all aspects of tenant relations. These include retaining tenants (4.59), negotiating leases (4.50), obtaining tenants (4.50) and handling tenant relations (4.39).

The lessons of the "Death Wish Paradox," the "Tenant Churn Index," and the various techniques for calculating the costs of poor service to residents and negative word of mouth, coupled with the admonitions to property managers contained in *Managing the Future,* make developing techniques for reducing resident churn an imperative for the apartment manager. We suggest that there are several ways to do this. However, a preliminary step in this direction is consideration of the cost of losing customers as you develop your marketing budget.

Budgeting for Retention Marketing

The "Death Wish Paradox," so simple in concept, yet so profound in implication, deserves to be framed and placed in a prominent location in every marketer's office. Its relevance for the apartment marketer is not diminished merely because such comparisons have been almost entirely overlooked in the rental housing business. Indeed, because the lessons of the paradox are generally yet to be learned, the trailblazing marketers who do so will not only automatically ensure the success of their properties, but also achieve market leadership for their companies. Heady stuff, indeed!

If the expressway to market leadership requires vastly increased attention to current-customer marketing—what the commentators call customer retention programs—it is vital to begin to allocate resources to the endeavor in a meaningful way. This means that the traditional apartment advertising budget, which has been the embodiment of acquisition or conquest marketing needs to be overhauled. Here is what Laura Liswood has recommended:

▶ For starters, the marketing budget should be split into two categories: (1) dollars spent on acquiring customers, and (2) dollars spent on keeping customers. There will be some overlapping because the same dollar in any given case may serve both purposes. But it's important for marketers and senior management to quantify the two basic roles separately, both for practical budgeting purposes and to ensure that the customer-retention role is given due recognition.

Most savvy apartment marketers know with great precision the costs attributable to attracting each prospect telephone call and visit to the property as well as the advertising expenses associated with each signed lease. All of these, of course, are exclusively resident-acquisition costs. The question is, how much does it cost to *maintain* current residents?

Most apartment marketers do not know, and few of them would even know how to devise a methodology to find out. Looking to the retail environment, however, you will find that the service commentators suggest an average *acquisition* cost, across all industries, of $118.76 per customer. On the same basis, the average annual cost to *retain* a current customer is $19.76. This means that it costs roughly *six times* as much to acquire a new customer as it does to keep a current one.

The precise ratio of acquisition to retention costs is unimportant. What is absolutely essential is to earmark a certain amount of the apartment advertising budget specifically for resident retention. A percentage of the overall budget, reflected in appropriate line-item categories, is perhaps the best way to make and display the allocation. Because it can become part of the property's standard operating budget preparation procedure, this approach tends to ensure that the retention effort will continue to receive attention in subsequent years. If the retail figures are correct, it is sensible to allot at least one dollar of the marketing budget to resident retention for every six dollars allocated for resident acquisition.

It is also important, as part of the budgeting exercise, to consider how the retention funds will actually be used. Market research among existing residents and analysis of the competition are likely to be funded in this manner. Examples of these applications are detailed in chapter 8. There are, however, resident retention strategies that do not require direct funding. They are what constitute the broad subject of resident relations.

Partnering as a Technique for Churn Reduction

One method for reducing resident churn is to consider applying to apartment properties the strategies that have been evolving within the retailing milieu. One of the most recent is "partnering," which recognizes that it is in the mutual interest of sellers and buyers to engage in long-term relationships, not only because the expenses associated with "customer churn"—so-called switching costs—are substantial, but also because it is economically beneficial to do so. The principles that underlie partnering represent a synthesis of many of the specific customer-responsive strategies—e.g., service, satisfaction, and value, among others—and have particular application in the apartment business.

Charles C. Poirier and William F. Houser defined business partnering as "a process of improvement that brings an organization and its constituent parts to the point where special benefits not found in competing networks can be created." They then described the benefits that can be realized from partnering relationships:

▶ The interaction between the organizations [of buyer and seller] does not occur in some field of combat, but in areas of mutual interest. Within this interactive zone, resources are pooled so conversations go beyond quantity and price. Consideration is given to all the potential interactions so problems can be solved and opportunities for improvement seized. The new relationship concludes with mutual winners, not with one winner and one loser from the traditional relationship.

The concept of business partnering encompasses linkages between a firm's outside vendors and the company on the one hand and the firm's "internal" customers on the other. In addition, the value of such partnering can be extended to the ways in which the organization relates to its clients.

It is conceivable that a company might pursue a philosophy of partnering for selfish reasons. In *Winning and Keeping Industrial Customers,* Barbara Bund Jackson recommended that businesses evaluate their customers in light of the customer's "switching" costs—i.e., the degree of risk that a customer perceives in entering into a commercial relationship with a vendor and the difficulty of changing to a new vendor if the relationship is unsatisfactory:

▶ At one end of the spectrum are the customers who can easily switch products or services (e.g., buyers of commodity chemicals or shipping services). At the other end are those who have an incentive to stay loyal (e.g., customers of costly computer and office-automation systems). In the middle are the majority, who are easily swayed (e.g., fleet buyers of company cars).

William A. Band elaborated on this as follows:

▶ When the perceived risk is high, and the changing of vendors difficult, buyers respond well to strategies that emphasize a close relationship between buyer and seller. However, when switching costs are low, buyers are less interested in a long-term commitment to vendors, and price carries more weight. Understanding switching costs is important in order to avoid building a costly relationship with a customer who does not need or want such a commitment, and to provide an adequate amount of vendor support to those who are in for the long haul.

Whether or not apartment owners and managers consider establishing partnering relationships from a position of self-interest, the applicability of this notion in the multifamily housing industry is apparent. Simply stated, owners and managers of apartment properties have an ongoing stake in the economic futures of their residents because the financial fortunes of residents enable them to pay rents and to absorb rate increases; what is less apparent—though no less real—is that apartment renters are similarly invested in their landlords' success, at least theoretically. When landlords prosper, chances that they will refurbish their properties improve correspondingly. Whether that correlation is exact, it is clear that when apartment properties encounter troubled economic times, the likelihood that their owners will upgrade them is remote.

Thus, the notion of "switching" costs is applicable to the apartment milieu as well. Apartment residents incur substantial expenses in moving from one place to another. These expenditures go beyond the financial burden of moving: There is also the "hassle factor"—packing up, arranging for utility shut-off and turn-on, changing addresses with business and personal correspondents, and all the rest—that adds to the perception of high risk. This dual investment is well-characterized by Donald R. Libey:

▶ Your customers don't want to go somewhere else. They have a desire
    to be loyal. . . . Bio-psychologically, The Customer's drive to survive
    is directly transferred to the supplier when the decision to trade is
    made. The Customer wants you to guarantee survival. The Customer
    is literally trusting you with a portion of personal survival.

Note that Libey has also addressed the psychological and emotional components of "switching." People develop strong attachments to what, for them, constitutes *home,* and most of them truly do *not* want to change this aspect of their lives.

Because apartment residents have made substantial financial and "hassle" investments in their landlords' properties, they are especially suitable candidates for partnering efforts by creative landlords who appreciate the breathtaking economic impact of resident retention and understand the overwhelming costs of resident defection. Apartment managers need to appreciate the fact that residents are not captive. A resident who will submit to the expense—and the hassle—of moving is really dissatisfied. That is why it is to the landlord's advantage not merely to satisfy residents, but to create incentives for residents to remain loyal customers.

One powerful partnering weapon that savvy landlords need to employ is solicitation of complaints from their residents. We turn to that subject in the next chapter.

5

The Complaint Revolution

Nobody likes to hear they've done a lousy job, but criticism from customers is more valuable than praise. You want your customers to tell you when you've screwed up, so that you can take care of the problem and take steps to ensure it doesn't happen again—to them, or anybody else. If they don't tell you, they'll just walk away shaking their heads and they'll never come back. Worse, you're likely to alienate somebody else in the future by doing exactly the same thing.

—CARL SEWELL and PAUL B. BROWN

Ironically, complainants are often valuable customers because they're giving the company a chance to make good before they take their business elsewhere. And if their complaints are handled to their satisfaction, 90 percent of them will stay. Most of us, as customers, are afflicted with the common human condition of inertia. We don't really want to move our checking account, change dry cleaners, take a chance on a different model car, or try the chairside manner of a different dentist. We prefer to stick with what's familiar, as long as we continue to get reasonable satisfaction from it. But there's a limit, and we *will* change when the satisfaction level drops too low or when we're offered a superior alternative. Thus, in a company that's truly service-oriented, any complaint is really an *opportunity*—an opportunity to correct a problem or do something better and a second chance to preserve a valuable customer relationship.

—LAURA A. LISWOOD

When you become a partner you break down the walls between yourself and your customer. You make a lasting commitment, and you invest in learning everything about your customer . . . . Your organization can truly become saturated with the customer's voice. You encourage your customer to fully understand what you can do, and you create a "value chain."

—RICHARD C. WHITELEY

Chances are, if you were to ask a roomful of site managers to name their best residents, you would get responses that sound something like this:

> Mrs. Cameron. Or maybe the Thompsons. No, definitely Mrs. Cameron. She's my best resident. Why, she's lived here for four years, she always pays her rent on time—maybe even *early*—and I never hear from her. *Never!* None of that whining about barking dogs, kids running in the hallways, or newspapers piled up in the lobby. And when it comes time to renew her lease, she never asks for anything. No new carpeting or new appliances—not even a touch-up paint job in the living room. Just takes the four percent increase every year, without any bickering. I'll tell you this: If I had 35 more residents like Mrs. Cameron, my job would be a lot easier, that's for sure.

On the other hand, if you asked the same site managers to name their best *friend,* the responses would be vastly different:

> My best friend? That's easy—Karen Morrison. She was a year ahead of me in high school. And when I got into leasing, she was a manager over at Bridgeway. We just naturally started comparing notes about the business. When her company put in that new Buffalo accounting system, she was having lots of problems, and she'd call me up at all hours, especially when she was doing her month-end reports. Now, we talk all the time, just to see how each other is doing.

Why is it that personal relationships are typically so different from professional ones? Why is it that we expect—even welcome—interactions with our friends that we would resent from our customers? For some reason, it might be perfectly acceptable for our friends to bang on our doors at midnight to complain about some aspect of their bosses' behavior, yet we bristle when a resident stops us in an elevator lobby to inquire timidly about a misdelivered package.

Professional Complaining Is Discouraged

Undoubtedly, one of the reasons for this discrepancy is that humans have different levels of *commitment* to their relationships with one another and, therefore, varying tolerances for the level of intensity and inconvenience they are likely to require. People are, in short, *differentially invested* between and within their professional and personal relationships. We believe that a major challenge for American business is to narrow the gap between the ways all the people in the company, and most especially frontline personnel, treat their friends and treat their customers.

Until this happens in the apartment industry, we are unlikely to be motivated to ascertain whether residents are satisfied or dissatisfied with their living situations. Karl Albrecht described it this way:

▶ Apparently, many people want to remain in a comfortable state of ignorance. "If I go around asking the customers how they feel about things," they seem to think, "they'll start complaining and I'll have to do something about it." That's exactly the point. The purpose of asking customers how they're experiencing your [product] is to find out how you can improve it and keep their business or get more of it.

Paradoxically, the U.S. Office of Consumer Affairs (USOCA) has found that the problems of noncomplainers are usually the easiest to resolve:

▶ If only given the chance, business could have retained the patronage of many of these customers. Therefore, this often large pool of non-complainants represents a significant lost marketing opportunity.

The fact is, customers are loath to complain, even though failing to do so virtually *guarantees* that their problems will not be fixed. The reasons for this apparent paradox are many. Probably the basic reason is that most people dislike contentiousness and haggling—the minor unpleasantness that sometimes escalates to wrangling, ultimatums, and even name-calling that characterizes complaining. When customers are pushed to the point that they complain, they risk encountering defensiveness, hard feelings, and even outright lying for their trouble. Customers would rather be treated equitably the first time and not be put in the position of having to insist on their rights.

Other factors conspire to discourage customer complaints. As reported in the *New York Times* (quoting research done by the USOCA):

▶ Seventy percent of consumers do not complain because they don't know where to call, don't think it's worth the effort, or don't think companies will respond.

Unfortunately, much corporate behavior tends to confirm consumer pessimism about receiving fair treatment.

Noncomplainers Vote with Their Feet—and Their Mouths.   Even if some or all of the above reasons discourage customer complaints, most consumers take decisive action when their expectations are unmet—they take their business elsewhere. Businesses that do not stay in touch with their customers are nonetheless subject to customer feedback: While buyers may choose to keep the offending vendor in the dark about their exasperation, they will not hesitate to let others know of their dissatisfaction. According to Davidow and Uttal:

▶ [Dissatisfied customers] are searching for opportunities to get even. They don't tell the retailers, manufacturers, and service providers that have served them poorly—they tell their friends and colleagues. As the bad word passes along, it creates a time bomb.

Lele summarized the deterioration of the buyer-seller relationship when customers feel disgruntled:

▶ Customer dissatisfaction presents a serious threat because many unhappy customers don't complain—at least, not to the company. Instead they tell family and friends about their dissatisfaction. A good number of them switch to other suppliers. If and when they do complain to the company, they are pessimistic about their chances of being satisfied. The company's response frequently confirms their worst suspicions. . . . The result is that the company and its customers become increasingly isolated from each other. Management thinks that because there are no complaints, there are no problems. Lacking information from the customer about the causes of dissatisfaction . . . the company repeats its mistakes. Customers, in turn, grow more frustrated with what they see as the company's indifference to their problems and needs, and switch to other suppliers.

Clemmer calculated the impact of the negative word of mouth from unhappy customers this way:

▶ Category	Number
The original customer who won't return	1
Potential customers not gained because the original customer didn't tell them how satisfied he or she was	8
Potential customers lost because the original customer told them how *dis*satisfied he or she was	16
Total customers lost from *one* unhappy customer	25

When we attempt to quantify the magnitude of customer dissatisfaction and its consequences, we find such disturbing statistics as these:

Approximately one in four purchases results in some type of consumer problem.

Nonetheless, nearly 70 percent of customers experiencing a problem *do not complain.* Some studies show the rate of non-complaining to be as high as *90* percent. This means that, for every complaint companies register, there are approximately three other customers with problems, some serious, that the firm never hears about.

Dissatisfied customers who don't complain are the ones least likely to purchase from the same supplier. Only 9 percent in this category do so.

Other sources confirm that the customers who actually complain represent only a minuscule portion of the number of customers who are dissatisfied. According to Davidow and Uttal:

▶ While complaints are useful in all sorts of ways, from pinpointing performance problems to selling collateral products, they're a remarkably feeble index of satisfaction levels. John Goodman of Technical Assistance Research Programs, Inc., who has studied the complaint process at over three hundred companies and government agencies, concludes that customers who complain to headquarters . . . represent a tiny fraction of all dissatisfied customers, somewhere between 2 and 4 percent.

Complaints are Golden Nuggets

While the estimates vary, the figures from the president of TARP in Washington, D.C., suggest that there is a vast sea of unhappy consumers, churning with unspoken discontent. The point was made by Stanley Marcus, Chairman Emeritus of Neiman-Marcus:

▶ Why do you think you have so many department stores in a mall these days? It's because each of them does such a poor selling job that they survive just by taking up each other's unsatisfied customers.

While there are no national studies on the subject of resident satisfaction, there is no reason to be complacent or to assume that the level of irritation in the apartment industry is lower than in other consumer trades.

Statistics also illuminate the reasons why it is vital to sellers to encourage complaints. Here is how Ron Zemke and Dick Schaaf have described the importance of customer complaints:

▶ According to John Goodman, TARP's president, complaining customers can turn into extremely loyal customers. Depending on the dollar value of their problems, only 9 to 37 percent of unhappy customers who *do not* complain will do business with the offending company a second time. But from 50 to 80 percent of those who *do* complain and subsequently have their complaint fully resolved (even if it doesn't turn out in their favor) report that they will ring the company's cash register again. Based on complaint resolution and repurchase records from a number of industries, TARP has even calculated a return on investment for successful complaint handling. The lowest ROI range is 15 to 75 percent for packaged goods companies; the highest, for retailers, is 35 to 400 percent.

Apparently, complaints—even if not resolved in their favor—can generate loyalty among customers and may eventually blossom into bottom-line benefits. Figures from TARP suggest that the *immediacy* of the seller's response to the customer's complaint increases the chances of repeat business: If the matter is resolved, as many as 70 percent of customers will do business again with the company that upset them. But if the complaint is resolved *on the spot,* 95 percent will do so.

More recently, Terry Vavra summarized the importance and vitality of customer complaints as, "the five things that can happen when a customer is unhappy." They are:

▶ *The customer suffers in silence.* The next time the customer buys the product or service, he will already have a negative attitude and will be expecting and looking for problems.

The customer switches to another marketer in silence. This is only a problem for the marketer who realizes she has lost a customer, but recognizing the loss provides no information [about] how or why.

The customer tells friends and neighbors about his dissatisfaction. In this case, the firm stands to lose several customers, the original unhappy one and all the other people he influences.

The customer talks to third parties. This is the worst outcome because it can lead to lawsuits or investigations and increased negative publicity.

The customer talks to the company. This is the only positive outcome. It gives the company a second chance, the opportunity to understand the customer's needs, identify the problem and correct it, and ultimately to win back the trust of the customer.

Because complaints are so vital to successful operations—they constitute the most valuable piece of a company's business intelligence—the best firms pay close attention to those that surface and take aggressive measures to stimulate others. This receptive attitude is reflected in the following from Milind Lele: "When one of our customers sneezes, our company catches pneumonia." Or, as Donald Libey noted, "In the extraordinary company, *every* customer problem puts the company on Red Alert."

The benefits of a strategy designed to surface and respond to complaints—i.e., what happens when complaints put a company on "Red Alert"—may be summarized as follows:

1. *It helps the company keep customers who might otherwise switch to competitors.* As Milind Lele observed:

▶ Many companies don't realize that customer complaints can be more than a grave problem. They are also a tremendous opportunity. If customers who complain are ignored or treated unsatisfactorily, they can become a threat to the company's franchise. On the other hand, if their needs are addressed effectively, these same customers represent significant future sales.

2. *It overcomes some of the effects of negative word of mouth.* As Jeffrey Disend noted, studies show that:

▶ Dissatisfied customers tell twice as many people as satisfied customers tell about their positive experiences.

3. *It enables the company to identify, and then eliminate, the cause of problems—what one commentator calls "ricochets"—that impede customer satisfaction.* (Ricochet-fixing—i.e., service recovery—is the subject of the next chapter.) Here's what Carl Sewell had to say about the benefit of complaints to his Cadillac dealership:

▶ Sure, we have to fix problems, but if that's all we do, we're going to keep having the same problems over and over again. It's more efficient to find out what caused the problem in the first place—we do what's sometimes described as a root cause analysis—and correct the problem once and for all.

4. *It provides a company with an opportunity to distinguish itself from the competition by demonstrating its commitment to customer concerns.* Goldzimer characterized this devotion in "moment of truth" terms:

▶ By encouraging your customers to provide feedback, particularly complaints, you are showing concern, interest, *and the desire to satisfy* your customers. The very act of soliciting feedback is a positive signal to your clients.

5. *It helps to empower a firm's employees, which in turn enhances their job satisfaction.* According to Patricia Sellers, writing in *Fortune* magazine:

▶ There is a surprising payoff for those companies that make a science of listening to the customer: When they make their customers happy, they make their employees happy, too. Contented workers make for better-served customers. And there is also mounting evidence that improvement in customer satisfaction leads directly to higher employee retention.

6. *It diminishes the feeling—and often the reality—of isolation that exists between buyers and sellers, and establishes bonds instead. The impression that a company creates of being "complaint-friendly" is an especially compelling way for a company to be responsive to its clients' concerns.* As Zeithaml and coworkers observed:

▶ Complaints can become part of a larger process of staying in touch with customers. In particular, they can provide important information about the failures or breakdowns in the service system. If compiled, analyzed, and fed back to employees who can correct the problems, complaints can become an inexpensive and continuous source of adjustment for the service process.

7. *It enables the company to formalize complaint-handling procedures, which in turn establishes the firm as a "learning organization" in which*

Guarantees

Retailers have long recognized that guaranteeing their products and services benefits both their external and internal customers. Guarantees encourage personnel to do the job right the first time. When that does not happen, corrective action becomes expensive—whether or not the work is guaranteed: The company will not only spend money to correct the error, but it may lose additional business due to customer dissatisfaction, and it may suffer from negative word-of-mouth advertising. One advantage of guarantees, then, is that they set clear performance standards for personnel that benefit the company overall. Indeed, guarantees strengthen performance standards because both customers and employees monitor compliance. As Christopher Hart, one of the leading authorities on this subject, has observed:

▶ A specific, unambiguous service guarantee sets standards for your organization. It tells employees what the company stands for. . . . And it forces the company to define each employee's role and responsibilities in delivering the service.

Second, guarantees have powerful marketing benefits. When they are advertised, they attract customers. As Hart said:

▶ *A guarantee builds marketing muscle.* Perhaps the most obvious reason for offering a strong service guarantee is its ability to boost marketing: it encourages consumers to buy a service by reducing the risk of the purchase decision, and it generates more sales to existing customers by enhancing loyalty.

the customer's voice is paramount. Over time, the company is considered by its clients to be a partner in their success. Jeffrey Disend summarized the characteristics of these organizations as follows:

▶ They can never know enough about their business. They're always trying to find out what their customers want: What problems are they having? How can our product or service be more useful to them? Executives work on the front line and 'shop' the company. Hourly workers regularly go out to meet with customers, see how customers use their products, learn about other customer needs. Ideas for improvements come largely from listening to customers.

Before a company embarks on a course that begins with complaint-responsiveness and evolves into complaint-generation, it needs to review and, if necessary, upgrade its complaint handling policies. The self-examination prerequisite is especially important in high-touch service industries such as

---

Guarantees (*continued*)

In the text, we have noted the prevalence of customer dissatisfaction with retail purchases and the perplexing shortage of consumer complaints. Government figures indicate that some 70 percent (or more) of dissatisfied customers *do not complain,* and for every complaint brought to a company's attention, approximately three other customers also experience problems—some of which are serious—that the company never learns about. In that discussion, we emphasized the value of customer complaints and suggested techniques for surfacing them.

Probably the most effective strategy for revealing customer complaints is to guarantee satisfaction. Guarantees force companies to produce a high quality product because anything less will induce customers to invoke the guarantee. The capacity of service guarantees to unearth customer complaints that otherwise would escape the attention of the company gives a substantial marketing edge to the firm that employs them.

The marketing muscle of guarantees is probably most evident in connection with goods whose value depends primarily on so-called experience qualities—those intangible characteristics that can best be discovered only postpurchase. (The distinction between "experience" and "search" qualities will be discussed in chapter 7.) Because the product's suitability can best be determined only after the customer has the opportunity to experience it, the perceived risk can likely be diminished by guarantees. Here is what Berry and Parasuraman have said about the search/ experience dichotomy:

▶ Customers must experience the intangible service to really know it. Intangibility makes services more difficult for customers to imagine and desire than goods. Customers purchasing professional tax advice have no knobs to turn, buttons to push, or pictures to see. Customers' perception of risk tends to be high for services because services cannot be touched, smelled, tasted, or tried on before purchase. Customers can test-drive a new automobile and kick the tires, but to try a new vacation resort they must first register as guests.

---

apartment management, because the fact that a firm takes corrective action when one customer brings a complaint to the attention of the firm—and that customer gets satisfaction in return—creates the anticipation of similar results on the part of other prospective complainers. Thus, whenever a company commits itself to a policy of customer-responsiveness, the resulting positive word of mouth challenges the firm to keep promises consistent with the expectations of all of its customers. Nothing could be more damaging than asking for complaints and then *not* doing anything about them.

The essential foundational elements for an effective complaint-handling

Guarantees (*concluded*)

Because choosing a particular apartment community as a place to live has primarily "experience" qualities, some apartment marketers believe guarantees are an appropriate component of their marketing efforts. Others, ourselves included, eschew the use of guarantees in this environment, especially those involving refunds. In our experience, many apartment residents consider guarantees to be a substitute for adequate performance. Too often, such guarantees involve a refund, and more value is placed on the refund than on corrective action—or the quality of service that precludes the need for action in the first place. Their negative reaction is akin to those of prospective buyers of laundry equipment:

▶ As Whirlpool, the leader in home laundry equipment, has said, "Consumers don't want their money back. *They want a product that works.*

The contrary view toward guarantees was similarly summarized by Peter Glen:

▶ Lip service is even worse than mechanical service. And we are having an epidemic. Suddenly service providers are starting to issue guarantees and pay their customers after providing them with bad service. The Marriott Hotels say that if your breakfast is delivered more than fifteen minutes late, it's free. The pizza place offers a discount if your order is not delivered within thirty minutes. The restaurant provides free desserts if entrees don't come in ten minutes, and the bank hands out five-dollar bills if customers wait in line more than five minutes.

This automatically gives all the employees permission to deliver your breakfast and your pizza late; free desserts are figured into the selling cost of the restaurant's shoddy operations and charged to the customer; and banks can now plan on keeping customers waiting in lines forever, as long as they come around afterwards and given them some money for their time.

Paradoxically, while guarantees are designed to insure customer satisfaction with a product, they have the potential to institutionalize its failpoints.

process are in place once the company has (1) hired nice people, (2) trained them in such customer-sensitive subjects as listening skills, and (3) empowered them to fix their customers' problems, whenever possible, on the spot.

The hiring-training-empowering triad was discussed in chapter 3. We turn next to service "recovery"—the end-product of customer service.

6

The Recovery Revolution

Customers don't expect you to be perfect. They do expect you to fix things when they go wrong.

—Donald Porter, Senior Vice-President, British Airways

Everything you need to know about handling mistakes you learned in nursery school: acknowledge your error, fix it immediately, and say you're sorry. Odds are, your customers, like your mom and dad, will forgive you.

—Carl Sewell and Paul B. Brown

The word "recovery" has been chosen carefully—it means "to return to a normal state; to make whole again." Though many organizations have service departments established to fix what breaks, the deliberate management of the recovery is typically a reactive, damage-minimizing function. We suggest recovery can be as proactively managed for positive outcomes as can service in general.

—Chip R. Bell and Ron Zemke

Apartments are assets that deteriorate and lose value over time. This wasting process is accelerated—or slowed—by such factors as physical age, climate, and construction quality, as well as the rate of tenant "churn" at the property. Apartment owners and managers predicate their budgeting for preventive maintenance and capital improvement, as well as much of the routine maintenance and repair efforts, on their assessment of the property's rate of aging. Their goal is to preserve the value of the asset and to maintain it in as nearly mint condition as circumstances permit.

Property managers appreciate the reality of physical obsolescence and handle it as routine. Decisions whether to replace or repair a refrigerator or a roof, to resurface a parking lot now or wait another year, to install new carpeting in an elevator or the lobby are everyday agenda items in the management business. Budgetary conditions, marketing considerations, and economic forecasts are only some of the forces that influence the decision-maker.

It is also true—although infrequently recognized—that apartment prospects and residents are very much aware that apartments deteriorate. On the basis of their own experiences, from what they have heard from friends and relatives who have been renters, and even from the various "moments of truth" they have compiled during their contacts with an apartment property, renters understand and accept the reality of breakdowns and inconvenience as an unpleasant consequence of apartment living. So Donald Porter's comment at the beginning of this chapter, while undoubtedly directed to the airline industry, applies to rental housing managers as well: Perfection is not achievable; appropriate response when the inevitable breakdown occurs— what Ron Zemke terms "service recovery"—is a necessary part of the apartment manager's arsenal.

The "Over-Promise/Under-Deliver" Trap

The resigned acceptance of the fallibility of apartments by both landlords and residents is likely to be one of the few times they agree about this issue. The second portion of Porter's admonition—"[Customers] do expect you to fix things when they go wrong"—raises the issue of customer expectations about the promptness and thoroughness of the work, among others. The simple fact is that most apartment owners and managers are not prepared to *delight* their residents when they need apartment maintenance. Indeed, quite the opposite is usually true: The apartment maintenance process is the point at which apartment owners and managers most typically make promises to their residents that they either could not possibly keep, do not intend to keep, or wish forlornly that they could keep. These misguided assurances result in profound levels of discontent on the part of their customers. This damaging approach—what might be called over-promising and under-delivering— pervades the multihousing industry and is a prime reason for the widespread mistrust and dislike of landlords. Milind Lele has warned service-providers to avoid this pitfall:

▶ The majority of firms fail to understand the importance of controlling or managing customers' expectations. That's putting it mildly; in many cases companies create their own problems by generating unrealistic expectations and ruining their credibility with customers. . . . They try to manage expectations dishonestly. And they work hard to hide bad news, rather than face facts and deal with the problem.

Mack Hanan and Peter Karp made the same point more vehemently:

▶ The best rule for customer satisfaction is *to deliver*. There is a vital corollary to this proposition. It is *not to promise what cannot be delivered*. Disappointment can be a lower low than fulfillment can be a high. . . . It is commonplace to forget an expectation that has been fulfilled. Hardly any customer forgets a disappointment. In the long run, what is expected but not received counts stronger negatively than fulfillment counts positively.

As insidious and misguided—and ultimately self-defeating—as the "over-promise/under-deliver" syndrome is, its popularity is understandable. Site personnel are frequently confronted by angry, unpleasant, sometimes obnoxious residents who make extreme demands. Nonetheless, in an effort to be responsive and responsible, site employees make ambitious promises—usually in good faith and often unnecessary—to placate their customers. Unfortunately, employee expectations often end up being overly optimistic, frequently for reasons that are beyond their control. For example, service requests typically involve parts and equipment in addition to labor. For a variety of reasons, these supplies may be temporarily unavailable; the "labor" component—i.e., the maintenance staff—may turn out to be equally unavailable, especially because their other duties conflict. The common situation is one in which routine resident needs collide with site emergencies. (This was elaborated in chapter 3: The Pareto Principle.)

The Importance of Questioning and Listening.   Another problem is that different people attach different meanings to the same words—in this case, the phrase "right away," which is a frequently used pledge in the apartment business. Here is how a misunderstanding might arise:

Resident (to manager): "Something's wrong with my dishwasher: Nothing happens when I turn the setting to 'Pots and Pans.' It didn't get the dishes clean last night when I tried to use it." (All the while thinking: "I'm having a dinner party that starts in less than an hour and I need to get those dishes washed so that I can use them again for my guests. This problem has to be taken care of *immediately!*")

Manager (responding): "I'll get somebody up to your apartment to take a look at the dishwasher *right away*." (Meanwhile thinking: "Jeff's on vacation, and he won't be back until tomorrow morning; we're really short-handed this afternoon. The only maintenance person I have available is Terry, and he's working on the boiler. I'll write a service request. Maybe Terry can get to the dishwasher later this evening. In any case, I'll make sure that either Jeff or Terry handles the problem first thing tomorrow.")

Resident requests, whether or not they are reasonable, inevitably ripen into expectations that often go unmet. The expectations themselves are either implicit ("This problem is obviously so serious that *anybody* would understand that it needs prompt attention!") or unexpressed ("This problem is so important *to me* that I'm sure it will be fixed immediately!")

The IRV Curve of Customer Satisfaction.   In retailing, the degree of fit between buyers' expectations and companies' performance is the primary measure of customer satisfaction. As Milind Lele described it:

▶ Customers judge their satisfaction or dissatisfaction with a product by comparing its performance against a reference level of expectations that they've created or that has been established in their minds. If performance is [slightly] below expectations, they're satisfied; and if performance exceeds expectations, they're very happy.

Indeed, customer satisfaction might be depicted in an equation:

$$\text{Customer satisfaction} \ = \ \frac{\text{Performance}}{\text{Expectations}}$$

Much of the antidote to the pervasive over-promise/under-deliver style that typifies many businesses is to adopt its antithesis as company policy: Under-promise and over-deliver is a sure way to satisfy customers. The singular benefit of this latter approach can perhaps be best understood from the following illustration:

The "Perception and Performance Principle"

Promise to Meet Customer Needs ⟶ Exceed
Promise ⟶ Customer Satisfied
Promise to Meet/Exceed Customer Expectations ⟶ Deliver 99% or
Less ⟶ Customer NOT Satisfed
Promise Less than Capacity to Meet/Exceed Expectations ⟶ Deliver
100% ⟶ Customer Satisfied

The foregoing diagram illustrates a fundamental principle that distinguishes customer-driven organizations from those that are not: These firms understand that their clients expect them to keep their word. Companies that go to the trouble to pin down customer expectations and then exceed them—while resisting the temptation to promise to deliver more than they can produce—invariably succeed. Their approach to the principle depicted above looks like this:

Promise 90% (or less) of Capacity to Meet Expectations $\longrightarrow$ Deliver 90% (or more) $\longrightarrow$ Satisfaction

On the other hand, those firms that routinely make promises to induce customer confidence, and then fail to deliver on their commitments, are destined to fail.

The second part of the antidote, then, is to find out what customer expectations really *are*—not intuit them—and then strive to satisfy them. Frontline servers cannot substitute their judgments for those of their clients in deciding what is an appropriate, timely response. This is especially true because satisfaction depends to a great extent on whether the customer considers the recovery to be punctual or not. As David Freemantle pointed out:

▶ As soon as a company hesitates in redressing a problem with a customer, a critical alienation will occur. Conversely, swift reparation can produce a perception of a higher standard of customer service than if the problem had not occurred in the first instance.

Speed of Response as a Component of Satisfaction.   The importance of speed as a factor in the adequacy of service recovery is attributed by Libey to an unlikely source: Federal Express.

▶ As a result of the advances in communications technology and the overwhelming acceptance and success of Federal Express, global time has been redefined and reconstituted. . . . Consider the magnitude and magnificence of that accomplishment. One visionary, Fred Smith, altered global time through the philosophy of customer-focused marketing. His creation of Federal Express and his magnificent obsession with his customers has actually altered *time!*

While it may be feasible to promise action within a certain time period, it may be unnecessary to do so: The customer may be less demanding than the service provider would have supposed. In these circumstances, delivering slightly less service than the company is capable of delivering may nonetheless WOW its customers. To restate the earlier point, there is no substitute for conversations with customers to learn their expectations. Here is an example based on the malfunctioning dishwasher situation illustrated previously.

Resident (to manager): "Something's wrong with my dishwasher: Nothing happens when I turn the setting to 'Pots and Pans.' It didn't get the dishes clean last night when I tried to use it."

Manager: "Terry, our maintenance man, is working on the boiler right now; we've been having some minor problems with it, and I want to get them fixed well before winter sets in. Jeff, our maintenance chief, is on vacation and won't be back until morning. Tell me: Would it be satisfactory to you if Terry takes a look at your dishwasher later this evening, or would it be alright if Jeff comes by tomorrow morning?"

Resident: "Well, I don't know whether I mentioned it, but I'm having a dinner party in about an hour, and I really need help with my dishwasher right away. You see, the dishes didn't get clean last night, because of the problem I'm having, and I need clean dishes for my guests."

Manager: "You're right. I didn't understand that you had a time problem. How about this: I'd be delighted to wash your dishes in *my* machine right away, so that you'll have clean dishes in time for your guests; and then, just as soon as Terry is free, I'll have him go up to your apartment. Either he or Jeff will have the problem fixed no later than tomorrow morning. I'll check with you about noon tomorrow, just to see that everything is satisfactory. Will that be okay?"

In this instance, if the manager succeeds in getting the resident's dishes clean within the hour following the complaint, and if the underlying problem with the dishwasher is resolved by the site staff (or an appliance repair contractor) before the following afternoon, the resident will doubtless be impressed by the swiftness of the repair. This is true even though the resident may initially have considered immediate attention to the dishwasher to be absolutely necessary. The fact that the manager chose to pose *alternative solutions* to the resident resulted in a satisfactory outcome for both landlord and tenant. In these circumstances, it is likely that the landlord benefitted from positive word of mouth—even though the manager did not produce immediate satisfaction, or even the most immediate resolution that would have been doable under the circumstances.

Avoiding Double Deviations.   Much of the success of the service recovery effort depends on whether it meets the timing requirements that customers have for it. Another imperative for a successful recovery effort is that the response actually *solve* the customer's problem. While this requisite seems obvious, recovery has the potential to exacerbate customers' distress. As Berry and Parasuraman have pointed out:

▶   When a service problem is followed by a weak recovery effort . . . the company fails its customers twice, creating . . . a "double deviation" from customer expectations. A double deviation will dramatically deflate customers' confidence in a company; when preceded by a history of unreliability, it will *devastate* customers' confidence and drive them to the competition.

Service recovery is risky. Disappointed customers are especially difficult to please; frontline employees are peculiarly subject to burnout in these interactions, although their sustained performance is crucial: The challenge facing the front line is to defuse the situation, discover customers' expectations, and renew their confidence in the company's ability to respond. Moreover, companies that disappoint their customers are particularly prone to exaggerate their ability to recover. Finally, it is vital to meet customers' expectations once a breakdown occurs and not allow the situation to further disintegrate with a feeble effort at resolution. In light of these hazards, companies need to *strategize* their recovery efforts.

Aspects of Service Recovery

Recovery logistics have three components: (1) resolving the immediate problem so the customer is satisfied; (2) preventing a reoccurrence so others will not encounter the same problem in the future; and (3) planning responses for recurring breakdowns that are unavoidable.

Apologize and Empathize. The service commentators offer several suggestions for accomplishing these tasks. First, the company needs to recognize that a successful resolution of the problem starts with appropriate, sincere treatment of the disillusioned customer. Scott Gross recommended that the frontline server, as the most immediately available representative of the seller, begin by offering a heartfelt—even outrageous—apology:

▶ When you say you are sorry, be so generous that there is no doubt that you mean it. You will create so much [positive] word of mouth that your mistake will be worth its weight in gold. An occasional screw-up handled outrageously may be just what the promo doctor ordered!

According to Kristin Anderson and Ron Zemke, the customer and the problem should be addressed separately, and a high-touch approach is indispensable:

▶ When a service provider wallows in a customer's misfortune, there are two victims instead of one. As a service professional, you need to see the clear difference between what happened and who it happened to—and work on the former to bring things back to normal.

They further recommended that the staff member display empathy for the customer in this circumstance:

▶ Showing empathy for customers actually allows you to be professional . . . [and] also makes customers feel like important individuals. Empathy cannot be handed out by a machine; it's something one person does for another. There is no substitute for the human touch . . . . Use empathy to let your customers know that you—and they—are more important than machines.

Empathy is expressed in many of the conversational vignettes between apartment manager and resident in this and earlier chapters.

The Personal Component

Because service recovery is innately a person-to-person activity, service commentators emphasize that the complaint-handling procedure hinges on staff who have exceptional human relations skills. Berry and Parasuraman said it this way:

▶ Excellent recovery requires excellence in the process dimensions of service. And this requires excellent people. . . . Employee responses to service problems cannot be left to chance. While some employees may be naturally responsive, reassuring, and empathetic in dealing with customers experiencing problems, most are not. Even employees who exhibit exemplary behavior during routine transactions may come unglued in dealing with problem situations. Inability or unwillingness of service personnel to respond effectively to exceptions is a pervasive problem.

Heskett and coworkers identified the optimum personality traits for those assigned to work at recovery:

▶ [The most important requirement] is the personal manner in which the recovery process is carried out. This requires assigning people with the best listening and human skills to the recovery process, giving them the most careful training, providing them with decision latitude for the use of good judgment, and rewarding them well for their good work.

Because these efforts are frequently high-stress as well as high-touch endeavors, other commentators recognize that the work of frontline staff is "emotional labor." Clemmer put it this way:

▶ Frequently, pre- or post-impact recoveries are heroic. That is, they require extra, sometimes superordinary, efforts to catch or make up to customers for problems created by ricochets. A steady routine of heroic recoveries is a prescription for stress and burnout.

Get the Boss Involved.   Gross—and others—suggested that recovery is legitimized if the *boss* participates actively in recovery:

▶ Every problem should belong to two people: the person directly responsible and someone with at least an impressive, weight-carrying title, preferably the owner. . . . Involving the boss in setting things right has several benefits:

- It lets the employee know that getting things right is important.
- It lets the customer know that getting things right is important.
- It lets the boss know about problems so that he or she can focus attention and resources on prevention.

This latter aspect of leader involvement in the recovery process has the larger advantage of helping the boss to avoid making decisions in a vacuum without understanding the needs and wants of the customers who make the business possible. More important, the *frontline involvement of the boss* in complaint-resolution tends to sensitize company leadership in general to customer expectations, which is a vital trait of customer-driven companies.

Objectives of Service Recovery

In strategizing the recovery effort, it is advisable to begin by setting goals, and to do so from the perspective of the disgruntled customer. Gross summarized the destination of the process this way:

▶ Complaining customers are looking for a resolution of what they see as a conflict. They may want something fixed, an apology after slow service, or restitution for missing, damaged, or shoddy product. They want justice, and justice delayed really is justice denied. Besides, every hour that you delay in setting things right is another hour for the customer to stew in his anger, and another opportunity for him to tell someone else about how awful he's been treated.

In addition to fixing the problem for one customer, service recovery has the potential to assist the company in preventing problems for other customers in the future, a procedure that is termed "root-cause analysis." Here is what Berry and Parasuraman said about this subject:

▶ Problem-resolution situations are more than just opportunities to fix flawed services and strengthen ties with customers. They are also a valuable—but frequently ignored or underutilized—source of diagnostic, prescriptive information for improving customer service. . . . A company can and should learn as much as possible from each recovery experience. Effective learning involves searching for and correcting the underlying cause of the service shortfall, readjusting the monitoring of the service process, and implementing an information system to track problems. . . . To be fully beneficial, the recovery effort must strive to ferret out and fix the root causes of the failures.

Service recovery also can be used as a planning tactic for multifamily housing managers. We noted earlier that preventive maintenance is actually a type of service recovery, even though it is undertaken in advance of a breakdown. A similar approach, what we might term a "failpoint strategy," enables apartment managers to design responses to malfunctions before they occur. For example, despite the best efforts of maintenance personnel, apartment HVAC systems often fail in the summertime—usually on the hottest days of the year. Recognizing the likelihood of such mishaps, savvy managers outfit common areas with fans; stock pitchers and fixings for iced tea, lemonade, and other beverages; and have sufficient staff available to serve cold drinks to residents until the problem is resolved. "Failpoints" usually are system defaults. They may include late or inadequate snow plowing—the "Rose in the Snow" vignette in chapter 3 was actually a failpoint—inconvenience caused by delays in sweeping parking lots, blaring fire alarms caused by power outages, and numerous other occurrences. Whether the appropriate response is a rose personally delivered to each inconvenienced resident or some other meaningful token that acknowledges responsibility and tenders an apology for the mishap, the site staff should brainstorm how they intend to handle predictable failpoints when they occur. (This type of brainstorming was discussed in chapter 2.)

Service Recovery Competence as a Marketing Tool

Yet another goal of service recovery—and one that is particularly appropriate in the multifamily business—should be to create competency in the company's recovery efforts. The firm may have sufficient confidence in its abilities to respond to service mishaps that it is willing to market its effectiveness in this area. In *The Complete Guide to Customer Service,* Linda Lash noted:

▶ Companies may be reluctant to advertise that [they have] solutions for service or product failures. It calls attention to the reality that products or services fail, that photocopy machines break down, that overbookings may occur, that staff may not always be friendly and unrushed. Yet customers are often well aware of these problems, either from personal experience or word-of-mouth advertising from their friends. Knowing that a company has solutions to these problems creates customer confidence, both in the company's dedication to preventing the problem from occurring routinely and in the company's commitment to delivering a helpful solution when the problem does occur. To put this into advertising is a bold step but one that has won customers and market shares for those who have done it. When customers know that they will be looked after when problems occur, or that they will receive continuing service on a major item, the assurance increases their intent to purchase that product or service again.

The ℞ for Service Recovery

Having established the purpose of the service recovery venture, the next step is to consider the components of the process. In *Delivering Knock Your Socks Off Service,* Kristin Anderson and Ron Zemke set out the following six-step prescription for service recovery:

▶ 1. *Apologize.* It doesn't matter who's at fault. Customers want someone to acknowledge that a problem occurred and show concern over their disappointment.

2. *Listen and empathize.* Treat your customers in a way that shows you care about them as well as about their problem. People have feelings and emotions. They want the personal side of the transaction acknowledged.

3. *Fix the problem quickly and fairly.* A "fair fix" is one that's delivered with a sense of professional concern. At the bottom line, customers want what they expected to receive in the first place, and the sooner the better.

4. *Offer atonement.* It's not uncommon for dissatisfied customers to feel injured or put out by a service break-down. Often they will look to you to provide some value-added gesture that says, in a manner appropriate to the problem, "I want to make it up to you."

5. *Keep your promises.* Service recovery is needed because a customer believes a service promise has been broken. During the recovery process, you will often make new promises. When you do, be realistic about what you can and can't deliver.

6. *Follow up.* You can add a pleasant extra to the recovery sequence by following up a few hours, days, or weeks later to make sure things really were resolved to your customer's satisfaction. Don't assume you've fixed the person or the problem. Check to be sure.

The quality of the service-recovery effort is one measure of the quality of the company that institutes it. It is one of the most important determinants of service quality, and it is a major driver of customer loyalty. Customer loyalty, in turn, has a direct, bottom-line impact on profitability. Nonetheless, many companies remain unaware of the extraordinary number of unhappy customers they stand to lose at any particular moment, and equally important, they treat those few who actually *do* complain with disdain or worse.

Improvements in complaint-surfacing and complaint-handling are impossible without stimulus from the top of the organization. For this reason, and because the quality of a company's service-delivery system depends on leadership, we turn to that subject in the next chapter.

7

The Leadership Revolution

Underneath all of the lists, rules, manuals and consumer insight is a core problem we need to address: that our spirit at the top has to change and our attitude toward front-line service be improved. Service is a spiritual and cultural issue. . . . Few on top have been frontline. American managers are still short-term, bottom-line focused. They got where they are generally without concern for spiritual values. They want competitive volume levels *today,* are often more motivated by how to look to the next job in the next company than what *this* company will be in ten years' time. Devoting energy and heart to internal morale, creating the esprit de corps, listening to each other is still considered a job for "personnel."

—MIMI LIEBER

Leaders who hope to motivate their employees to create value for their customers must also generate a spirit of excitement, pride, and *esprit de corps.* Companies with a strong, positive corporate culture have an almost tangible spirit of excitement. In these enterprises, employees know how to work together as a team toward the common aim of serving customers, and their pride comes from setting and meeting challenging goals. This kind of pride begins at the top of the organization.

—WILLIAM A. BAND

Commitment and dedication on the part of your people only happens when there's the same commitment and dedication on the part of the boss. Top management must confront the realities of the marketplace daily. I don't sit on some mountaintop, telling the American Airlines passenger service department how to deal with problems. I get out there and watch them work. I take regular trips on American—not because I have to go somewhere, but because I want to see for myself how we're doing.

—ROBERT CRANDALL, CEO of American Airlines

If the chief executive officer isn't the number one champion of The Customer, you're in trouble.

—DONALD R. LIBEY

Real estate management as a profession is a latecomer to customer service for several reasons. First, owners of apartment properties are naturally predisposed to so-called acquisition marketing, that is, finding and closing new business rather than satisfying—and thereby retaining—existing customers (the "Death-Wish Paradox" quoted in chapter 4). Whatever the terminology, the defining characteristic of this strategy is the devotion of the bulk of a company's advertising and marketing budget to capturing new business, despite the fact that to do so is demonstrably more expensive and less fruitful than earmarking funds specifically for business retention.

Acquisition Marketing in the Apartment Industry

In fairness, the preference for acquisition marketing, with its attendant, unsurpassed thrill of deal-making, is no more prevalent in the apartment industry than it is in other enterprises. Indeed, Laura Liswood set these alternative marketing styles into a historical context as follows:

▶ In the past, acquisition and retention marketing went hand in hand. Selling and service were part of the same ongoing company-customer relationship. By doing business with an establishment, a customer was automatically entitled to certain service rights: the rights to fair, courteous, and friendly treatment and the assurance that the proprietor would make good on anything that went wrong. However, as we matured into a more mobile, industrialized, technocratic society, a distinction arose between selling and everything that came after the sale. Selling became so specialized that it got to be called "marketing," and the job of attracting attention to a company or product evolved into "advertising and promotion." With the relentless growth in population, consumer demand, and purchasing power, everybody got so busy selling, promoting, and keeping score that owners and managers began to neglect the second half of the sale: the half where customers were supposed to be happy about turning over their money. We relegated the second half of the sale to "customer complaint departments," "service departments," and "warranty departments." That situation might have turned out fine, except that the job of providing service didn't furnish the glamour, excitement, and income associated with marketing and promotion.

Among other places, the passion for acquisition marketing in the apartment business is exemplified by the reward system that apartment managers have designed, negotiated, budgeted, and refined for their employees: Leasing velocity is the centerpiece of the bonus structure, and the sole claimants of these perks are the leasing staff. This practice validates and enshrines acquisition marketing to such an extent that, taken to its logical (but unlikely) extreme, leasing personnel might be inclined to churn residents through apartments so as to target these units for future customer acquisition.

We believe that reward systems in the apartment business—if any—should be employed to compensate behavior that we want to encourage: Conduct, once rewarded, tends to be replicated. Bonuses to a property's site staff, in our view, ought to be based on increments related to a property's net operating income (or reductions in expenses associated with resident churn, or other consequential measures that reflect improvements in a property's value), and should be spread among *all* members of its staff. Since all employees at the site have frontline contact with residents, lease renewal is everyone's responsibility and concern; churn-reduction ought to benefit everyone who effectively combats it. To make this important point in a slightly different way, owners hire property managers to improve the performance of their buildings, and a prime measure of achievement is upward movement in NOI. Because one technique for improving NOI is to propel rent and occupancy numbers while simultaneously reducing expenses—those items contained in a "Tenant Churn Index," for example—everyone who actively participates in these endeavors ought to be rewarded when their efforts are successful. (See chapter 4 and exhibits 4.1 and 4.2 in particular.)

The second reason for the delay in recognizing the importance of customer service in the apartment industry is fundamental and attitudinal, an unfortunate relic of those tranquil days when renters were in unending supply—plentiful, placid, and prosperous. While businesses generally, and retailers specifically, were vigorously—and noticeably—upgrading their appreciation of their customers, apartment owners and managers did little more than acknowledge their indebtedness to their customers by referring to them as "residents" rather than "tenants." However, just as units are units—whether we call them "apartments" or "apartment homes"—residents are "tenants," and they will continue to have second-class status unless and until their treatment is enhanced commensurate with their new title. We believe that only when apartment owners and managers refer to their tenants as "customers" or "clients," and only when they treat them as friends (or honored guests), will they have begun the process of fashioning a new belief system within their organizations, one that—as it matures and blooms—will be customer-based and customer-zealous.

The third reason for the delay in resident focus is itself a paradox: Owners and managers tend to punish site personnel for deficiencies in a property's performance, and the staff in turn tends to discipline residents. In addition, "churning" the owner's internal customers at an apartment site—typically beginning with the manager—is a panacea for a variety of ills (paltry site traffic, disappointing leasing velocity, elevated resident turnover).

Your Employees Are Your Customers, Too

Some real estate management companies "spin" employees to the point that they continually advertise the same positions in the "Help Wanted" section of the classified pages. Firms with a revolving-door attitude toward staffing fail to understand the linkage between contented workers and company success. This is characteristic of the leading service industries—including, and most especially, multifamily housing—in which establishing bonds between customers and companies is a necessary prologue to long-term relationships and repeat business.

The antithesis of this revolving-door attitude toward a firm's internal customers is exemplified by Hal Rosenbluth. His company's objective is to delight its employees, who in turn strive to delight the firm's external customers. As Rosenbluth put it:

▶ Companies earn the bad attitudes of their people. Does anyone ever begin a new job with a bad attitude? No. They are "bright-eyed and bushy-tailed," filled with anticipation, excitement, and ambition. But companies with little regard for the happiness of their people find that their enthusiasm and open-mindedness are soon replaced by apathy and bitterness.

Employees whose enthusiasm for their work has evaporated can hardly be expected to fulfill the company mission—which, at Rosenbluth Travel, is as follows: "Our goal is to spoil our clients beyond the point where anyone else's service will do."

Employees who are apathetic and bitter quickly become disgruntled. Thereafter, as Paul Goodstadt, director of service quality at NatWest Bank, has warned:

▶ Disgruntled employees [become] terrorists. They're out there sabotaging the customer's experience by their alienation, anger, and resentment. We must get to them and turn them around. We must get them on our side, and (more importantly) on the side of the customer.

Rosenbluth admonished the business manager to remember:

▶ *Happiness in the workplace* is a strategic advantage. Service comes from the heart, and people who feel cared for will care more. Unhappiness results in error, turnover, and other evils. To strengthen happiness you have to measure it . . . . Finally, companies have to have fun. When was the last time you excelled at something you disliked?

In chapter 2, we briefly explored the Japanese concept of "shared fate," the notion that employers and employees, whatever their job titles and respon-

---

Empowerment and "Giving Away the Store"

Resident-passionate, fully empowered frontline employees will very likely be more—or less—beneficent toward their customers than either business considerations alone would recommend or their employers would want them to be. Because frontline servers in the apartment industry are supervised by owners or management company central office personnel, their decisions are subject to review—and perhaps reversal—as in any other business. This tension, of course, can negatively impact the relationships of site personnel with residents. Here is an example of a typical situation:

> Joan (a resident) telephones Cheryl (the manager of her apartment community) to complain about the lack of air conditioning in her two-bedroom apartment. The problem has been ongoing for several days despite the efforts of maintenance personnel to correct it. Joan acknowledges that "the maintenance guys have done their best," but relief has been temporary, at best, and the results unsatisfactory. Joan is especially upset because her two small children, both of whom are suffering from chickenpox, have been unable to sleep because of the heat. "They're just miserable," Joan protests, "and I want something done about this *right now!* And while you're at it, Cheryl," she continues, "I think it's only fair that I get a month's free rent for all this aggravation."

What can Cheryl do? Well, in addition to employing her empathetic listening skills with Joan, there are several options available. Assuming that she cannot immediately remedy the underlying problem, Cheryl might purchase several small fans and deliver them to Joan personally, meanwhile offering additional apologies. Alternatively, Cheryl could invite Joan and her family to use a model apartment or a vacant unit until the air conditioning is fixed. If that is not an option, Joan might be offered temporary lodging in a nearby motel (at the property's expense). So far, so good: Most companies would permit an empowered site manager to take any of these actions.

---

sibilities, are equally invested in the success of their companies, and equally aware that success can be affected by downswings in staff performance and productivity. In companies whose personnel at every level have internalized the principle of shared fate and the truth of the axiom, "The Customer Comes First," customer service becomes the battle cry of every employee, from the CEO to the front line and back again. Because individual accountability is intertwined with delighting customers, every employee has the authority to become a sole-source customer-satisfaction company. When this transforma-

Empowerment (*continued*)

However, what about the matter of free rent? Jan Carlzon may not be concerned about the economic impact of SAS employees' generosity, but the issue of free rent as a means of making an apology—or as a substitute for one—generates substantial controversy in the apartment business. Here is how the predicament might evolve:

> *Cheryl:* "I understand, Joan, that you and your children have had a lot of discomfort because of the air-conditioning problems in your apartment. My family always gets cranky and upset when they're too hot or too cold. But I'm certain we'll get the problem fixed no later than noon tomorrow. Meanwhile, you'll be very comfortable while you're staying in the model apartment. Also, I would like to offer you five days' free rent to make up for the hassle you've experienced."

Alternatively, of course, Cheryl might decline to extend Joan any free rent at all, offer free rent for a lesser period (e.g., only three days), or present some other option altogether. Such a decision probably would add to Joan's upset and might well impel her to telephone Cheryl's supervisor, Kate, to complain.

Opinions differ about what ought to happen at this point. Some customer advocates would recommend that Kate make every effort not to disappoint Joan, even if, as in this situation, Kate's decision would necessarily be contrary to Cheryl's. The rationale for this result, of course, is "the customer is always right"—a policy that can extend to allowing customers to adjust their own grievances. (In chapter 3, we quoted Hervey Feldman, president of Embassy Suites hotels, who does just that; and the satisfaction of one hotel customer may cost only the equivalent of a single night's lodging, whatever that may be.) Moreover, the economic consequences of a month's free rent granted to one resident may be relatively insignificant, surely less than the economic damage that would result if the incident were to prompt Joan's decision to move out. Indeed, Joan's displeasure might result in negative word of mouth that itself would have measurable economic implications (recall the calculations in chapter 4). In apartment management, however, the problem is not merely the potential loss of a single month's rent; it includes, as well, the consequences of Joan telling her friends and neighbors in the building about the incident and other residents demanding similar treatment as a result.

There are other unfavorable consequences that ensue when a manager overturns an employee's decision. Customers who discover sympathetic supervisors are unlikely to trust decisions made at the front line: They will seek to deal directly with a manager, and will recommend that others do the same. A site manager whose judgments are routinely overturned has no authority and will become ineffectual. An empowered frontline server, if not appropriately supported, is inordinately subject to burnout.

Empowerment (*concluded*)

We believe free rent is an undesirable option. We think it tends to become an automatic response to problems—an unacceptable "knee-jerk" alternative to fixing them. There is no doubt, however, that supervisors need to do whatever is necessary to support their frontline employees, even if they disagree with them. Consequently, after Joan telephones Kate to explain her version of the situation, Kate should talk with Cheryl before making a unilateral decision. The best outcome, of course, would be for either Kate or Cheryl to call Joan back and let her know they have agreed that Cheryl's determination will stand.

The best companies use situations such as the one portrayed in this vignette as a type of preventive maintenance—i.e., as learning experiences—that will allow them to structure responses to the problems that inevitabily arise in serving customers. In the example cited here, Kate and Cheryl ought to take time—in private—to rethink how situations involving unhappy residents should be handled in the future. They might decide, for example, that free rent in *any* amount is an inappropriate response when customers are unhappy. Instead, they could cooperatively prepare a list of acceptable alternatives. In addition, Kate and Cheryl might agree that because there could be circumstances in which deviations from this list might be appropriate, they will discuss the situation prior to making any departures from it.

We believe that empowered employees are essential in a customer-driven company. On the other hand, because investment real estate is a business in which there are inevitable checks and balances, certain parameters need to be set to guide the exercise of this desirable discretion. These should become part of the training provided to staff members, whether they are new hires or long-term employees.

---

tion occurs, as Jeffrey Disend exclaimed, "Everyone believes, 'I'm it! I'm personally responsible for the quality and service our customers get.' " Until this understanding permeates the entire organization—the notion that every employee, whether physically situated at the frontline or in the corner office is independently responsible for the satisfaction of each of the firm's customers—the customer service ethos that the company is seeking will be a mirage. *Customer-first* behavior is a joint and several responsibility.

Service Is a Personal Undertaking

While it is important to understand that there is a distinction between internal and external customers, this differentiation between a company's clients tends to overshadow the essential quality of the attitude that the company needs to manifest to *all* of its customers. In the service culture, every employee has a customer. Every department, whether or not it has contact with the (external) paying customer, has a client who must be served if the overall mission of the company is to be realized. William Band put it this way:

▶ If there is one dominating challenge facing business enterprises in the next decade, it can be summed up in a single word: *people.* As companies struggle to become more customer-focused, they often find that their organizational structure and their employees' attitudes, beliefs, and habits present the greatest barriers to success. Ironically, part of the problem is that while businesses are attempting to treat their external customers with more care and respect, they sometimes fail to put the same value on their *internal* customers: their employees.

This essential, people-sensitive aspect of customer service is imbued with the flavor of the Golden Rule and the aroma of the Boy Scout Oath. Providing excellent service to customers is an everyday person-to-person activity. Delivering *exceptional* service is doing something remarkable for the customer—whether internal or external—as a *person.* This requires seeing each of the firm's customers as a person, as a thinking, feeling human being with needs. It means challenging all employees to be empathetic (rather than sympathetic)—i.e., to ask themselves about every customer: If I were this customer, what would *I* want? What else might this person need? How can I do things better for this customer? As Karl Albrecht observed:

▶ The outstanding service organization is one in which all "servers" know clearly who their customers are; they know what constitutes value for them; and they work continually to deliver that value. Whether a particular department serves external customers or internal customers, or both, its mission is essentially the same: to deliver value to those customers.

Top-Down Customer Service

Customer reverence as well as the shared-fate philosophy—the notion that "we're all in this together"—necessarily begins with the boss, whose gut-level understanding of these imperatives is exemplified by the reduction of internal customer (i.e., employee) churn, substituting for it a program with employee empowerment as its centerpiece. In *Business Partnering for Continuous Improvement: How to Forge Enduring Alliances Among Employees, Suppliers, and Customers,* Charles Poirier and William Houser put it this way:

▶ The reality of the past decade's efforts is that American managers prefer a quick fix, often characterized by the inevitable downsizing in personnel. They talk at length of the merits of a long-term orientation, of the importance of quality, a customer focus, and innovation as critical to success, of their willingness to adopt successful ideas, and the fact that people are their most important assets. Such talk has a hollow sound to the growing thousands of displaced people who decry the lack of any semblance of consistency in their former organizations, where the "survive-the-month" attitude was worshipped in deference to long-term success. . . . The solution to this problem requires that leaders develop a greater understanding of the criticality of their continued, oriented, and supportive posture as a factor in successful implementation of a *continuous* improvement process, which has now become a business imperative.

Creating a shared-fate, customer-passionate environment should be the first priority for every employer. Jan Carlzon, one of the pacesetters who understood the pivotal role that internal customers play in achieving this company goal, described the obligation of its leadership as follows:

▶ It is up to the top executive to become a true leader, devoted to creating an environment in which employees can accept and execute their responsibilities with confidence and finesse. He must communicate with his employees, imparting the company's vision and listening to what they need to make that vision a reality. To succeed he can no longer be an isolated and autocratic decision-maker. Instead, he must be a visionary, a strategist, an informer, a teacher, and an inspirer.

Carlzon evidently took his own advice—that the boss must be a visionary—very seriously. Realizing that he was entirely powerless to control, let alone supervise or even be in attendance at each moment of truth that SAS personnel might have with the airline's passengers, Carlzon wisely chose to *empower* his employees to act on his behalf in the best interests of SAS customers. In doing so, he recast the essence of his organization to represent its revamped ranking of concerns. This transformed the organization from a hierarchy, which had prioritized the upper echelons of internal customers, to a "flattened" structure, which accurately depicted the revamped, customer-driven SAS. Carlzon described the transformation this way:

▶ Any business organization seeking to establish a customer orientation and create a good impression during its "moments of truth" must flatten the pyramid—that is, eliminate the hierarchical tiers of responsibility in order to respond directly and quickly to customers' needs. The customer-oriented company is organized for change.

While Carlzon was describing a "decentralizing" process, others characterized this change as an "inverted pyramid." Disend put it this way:

▶ In customer-focused organizations, the [hierarchical] pyramid is exactly the opposite . . . [and] the people most important to the success and survival of the company *aren't* the owners or executives; rather they're the customers. The customer is the real boss, and these organizations recognize that fact. The people in the organization believe they "work for" the customer. The customer has the highest status, importance, and power.

Band added another dimension to the characterization:

▶ The "inverted pyramid" represents a change in attitude, whereby managers and supervisors act more as coaches or counselors than commanders.

Learning Organizations Are Localized.   Peter Senge characterized the so-called learning organization in his book, *The Fifth Discipline: The Art and Practice of The Learning Organization.* Such a firm adapts to changing circumstances as if it were actually assimilating information. It then acts on what it has discovered, thereby continually expanding its capacity to create its own future. Senge has suggested that such companies will increasingly incorporate Carlzon's organizational paradigm, including employee empowerment:

▶ Learning organizations will, increasingly, be "localized" organizations, extending the maximum degree of authority and power as far from the "top" or corporate center as possible. Localness means moving decisions down the organizational hierarchy; designing business units where, to the greatest degree possible, local decision makers confront the full range of issues and dilemmas intrinsic in growing and sustaining any business enterprise. Localness means unleashing people's commitment by giving them the freedom to act, to try out their own ideas and be responsible for producing results.

Jan Carlzon's revolutionary idea—to turn the organizational structure of the personnel of his airline literally upside-down so that it would be immediately responsive to its passengers—became transformed into a mission statement for SAS employees. Karl Albrecht described Carlzon's directive as follows: "If you're not serving the customer, you'd better be serving someone who is." This concept, in turn, generated an awareness of the significance of a company's so-called internal customers—i.e., its employees—which sensitized Hal Rosenbluth and others to the importance of nurturing a firm's own personnel as a means of stimulating service-delivery to its "external" customers.

While Carlzon and Rosenbluth, among others, envisioned their functions in their respective companies as decidedly secondary to, and supportive of, frontline personnel in their firms, their efforts to define the organizational missions of SAS and Rosenbluth Travel were essential to their companies' success. The personal visions of these extraordinary leaders, while different from one another, were nonetheless complementary. More important, they were metamorphosed into forward-looking, customer-responsive missions for their organizations that can prove instructive for real estate management firms today.

"History," as Donald R. Libey observed, "is very clear and loaded with common sense in one principal area of commerce: pay extraordinary attention to your customers and they will pay extraordinary attention to your business." Combining this vital lesson of history with Carlzon's and Rosenbluth's visions yields an understanding of what commercial reality is to the top leadership of a service provider: Customers are the essence of a company's success; continuing to do business with a firm's current customers is the gist of marketing; and therefore the company needs to act in ways that demonstrate responsiveness to customer needs and preferences. Libey put it this way:

▶ The survival philosophy of the future must begin and end with The Customer for there is no other possible object of competitive primacy. If you will be first among competitors, you must first have the greatest share of The Customers. Without customers, you are but dust in the wind; with customers, you are primal.

Customer Focus in Apartment Management

In the apartment industry, this reality—that residents are the only reason for the company to be in business, and the only reason that it can stay in business—will be the defining and differentiating characteristic of the service organization, comprising its mission, its core value, through the millennium. The proper role of leaders in this environment is to express this reality in a mission statement for the organization, and thereafter to live and exemplify the mission statement in their business lives.

Michael Hammer and James Champy, authors of *Reengineering the Corporation: A Manifesto for Business Revolution,* linked corporate mission statements, leaders' actions, and company success in this powerful statement:

▶ Creating a corporate value statement alone is useless and just another faddish exercise. Without supporting management systems, most corporate value statements are collections of empty platitudes that only increase organizational cynicism. To be worth the paper it's printed on, a value statement must be reinforced by the company's management systems. The statement articulates values; the management systems give those values life and reality within the company.

And, of course, senior management must live these values themselves. If an executive says it's important to care about customers and then spends an hour a week on the phone with customers, the value of that time to customers may be minor, but its value to the organization is immeasurable. The hour is a symbol and a demonstration

---

Customer-Focused Marketing *(After Libey)*

- Must come from the top down—beginning with the policymakers
- Requires support—money, people, deep personal involvement, proper tools
- Requires knowledge—of the customer, of the product or service, of the company, in general (personal development)
- Demands speed—of response, of results
- Must be accessible—available to all, equally
- Requires personal contact—empowerment

---

of management's personal commitment to the values by which they expect everyone to live.

Another truism that is broadly applicable in the business world—and typical of the apartment industry in particular—is that most companies operate in environments that have been created more by happenstance than by design. Because real estate management has frequently been an offshoot of allied activities—development and finance are but two—management as a stand-alone discipline has often been considered to be a secondary activity in relation to the central business of the firm.

In the 1990s, however, real estate managers cannot afford to maintain the status quo. Not only economic changes (e.g., defaulted mortgages putting large properties into the class of "troubled assets" and the general lack of development because it is less profitable now) favor improvement of existing properties. There have been wide-ranging social and societal changes as well. With the end of the "baby boom," no more large groups of "new" customers will be coming of age, and the growth of two-income households has reduced some of the economic uncertainty that might favor renting over buying. Indeed, low interest rates and excess existing housing stock give people a real choice between homeownership and renting and a wide selection among available apartments. In addition, growing numbers of double-income households and single-parent families mean greater desire and need for specific services. Not only are there fewer new customers for rental apartments, but those customers are changing. As reported in *Managing the Future* and *Emerging Trends in Real Estate: 1994*, property management is a necessary ingredient in the success of apartment properties. Resident retention is critical to management success, and being customer-focused is the foundation of resident retention.

The Company Culture.   Historically, real estate management companies evolved in response to price-sensitive market conditions rather than according to long-range plans. However, they are beginning to experience a business culture that, while somewhat less price conscious than its predecessors, has become, seemingly overnight, extraordinarily customer-responsive. As consumers, your residents are already encountering increasing pressures to make choices in their everyday business lives on the basis of claims that many expensive products offer superior quality, value, or service, or a combination of these features, that overwhelms mere price considerations. As Zeithaml and coworkers noted:

▶ In every nook and cranny of the service economy, the leading companies are obsessed with service excellence. They use service to be different; they use service to increase productivity; they use service to earn the customers' loyalty; they use service to fan positive word-of-mouth advertising; they use service to seek some shelter from price competition.

Moreover, competing owners and management companies, however tentatively, are beginning to introduce customer-responsive techniques into their own businesses, and are experimenting with marketing their portfolios—or even their entire firms—with a service emphasis. Having established the outlines of a service culture, these companies use it to crush their competition. Davidow and Uttal have described this phenomenon as follows:

▶ The service winners know that customer service is both a potent competitive advantage and a particularly defensible one. Because customers perceive service in relative terms, a competitor who wants to beat a company that offers relatively superior service can't play catch up. He has to leapfrog, to outdistance the competition. But since providing great service tends to be expensive, leapfrogging can break the bank.

The real estate management literature is ablaze with admonitions to practitioners to introduce service features into their product bundles. It's almost as if there is a *conspiracy* afoot to force apartment owners and managers to renovate and redesign their companies with a customer focus. Frankly, Davidow and Uttal consider the current state of customer service to be a disaster:

▶ "Crisis" is a strong word but no exaggeration. Most customer service is poor, much of it is awful, and service quality generally appears to be falling. At the same time, the penalty is growing for companies that render inferior service. Customers . . . are getting smarter about the value of service. They're increasingly frustrated and more willing than ever to take their business elsewhere.

Strategic Planning—Stating the Vision.   Revolutionary circumstances are extraordinarily demanding of company leadership. Someone at the uppermost level of the firm—whether it is a children's hospital, a video store or a real estate management company—must respond to the challenges that this new customer uprising poses to the company's very survival. These leaders may choose to begin their customer-service odyssey by reading some of the outstanding literature in the field (see the Bibliography at the back of this book); when they do, they will need to resist the temptation to instantly implement everything they have learned. As Jeffrey Disend has counseled:

▶ Becoming service-oriented is a process, not an event. Transforming an organization is not something that occurs quickly. Exceptional service is not something to get fired up about for a few months or a year and then forget about. It's a commitment to a lifelong approach to making customers the focal point of the organization.

The literature, besides heightening their enthusiasm, will provide sufficient information to enable company leadership to create a strategic plan for the organization, for which the company mission statement serves as the foundation. Such a plan is a necessary introductory step in the process of a company's becoming service-sensitive; in the apartment business, it is designed to answer the question, "Why should prospective apartment residents choose us, and having done so, why should they decide to stay?" Senge defined a mission statement this way:

▶ [It is] the organization's answer to the question, "Why do we exist?" Great organizations have a larger sense of purpose that transcends providing for the needs of shareholders and employees. They seek to contribute to the world in some unique way, to add a distinctive source of value.

Few apartment managers have ever crafted such an ambitious plan, and fewer still have done so with the goal of generating a vision statement that will be used both as a compass and a map—first to guide, and then to measure, the company's long-term progress toward meeting its goal of becoming customer-passionate.

Participants in the strategic planning process may comprise the company's entire personnel roster, its management team, or a committee representing the various divisions within the firm. Because the first step, the task of developing a mission statement, necessarily involves imbuing the entire company with a personal vision, we believe that participation by as many employees as possible is crucial. Senge recommended a broad composition of the group:

▶ The first step in mastering the discipline of building shared visions is to give up traditional notions that visions are always announced from "on high" or come from an organization's institutionalized planning processes.

The result of the process will be a collective conceptualization designed to inspire and provide direction for everyone in the firm, as Senge pointed out:

▶ At its simplest level, a shared vision [answers the question] "What do we want to create?" Just as personal visions are pictures or images people carry in their heads and hearts, so too are shared visions pictures that people throughout an organization carry. They create a sense of commonality that permeates the organization and gives coherence to diverse activities. . . . When people truly share a vision they are connected, bound together by a common aspiration. Personal visions derive their power from an individual's deep caring for the vision. Shared visions derive their power from a common caring. In fact, we have to come to believe that one of the reasons people seek to build shared visions is their desire to be connected in an important undertaking.

Define the Business.   The planning group should begin by conceptualizing the nature of the company's business.

- What does our company do?
- Where is our real opportunity in the market?
- What is our special competence? What are our customers' real needs?
- What motivates them?
- What can we do with our service that our customers will really notice and pay a premium for?

The answers to these questions—whom the business is satisfying, what customer needs it is meeting, and how distinctively it is doing so—will define the nature and quality of the company's business.

Because companies have both internal and external customers who may have different expectations and needs than their counterparts, it is helpful to distinguish between a company's internal and external focuses. In addition, adopting an expansive view of the company's mission—how it intends to market itself to its external customers—helps the firm to adopt a sufficiently comprehensive approach. As Jeffrey Disend pointed out:

▶ An organization can . . . shape what people think about by deciding what business it's in. That may sound naive and blindingly obvious, but many organizations don't have a clear picture of this. The business you think you're in affects what your organization does, how it's organized, and what your people do. Identifying an organization's primary business provides focus and direction.

The importance of selecting an external focus is perhaps best illustrated with a few examples. In the early 1970s, Smith Corona fashioned a strategic plan based on the determination that the company was in the business of manufacturing typewriters. Meanwhile, IBM, whose primary product at the time was the Selectric typewriter, envisioned itself in the business of providing business solutions. Despite its recent financial problems, Big Blue has significantly outperformed its former competitor, and has done so in part because it initially formulated a vast business purpose to pursue. *Too narrow a focus can doom a company to mediocrity.*

Here are some other examples. What is Coca-Cola's business purpose? Viewed from an internal perspective, the company produces and markets soft drinks; considered more expansively, however, Coke is in the refreshment and nostalgia business. How about the American Automobile Association? Some might say that Triple-A provides emergency car repair service; a broader view is that it provides security for automobile owners. Similarly, a university continuing education department might conceive of its business as delivering college courses; the more inclusive approach would be to characterize its mission as designing vehicles for people to improve their lifestyles and thereby feel better about themselves.

Create a Mission Statement.   The variety of customers whom apartment managers serve complicates the formulation of a business purpose in the apartment industry. On the one hand, owner-clients expect the management company to maximize their properties' income and minimize its expenses, to maintain them to the highest standards, and to provide comprehensive reports of progress in meeting these goals. On the other hand, apartment residents require management to provide a secure, comfortable, well-maintained environment; to respond promptly to their needs; and to treat their requests with respect. Finally, site and central-office employees want an environment that will be conducive to their productivity, one that rewards them appropriately for their efforts, respects their opinions, and recognizes them for their contributions. While these expectations are not internally inconsistent, they are so diverse that addressing them by means of a one-sentence mission statement presents a real challenge. Indeed, because of this proliferation of customers, the leadership of the real estate management company may elect to urge the planning group to concentrate on one or another of them in its mission statement. For example, a firm that trumpets, "We make you feel right at home!" is undoubtedly making a statement to its prospective residents, while another that proclaims it is "Building unparalleled value for the '90s" is more likely seeking management business from owners of income-producing real estate, including apartments. (Because the central objective of this book is to encourage managers to develop programs for retaining residents, we have not concentrated on the property owner as a customer of the management company. Programs that retain residents will ultimately maximize rental income by reducing the costs incurred due to resident churn, poor service, and negative word of mouth. Successful resident retention ought to contribute to retention of owner-clients; calculations such as those in chapter 4 should be sufficient evidence to convince them of the vital importance of churn reduction to improving the economic performance of apartment properties.)

The process of formulating a mission statement and deriving a strategic plan for a management company—or a component of the company, such as the personnel at an apartment property—is designed to assist the entity in preparing a blueprint that will guide it successfully through the competitive underbrush that it undoubtedly confronts.

Assess the Competition.   One starting point in developing a strategic plan is to find out the number of competitive firms or entities within the market area. Couple this with the historical demand for management services (or apartment usage) in the same area, and these data should help the planning group arrive at a conservative forecast of future demand for the firm's product.

By focusing on the market, the group will be able to identify the new entrants providing competitive services, together with the number of firms that have emerged during the past 24 months. Moreover, it may be possible to forecast likely players that will emerge during the succeeding two-year period. An accurate assessment of the amount of competition, together with an evaluation of the company's own capabilities, will assist it in charting a new course and positioning its products and services against opposing offerings.

Identify Distinctive Competencies.   Addressing the way a management company responds to the various needs of its diverse clientele of external and internal customers determines its distinctive competencies—its uniqueness in its markets—which in turn tends to create customer loyalty to the firm. The relationships that a company initiates and cultivates with its constituencies determine its peculiar positioning within the apartment industry. Because each of these clients has unique expectations, company leaders can determine what they are and strategize ways to meet them. If the company consistently *exceeds* its clients' expectations, the leaders can establish a special competence for their companies. Here is an example:

> Assume that the management company has a client who expects her property to achieve a five-percent annual increase in net operating income—a figure that would exceed its past performance. If the company can deliver a nine-percent increase, it will have demonstrated to the owner that it possesses a "distinctive competence." Similarly, if apartment residents have become accustomed to a one-day turnaround in work-order processing, a one-hour response time exhibits the distinctive competence of the maintenance personnel at the property. Finally, for site employees whose labors

Mission Statements

A mission statement is the foundation document of a company. Properly crafted, it sets out what business you are in, what market you serve, what distinctive quality you bring to the market, and the special way you approach it.

Mission statements should define the shared vision of a firm's internal customers about their professional future and how they will serve their external clients. Everyone in the company should participate in drafting the company's mission statement. If logistics make such extensive involvement impractical, the statement should at least connect the visions of people throughout the organization, rather than merely institutionalize the opinions of those at the top.

The purpose is to establish an overarching goal that participants in the process consider to be truly desirable. The loftiness of the target ennobles the entire enterprise, creating a spark that enlivens the organization and uplifts the aspirations of its employees. Great organizations have a purpose that transcends providing for the needs of their staffs: By means of synergistic, harmonious efforts, they seek to contribute a distinctive source of value to a particular market.

A mission statement answers the following questions:

1. What function are we trying to fill in society? What unique capacities does our company bring to this task?
2. For whom do we perform our functions? What do we want to communicate to our customers that will let them know how important their satisfaction is to the future of the enterprise?
3. How do we go about fulfilling these functions?

We believe the commitment to customer satisfaction as the company's ultimate product must be built into its mission statement. Indeed, *customer satisfaction must be the mission.*

Our own company's mission statement is deceptively simple: "We're resident *passionate!*"

typically go unnoticed, if the president of the management company publicly recognizes their achievements at a monthly staff meeting or a holiday get-together, this also demonstrates the employer's distinctive competence in the minds of the staff.

This concept of "distinctive competence" is especially useful to leaders in apartment management firms that are faced with significant market pressures. The ability to develop "brand loyalty," which certain retailers have succeeded in doing, is a devastating competitive advantage that is available in the apartment business as well.

The customer service revolution that is just now beginning to reach the apartment industry will undoubtedly result in brand loyalty to management companies that have developed a reputation for delivering uncommon value to apartment residents. Its clearest manifestation will be residents who, when circumstances require them to leave a particular apartment community at the expiration of their lease terms, inquire whether the firm manages another property in the city to which they are moving. *Portfolio loyalty based on product differentiation* will be the defining competitive advantage in the apartment business in the future.

Distinguish Your Apartment Product.   Product differentiation is the strategic goal of the planning process for the leaders of the real estate management firm. In one sense, seeking a competitive edge by devising a means of differentiating a firm's product from the thicket of competing goods is an effort to rob customers of their power to make choices. Because rental amounts vary within the community, and because there is usually a glut of product, apartment renters have a substantial amount of discretion (read: "power") available to them. In such an environment, which has typified the apartment industry in most markets periodically (and which almost certainly will return at some time in the near future), prospects' selections are usually random and frequently are determined *primarily* on the basis of price considerations. Consequently, the success of any particular apartment community, as well as its managing entity, is more likely to be determined by chance than any other factor.

On the other hand, if the property can be successfully distinguished from its competition on the basis of some consideration *other than price*—the quality of the service orientation demonstrated by the site staff, for example—it will attain a competitive advantage, and its managing agent will achieve similar preeminence. The problem is that "service" is a difficult concept to employ as a sales proposition. Because of this fact, leaders of companies who are attempting to differentiate otherwise interchangeable products are confronted by a somewhat greater challenge than others whose goods are easily distinguished from those of their competitors.

Economist Philip Nelson has categorized products as possessing so-called *search* and *experience* qualities. The former are qualities that a consumer can evaluate *prior to* purchase, while the latter are those that can be determined only *after* the purchase. The central, albeit unfortunate, characteristic of service is that it possesses primarily "experience" qualities: Service is intangible, which means that it cannot be inspected prior to purchase. Service is delivered to customers at the same time it is produced. If the leasing agent does not smile during the course of an apartment showing, there is no way to add that missing smile to the sales presentation later on.

The fact that service is an intangible quality makes it an especially difficult characteristic to market. A real estate management company may assert that it is "resident-driven" or "resident-passionate," yet prospective renters cannot determine the truth of the claim until they experience the environment that the firm has established, that is, until *after* they become residents.

Because marketing service as a competitive advantage is such a formidable challenge, some may wonder whether the process of becoming a service-oriented company or entity is worth the trouble. In fact, we believe that management firms, as well as divisions of such firms, ought to undertake this arduous journey at least in part *because of its unparalleled marketing potential.* Here is what Berry and Parasuraman have written about this subject:

▶ Services are dominated by experience qualities, attributes that can be meaningfully evaluated only after purchase and during production-consumption. In services, both *post-sale marketing* through orchestrating a satisfying experience for customers during production and *word-of mouth communication* (which is surrogate and supplement for customers' direct experiences) have prominent effects in winning customers' loyalty.

Reasons Why Customer Satisfaction Is a Company's Salvation

Four factors coalesce to make customer satisfaction the driving force for an organization. First, customers are the lifeblood of a business (this has been noted at several points elsewhere in this book). Without them, a company has no reason to exist. As Donald Libey pointed out:

▶ The only path to long-term, profitable survival is customer-focused marketing. All business begins and ends with The Customer. In the beginning, there was The Customer. In the end there will be The Customer. The company with the most customers wins.

Second, when a firm establishes customer service as a "distinctive competence" it sets itself apart from, and far ahead of, its competitors. Again, as quoted from Davidow and Uttal earlier in this chapter:

▶ The service winners know that customer service is both a potent competitive advantage and a peculiarly defensible one. Because customers perceive service in relative terms, a competitor who wants to beat a company that offers relatively superior service can't play catch up. He has to leapfrog, to outdistance the competition. But since providing great service tends to be expensive, leapfrogging can break the bank.

For apartment managers who operate in a marketing milieu in which devotion to customers is a rarity, constructing a credible service program will result in a competitive advantage that will be unbeatable.

Third, once it has established a reputation for delivering superior service, the firm can capitalize on the positive word-of-mouth referrals that every company craves. Because prospects seek out and rely more on information from personal sources (i.e., the experiences of others) than impersonal ones (for example, newspaper and magazine advertisements), word-of-mouth advertising over time can become the central marketing strategy for the firm, resulting in significant cost savings. As Hanan and Karp stated in *Customer Satisfaction: How to Maximize, Measure, and Market Your Company's "Ultimate Product"*:

▶ At its best, [advertising] replicates an exchange of confidences between a trusted source and a trusting prospect. Who can be trusted? The most trustworthy source is never you, the manufacturer or supplier. *The most credible persuader is another customer who has already been satisfied.* This permits new customers to identify with the same satisfaction, apply it to their own situation, and rehearse their enjoyment of its benefits for themselves.

Indeed, the availability of testimonial advertising demonstrates to a prospective customer the firm's commitment to manufacturing satisfied customers, which is the company's true bottom line. As Hanan and Karp observed, *satisfied customers are the most effective salespeople for the organization's goods and services,* in effect becoming partners who help to grow the business.

Finally, providing exceptional service to a company's external clients benefits its internal customers as well. As Scott Gross pointed out:

▶ There is a surprising payoff awaiting these and other companies that imbue their customers with the service ethic: When they make their customers happy, they make their employees happy, too. Contented workers make for better-served customers, and there is mounting evidence that improvements in customer satisfaction lead directly to higher employee retention.

When the firm consistently delivers excellent service to all of its customers, a reinforcing process sets in: Small positive changes based on small positive actions tend to snowball, producing what might be called "virtuous cycles" of service that fortify and amplify each other. (See chapter 3 for a more detailed discussion of employee empowerment and satisfaction.)

For the leadership of a real estate management firm, becoming resident-passionate presents significant risks and opportunities. The metamorphosis from an inward-looking company that is preoccupied with its own narrow bureaucratic concerns to a vibrant, outward-focused, customer-centered organization is an arduous, time-consuming process. Visionary leadership is the essential distinctive characteristic, as well as the driving force, of this dynamic transformation.

8

The Benchmarking Revolution

Society is always taken by surprise at any new example of common sense.

—RALPH WALDO EMERSON

Benchmarking is the continuous process of measuring products, services, and practices against the toughest competitors or those companies recognized as industry leaders.

—DAVID T. KEARNS, CEO of Xerox

If you would like to be an outstanding guitar player, cabaret singer, tennis player, sculptor, novelist, surgeon, stand-up comedian, interior designer, or anything else, it makes sense to study the best in your chosen field. How do they do what they do? What are their critical skills? How do they approach the challenge of excellence? How do they think? What are their success attitudes? How did they get to be the best?

—KARL ALBRECHT

Benchmarking is one way to cut the ties of the past. By carefully revealing reality to the organization in digestible pieces, it inserts new views, objectives, and models into the murky waters of the past. Once gathered, benchmarking data do not go away, even if placed in a locked safe or shredded. Every individual who came in touch with the message is forever changed; they will never again see the organization in the same light. These individual revelations can build toward internal revolution, even while the security system is reporting that all is well. Change cannot be prevented or contained once it begins.

—KATHLEEN H. J. LEIBFRIED and C. J. MCNAIR

Competition, though unwelcome, is healthy for any business. While most companies would probably prefer to have a monopolistic position in their industries, the benefits of competition are undeniable. Competition requires a firm to bring its best products to market, to price them fairly, and to service them faithfully. Competition challenges companies to stretch capacities, to refine products and pricing structures continuously, and to vie with competitors at the highest, most productive, most cost-effective levels of which they are capable. In short, competition impels a company to excellence and forces the ones that cannot meet this standard out of the market. This is not new. Rather, it is "the American way" of doing business and one of the reasons the Japanese have been so successful in recent years.

In the apartment business, successful developers have analyzed those product features in the competitive market that prospects prefer—and are willing to pay premium rents to obtain—and then incorporated these features into their unit designs. This concept, which might be termed "follow the leader," also challenges owners and marketers to study rival buildings— to "go to school on the winners," as Richard Whiteley puts it—to determine suitable rent structures for their properties. Finally, although somewhat belatedly, apartment marketers can begin to refine their rent-setting procedures by supplementing traditional amenities listings and price adjustments with certain "intangible perquisites" contained in the product "bundle" in a particular apartment market—e.g., quality of staff, construction and security features.

It is *competition* that drives these behaviors, after all, and competition is the foundation for "benchmarking," a novel concept pioneered by the Xerox Corporation to meet the Japanese competitive challenge of the 1970s and refined and perfected by Xerox, Avon Products, Exxon Chemical, AT&T, and others thereafter. The underlying principle of benchmarking, according to Robert C. Camp, one of the inventors of the concept, is "the search for those best practices that will lead to the superior performance of a company."

When these "best practices" are collected and analyzed, they can be incorporated into a company's own operations; the underpinnings of benchmarking are therefore similar to mimicry or imitation—i.e., copycatting. Karl Albrecht is one commentator who recognizes this implicit criticism. He explained it this way:

▶ It makes good sense for the leaders of any business organization to study the best practices of the champions in their own field. The goal is not to try to make an organization a carbon copy of any other, but to discern the truth of their success and implement that truth in their own unique way.

To this we would only add the old cliche: Imitation is the sincerest flattery.

Routine Benchmarking Applications

Consumers benchmark continuously and relentlessly. Comparison shopping, for instance, is characteristic of benchmarking. Before purchasing an automobile, shoppers compare and contrast the features of various brands (domestic and foreign), try to measure values of each in economic and other terms, and routinely calibrate their findings against some "absolute"—a Mercedes, a Cadillac, or a Lexus, for example, or perhaps the first car they ever owned or the "perfect" vehicle they have conjured up in their imaginations. Whether shopping for perfume, a new suit, a new apartment, or professional assistance with tax preparation, consumers weigh costs against product attributes and frequently consider the "bundle" of adjuncts that competing products offer—such as their guarantees, reputations, and ease and access of service—before they make a decision to buy. For consumers in the waning years of the twentieth century, effective benchmarking, although not identified as such, is almost second nature.

Benchmarking in the Apartment Industry

Benchmarking is also frequently involved when apartment managers design an advertisement, market a product, communicate with a client, negotiate with a vendor, or handle any one of the infinite number of commercial moments of truth that are required in residential management. Whether consciously or not, you probably emulate people whom you believe are most effective at performing these routine management and marketing tasks. Because the styles of the leading retail managers and marketers who dominate their respective industries are seen on television or billboards, in newspaper or magazine advertisements, they are readily adopted and adapted.

Although the best efforts of others may be routinely benchmarked, this does not necessarily restrict the scope of such imitation to any particular industry. You may choose to incorporate certain aspects of a fast-food advertisement into one of your own ads, or to copy decorating details you admired in an upscale hotel in the common areas of an apartment building you manage, or even to adapt the sales techniques of a particularly talented stockbroker as part of your own selling methodology. The opportunities to appropriate excellence from outside sources are potentially limitless. The willingness to seek out and emulate the "best of the best"—what the Japanese call *dantotsu*—extends across industries and is not restricted to any one. "Dantotsu" is another ingredient of benchmarking.

Yet another characteristic of benchmarking is that it helps a company realize its ultimate potential in a perilous competitive battleground. Robert Camp likened its utility to warfare:

Exhibit 8.1
Example Marketing Grid Form
(The Traditional Approach)

Type of Unit _____ Date of Analysis _____

Property	Subject	Competitor #1		Competitor #2		Competitor #3	
Monthly Rent							
Concessions							
Address							
	Description	Description	Adj	Description	Adj	Description	Adj
Location							
Age							
Curb Appeal (1)							
Square Feet							
Baths (number)							
Patio/Balcony							
View							
Fireplace							
Wallpaper							
Carpet							
Drapes/Blinds							
Washer/Dryer/Microwave							
Dishwasher							
Disposal							
Air Conditioning (2)							
Cable TV							

▶ In the year 500 B.C., Sun Tzu, a Chinese general, wrote, "If you know your enemy and know yourself, you need not fear the result of a hundred battles." Sun Tzu's words could just as well show the way to success in all kinds of business situations. Solving ordinary business problems, conducting management battles, and surviving in the marketplace are all forms of war, fought by the same rules—Sun Tzu's rules.

Pricing is a powerful weapon in commercial warfare, and benchmarking techniques can assist you in arriving at a proper pricing matrix for apartment properties.

Exhibit 8.1 (*continued*)

Elevator								
Pool								
Sauna/Exercise Room								
Tennis								
Party Room								
Security								
Garage (3)								
Parking Fee								
Tenant Pays Heat								
Rental Rate								
Less Monthly Discount								
Effective Rent								
Adjustments (Total Net)								
Adjusted Comp Rent								
Adjusted Rent/Sq Ft								

(1) 3 = poor; 4 = fair; 5 = good; 6 = excellent curb appeal
(2) W = wall unit; C = central AC
(3) R = aboveground, open ramp; U = underground parking

Reproduced with permission from *Contemporary Apartment Marketing* by Kathleen M. McKenna-Harmon, CPM®, and Laurence C. Harmon, CPM® (Chicago: Institute of Real Estate Management, 1993), p. 16.

NOTE: This example was adapted from a grid used by the authors. For any specific evaluation, the comparison items for the subject property and its competition might include such things as specific utilities, other parking options, and vacancy rates.

Benchmarking and Rent-Setting

The technique that is generally accepted in the apartment industry for evaluating a competitive market and ascertaining appropriate rental rates is the marketing grid. In *Contemporary Apartment Marketing: Strategies and Applications,* we described this rent-setting approach (see exhibit 8.1). Briefly, the grid format permits direct comparison of rental rates and amenities at the property that is the subject of the study with those of other properties in its competitive market. The left-hand column lists the features or qualities of the apartments in the study, and blank columns are provided for each of the buildings to be compared. The subject property is described in the column adjacent to the features list, and its competitors are evaluated in successive

Exhibit 8.2
Example Unit Benchmarking Grid (The Marketing Grid Updated)

Type of Unit _____   Date of Analysis _____

Property	Subject	Competitor #1		Competitor #2		Competitor #3	
Monthly Rent*							
Concessions							
Address							
	Description	Description	Adj	Description	Adj	Description	Adj
Location							
Age							
Construction Quality							
Staff Quality							
Building Reputation							
Security Quality							
Curb Appeal (1)							
Square Feet†							
Baths (number)							
Patio/Balcony							
View							
Fireplace							
Wallpaper							
Carpet							
Drapes/Blinds							
Washer/Dryer/Microwave							
Dishwasher							
Disposal							

columns to the right. Note that the grid includes two columns for the competition—one to describe qualities and features and the other to adjust rental amounts upward or downward in dollar increments. The adjustments are intended to reflect whether the subject of the study is superior to the competitor with respect to a particular feature or quality. If so, the figure will appear as a positive; if not, the number will be listed as a negative. The sum of the various adjustments determines the net adjustment to the competitor's rent. In effect, the rent of each competing unit is adjusted up or down relative to the subject property in an attempt to represent the competitor—and the rent it commands—as more nearly comparable to the subject property.

Exhibit 8.2 (*continued*)

Air Conditioning (2)							
Cable TV							
Elevator							
Pool							
Sauna/Exercise Room							
Tennis							
Party Room							
Security							
Garage (3)							
Parking Fee							
Tenant Pays Heat							
Rental Rate							
Less Monthly Discount							
Effective Rent							
Adjustments (Total Net)							
Adjusted Comp Rent							
Adjusted Rent/Sq Ft							

*Rental rate should be lowest monthly rent as of the specific date of the comparison.
†Area for comparison should be for smallest unit of the type in all properties being evaluated.

(1) 3 = poor; 4 = fair; 5 = good; 6 = excellent curb appeal
(2) W = wall unit; C = central AC
(3) R = aboveground, open ramp; U = underground parking

NOTE: This example was adapted by the authors from the marketing grid presented in exhibit 8.1 to include an evaluation of some specific *qualitative* components of units in the market. For any specific evaluation, the comparison items for the subject property and its competition might also include such things as specific utilities, other parking options, and vacancy rates.

Setting Rents and Assessing Competitiveness in the Future. Exhibit 8.2 is a futuristic version of the marketing grid in exhibit 8.1. Note that in addition to location and curb appeal, it includes a number of "intangible perquisites" related to the property as a whole—e.g., construction quality, staff quality, building reputation, and security quality—that can be considered in making a rent-based comparison. This is benchmarking applied at the unit level.

An even more ambitious approach is to evaluate the relative competitiveness of the properties themselves—rather than merely compare unit types in competing properties in a particular neighborhood. The example building (or property) benchmarking grid in exhibit 8.3 differs from most marketing grid formats because it includes several items that require *qualitative* judg-

Exhibit 8.3

Example Building Benchmarking Grid (Determining Market Competitiveness)

Date of Analysis _____

Quality Assessment*	Subject	Competitor #1	Competitor #2	Competitor #3
Construction				
Site Staff				
Building Reputation				
Entry/Foyer				
Common Areas				
Hallways (lighting/spaciousness/ decor)				
Unit Size and Design/Space Utilization				
Exercise Facilities (equipment, locker rooms)				
Indoor/Outdoor Pool/Surroundings				
Sauna/Whirlpool/Tanning Beds				
Party Room				
Building/Garage Security				
Location/Accessibility[†]				
General Appeal and Overall Cleanliness				
Amenities*				
Concierge Services[‡]				
Window Coverings				
In-Unit Washer/Dryer				
Underground Heated Parking				
Guest Suites				
Skyway Connection				

*For *quality assessment,* the authors rate their properties according to the quality of 15 attributes using a scale of **1** to **5** with 5 = excellent; 4 = very good; 3 = average; 2 = fair; 1 = poor. For *amenities,* they list the number **5** if the amenity is present, **0** if it is not. The total possible rating is 100 points. Usually one of the competing properties receives the highest score; this is therefore the "benchmark." The subject property total rating is thus a percentage of the benchmark.

[†]Location/accessibility relates to such things as shopping, dining, entertainment, and highways. It might also include public transportation, schools, and recreational facilities if appropriate.

[‡]Identify array of services offered, including dry cleaning pick-up/delivery.

ments about overall property characteristics—e.g., quality of construction, staff, building reputation, exercise or fitness facilities, and the security of the building and garage—rather than mere quantitative listings, and it uses a numerical rating scale. Thus, it considers not only whether the properties have such things as tennis facilities or central air conditioning, but also whether these items are good or excellent or only fair.

Benchmarking Involves Qualitative Assessments. Rating characteristics based on qualitative judgments admittedly adds greater subjectivity to a process that is inherently idiosyncratic. However, we believe there are a number of values of the type described here that prospects are likely to consider in making renting decisions. As a consequence, these values need to be included in marketing grids. Indeed, we believe that qualitative attributes are likely to be increasingly important in determining the distinctiveness of apartment properties. Consequently, some properties will deserve steeper dollar adjustments in a traditional marketing grid analysis than those derived from unit features and amenities alone.

A grid of the type depicted in either exhibit 8.2 or 8.3 helps to determine the actual *market leader* in a competitive apartment neighborhood. If a unit benchmarking grid like the one in exhibit 8.2 is used, the market leader—the market's "best-of-class"—is the property that emerges as the one whose "adjusted/comparable real rent" is the highest. If a building benchmarking grid like that in exhibit 8.3 is used, the market leader is the one receiving the highest score. It should be noted that the "best-of-class" property derived from this exercise is often not the subject property. The purpose of grid analysis is usually to measure whether the subject property is performing as well as may be expected in light of market conditions that typically include at least one competitor that is judged superior to the subject overall.

Completion of a building benchmarking grid helps the analyst determine the competitiveness of the subject property relative to the market leader on some particular quantifiable basis. For example, exhibit 8.3 isolates 20 "quality" and "amenity" factors that contribute to the value of an apartment property in a specific neighborhood. Based on the five-point rating system in the exhibit, the market leader can receive as many as 100 points. Conversely, the subject property—assuming it is not the market leader—will be competitive in a certain percentage amount compared to the market leader.

Exhibit 8.3 (*concluded*)

NOTE: The authors developed these lists of representative attributes and amenities based on competing properties within their specific market. For any particular benchmarking evaluation, it is imperative to identify property characteristics and specific features and amenities within your competitive marketplace (i.e., what the direct competition, in particular, has to offer).

Economic Aspects of Apartment Benchmarking.   Benchmarking quality attributes of the kinds contained in exhibit 8.3 can also facilitate measurement of the financial benefit—if any—that can be realized after making improvements to a property. It provides a useful starting point in valuing properties "as-is" versus "as-improved." Camp described the generic benchmarking process this way:

▶ Benchmarking is not just a study of competition but a process of determining the effectiveness of industry leaders by measuring their results. . . . [It] is basically an objective-setting process. *Benchmarks, when best practices are translated into operational units of measure, are a projection of a future state or endpoint.*

Once a building benchmarking appraisal is completed, the analyst will be in a position to make decisions about specific improvements to the quality features or amenities of the subject property that will enhance its competitiveness in a measurable way and determine whether they are achievable— i.e., physically possible and economically feasible. Such "improvements" are either those grid features for which the market leader outscores the subject property—but which can be improved at the subject so that it will be more competitive at the top of its market (i.e., the benchmarks)—or those features which can be improved at the subject property so that it can actually *outperform* the market leader. (Here, improvements include both physical attributes and "intangible perquisites.")

A completed building benchmarking grid of the type depicted in exhibit 8.3 will allow the analyst to evaluate the ability of the subject property to attract increased rents. The extent of this capacity can be measured by means of the typical marketing grid evaluation. Assuming, for example, that the market leader received 100 points and the subject property received 75 points on the building benchmarking grid, and assuming that the market leader rents one-bedroom apartments for $750 per month, it should be possible to increase rental rates for the same type of units at the subject property based on achievable improvements in the "quality" and "amenities" listings contained in the grid. By determining the costs of these achievable improvements, the analyst can calculate the payback period required to recoup the investment, as well as the post-enhancement improvement in the subject property's net operating income. However, such computations are the province of investment analysis, which is beyond the scope of this book.

Renter Psychographics and Apartment Benchmarking.   We need to add a cautionary word to this discussion. As we will explain later in this chapter, one of the deficiencies of marketing grids in general, including the enhanced versions we have described, is that *they fail to measure the true preferences—the so-called buy factors—of prospective residents* and instead reveal only the partiality of the market analyst. The propensity of apartment marketers to assume that their own likes and dislikes are the same as those of apartment prospects is almost certainly fallacious, and listing only those buy factors that the marketers themselves find appealing renders the results of such grid analyses almost meaningless. John Sharpe, Executive Vice President of Operations for Four Seasons Hotels, has pointed this out succinctly:

► Customers don't buy a product, they buy what the product does for them. Quality in product or service is not what *we* think it is.

Jim Clemmer had this to add:

► Too often the features, attributes, or service/quality expectations of the customer are out of sync with what the organization considers to be important and is focused on delivering. As customers, we have all dealt with organizations that have done an outstanding job delivering a service or product feature we could care less about.

While marketing grids represent an effort to provide an objective basis for rent-setting, they are innately compromised by the subjectivity of the analyst. The objection is two-sided: First, because the components of the grid analysis (the buy factors) reflect the analyst's predilections rather than actual preferences of apartment prospects, dollar corrections based on them are likely to be inaccurate (and incomplete). Second, regardless of whether the buy factors mirror the predispositions of prospective residents, the process of adjusting for them will be so reflective of the analyst's own prejudices, and so unlikely to echo the propensities of the market, that any rental adjustment at all is likely to be deceptive.

We understand and agree with much of this argument, but we also believe that market forces and prospects' preferences deserve primary consideration in determining suitable rent levels in an apartment neighborhood. The heart of the problem may be that the adjustments, taken in their totality, automatically distort likely market inclinations. In addition, relying on the sum of adjustments in rent-setting, even if these adjustments are made in very small increments, only compounds the error. The real issue is that prospects' preferences—their perceptions of value—are so individualized, so specific, and so quirky that the inability to know them, and thus to reflect them in a marketing grid, potentially renders grid analysis meaningless.

The Impact of Perceived Value.   The problem is that value consists of more than mere price. Consumers make purchases to satisfy specific wants and needs. These needs and wants are very personal. They are related to the individual's survival and well-being, both physically (materially) and psychologically (emotionally). The value of any product, as perceived by consumers, incorporates notions of utility and esteem (i.e., status or image) in addition to purchase price. In his book, *Value Selling,* Louis De Rose characterized perceived value in this way:

Exhibit 8.4
The Value Selling Checklist

Customer Requirements	Value Contributions	Customer Assessment of Value	How Do We Measure Up?
• Specified and implied • Weighted as to importance to the customer	• Product and service features • Benefits and capabilities that satisfy requirements with cost-effectiveness	• Acknowledges • Perceives • Sees benefit • Sees no value	• Clearly superior • Better than most • On a par • Inferior

Reproduced with permission of the publisher from *Value Selling—The Strategy for: Reaching the Industrial Customer, Satisfying Customer Requirements, Competing in a Cost-Conscious Market,* by Louis De Rose (New York: AMACOM, 1989), p. 82. Copyright 1989 by AMACOM, a division of the American Management Association. All rights reserved.

▶ Value resides in the perception of the buyer. It is not intrinsic to the product. . . . Perceptions of value are objective when value is seen only in the competitive price—that is, value in exchange—but highly subjective when seen only as a gratification of esteem or psychic urge. However, both objective and subjective considerations are entailed when perceptions of value involve a product's usefulness or utility—that is, value in use. . . . When value is seen only as value in exchange, price is the only cost the buyer acknowledges. When value is seen only as esteem value, not even price will be given much weight in the buying decision.

In support of this concept of value, De Rose developed a "value selling checklist" (exhibit 8.4) that suggests how retailers can catalog value in terms of supplier capabilities as they relate to customer requirements—*in addition to* product features and benefits. The step-wise approach to completing such a checklist is analogous to that of marketing grid analysis, but the components of the checklist are clearly the substance of benchmarking comparisons. Here's how De Rose put it:

▶ Value is a relative concept. The customer's acknowledgment or perceptions of value are developed by comparison. They are influenced by competition. What the customer recognizes as a value contribution is only meaningful if the offerings of one supplier can be compared with those of another. . . . Where your product or service offering contains no feature that directly relates to a specified requirement, . . . your rating [will be] an unfavorable one.

- In the first column we list customer requirements as they are expressly defined or specified. To enhance their meaning, the salesperson might weigh the importance of each requirement as he thinks the customer evaluates it. . . . [T]he salesperson should then consider those requirements that are implied. They are for quality and availability assurance. . . .
- In the second column the salesperson matches value contributing product and service features to customer-specified requirements . . . on as direct a basis as he can. [Similarly] he matches those quality and availability capabilities that he believes contribute value toward satisfying the customer's implied requirements. . . .
- In the third column the salesperson evaluates the customer assessment of value contribution in those product and service features and those supplier capabilities he has identified.
- In the fourth column, the salesperson evaluates how he compares with competitors in providing value contribution as the customer assesses it . . . product feature by product feature, capability by capability. . . .

The Value Selling Checklist identifies how product features and service capabilities satisfy customer requirements, competitively. To complete the value selling exercise, . . . you must demonstrate that relationship in cost terms. . . . For each factor [in columns 1 and 2], you will enter cost as you know it or can estimate it . . . under the ratings assigned in columns 3 and 4.

The extent to which retailers can—or actually do—measure value this way validates the benchmarking approach to apartment analysis and rent setting that we recommend here.

Brainstorming Buy Factors

As should be clear from the preceding discussion, we think it is vital in the apartment industry to be able to derive rental rates in a way that reflects renters' opinions about the value and quality of apartment features and amenities. Without the ability to make adjustments in rents based on market preferences, apartment marketers can merely make "head-to-head" comparisons—i.e., match individual unit prices at their subject properties against those at each of the competitors in the market. Although price may be a very important force that influences apartment prospects—and price is arguably the primary driver for some property types in good times as well as during economic downturns—it is by no means the only one. We think apartment marketers need a methodology that can take other motivators of renters into account.

A useful starting point for the apartment marketer to inject objectivity into any type of grid analysis is to brainstorm buy factors in a group exercise. Participants should comprise everyone the marketer can convene who is conversant with the particular apartment market under study, including members of the leasing and management staff, representatives of apartment referral agencies, and even apartment residents if they can be induced to attend the session. The contributions of maintenance and housekeeping personnel to this process should not be overlooked: Their insights are based not only on their own knowledge and intuitions about what renters prefer, but also on conversations among residents that they may overhear during the workday. On-site staff who live at the property are usually in the best position to assess the popularity—and thus the value—of amenities such as swimming pools and parking facilities because they share these experiences with the residents. As Sam Walton, founder of Wal-Mart, is known to have said, "Our best ideas come from delivery and stock boys."

Prior to attending the brainstorming meeting, as many of the participants as possible should "shop" competing properties to familiarize themselves with the competitors' features and amenities. Moreover, members should be instructed to report their opinions about the cleanliness of the properties, the friendliness and professionalism of the personnel they encounter, and their overall impressions about construction, security, and other matters that might be important to them as prospective renters at these properties. Their evaluations, particularly as compared to their assessments of these factors at their own buildings, will be especially useful.

Of course, the purpose of this brainstorming effort—in effect, a type of focus group—is to compile an exhaustive list of the various buy factors that are present in the market being evaluated, as well as ascribe accurate dollar values to them. We have found that, the more knowledgeable the observers who can take part in this process, the more useful the results. Apartment-referral agents are especially valuable participants. [NOTE: A proper "focus group" session would be conducted by a preferably disinterested third party and bring together actual and potential apartment renters—possibly including some prospects who did not rent at the property or even some former residents—to develop a true "consumer" perspective. The insights of residents and frontline personnel are potentially the most valuable in identifying qualities and parameters for marketing grid analysis.]

The Levitt Paradigm

In chapter 2, we introduced Ted Levitt's paradigm of product attributes—their so-called generic, expected, augmented, and potential characteristics. In describing Professor Levitt's model, we observed that the "generic" product (the inner ring) offers purchasers the minimum qualities that they expect to find in a product of its type; their expectations, as well as the price of these goods, are correspondingly low.

Levitt's design of the "expected" product (the second ring) contains all of the attributes of the "generic" offering and adds others (usually those constituting the support system) which are bundled into the product as additional elements of value, enabling it to command a higher price.

The "augmented" product (the third ring) contains the features of the preceding types, but adds qualities that make the goods *unique*—and uniquely *valuable*—in their market. "Augmented" products are "best-in-class" goods that *delight* customers and induce buyers to pay a premium price to obtain them.

We observed in chapter 2 that the progression from the "expected" to the "augmented" product requires surprisingly small investments for the payoffs that can be realized by making the requisite improvements. (The "potential" product—the outer ring, according to the Levitt model—is the ultimate expression of the imaginable product type and may or may not even be in existence.) Jim Clemmer, one of the proponents of the Levitt matrix, described the third ring this way:

▶ The third ring is much more intuitive and irrational. At its best, the third ring is a series of tiny gestures and insignificant signals that make dealing with an organization a rare delight. It is a sense of warmth and attention that makes for true user-friendliness. . . . The third ring is made up of thousands of little things that either add up to a high "wow index" or that bit by bit drive customers nuts.

Clemmer also provided a conceptual understanding of the characteristics of Levitt's three rings of perceived value. This is shown in exhibit 8.5. Note that he does not distinguish between the augmented and the potential product.

The Paradigm of the Rings and Apartment Marketing Grids. We contend that Levitt's paradigm of the rings may serve as a prototype alternative to the traditional apartment marketing grid—in particular, we subscribe to Clemmer's characterizations. Our goal in suggesting this substitute is to outline an approach that will be a *more accurate and user-friendly* means of considering apartment pricing. More important, this model is potentially *less subjective* than its predecessors.

The revised "grid" would consist of three concentric circles labeled, respectively, *I* (the inner circle), *II* (the middle circle), and *III* (the outer circle). The inner circle would be used to characterize what constitutes a "generic" or Level I apartment of a particular size—the basic product as it exists in a typical apartment community in the local market—i.e., four white walls and a rug, with standard bathroom fixtures and basic appliances (stove, refrigerator) in the kitchen, all clean and in working order.

In describing a Level II or "expected" apartment, some or all of the elements of the traditional marketing grid may be listed. For purposes of comparison here, we could say that such an expected unit, in a downtown market,

Exhibit 8.5

**The Three Rings of Levitt
(Adapted from Clemmer)**

	Generic Product	Expected Product	Augmented or Potential Product
Focus	Core products and services	Administration/field support	Moments of Truth
Objectives	Requirements	Satisfaction	Delight
Key Elements	Technical expertise (high tech)	Systems, processes, practices, and structure (high tech)	People (high touch)
Control	Management and professionals	Management and professionals	Frontline performers
Costs	Large and visible	Huge and hidden	Small and seemingly insignificant

Reproduced with permission from *Firing on All Cylinders: The Service/Quality System for High-Powered Corporate Performance* by Jim Clemmer (Homewood, Illinois: Business One Irwin, 1992), p. 39.

might be in a building between two and seven years old, have an area of 575–650 square feet, and include one to one and one-half baths, a microwave, drapes or blinds, and a balcony. The common areas of the building may include elevators, an outdoor swimming pool, an exercise room, and similar features or amenities. The pricing level for this apartment type might be between $540 and $600 per month.

By contrast, one-bedroom apartments in the subject property—we will call it "Lincolnshire"—may be somewhat smaller than the overall competition (say in the range of 530–620 square feet), and have fewer unit and common area amenities than the competition, yet it possesses superlative construction and security features. In a brainstorming session, the group might conclude that the Lincolnshire staff is exceptional, considering them much superior to the personnel at competing properties.

Using a traditional marketing grid approach (such as that presented in exhibit 8.1) and the "factual" data provided here, the person conducting the analysis might conclude that one-bedroom units at Lincolnshire should be priced well below the competition, perhaps less than $540 per month. On the other hand, armed with the Levitt prototype, the analyst might decide that the Lincolnshire one-bedroom unit actually transcends the "expected" apartment of this type in its market and is, in fact, an "augmented" or Level III apartment and therefore entitled to be priced somewhat above the top end of the range for expected apartments.

We believe that the Levitt paradigm has the capacity to supplement or, for some purposes, supplant the format of traditional marketing grid analysis, whose mechanistic underpinnings tend to overlook—and can therefore defeat—the types of qualitative judgments that we think are essential in modern apartment marketing. (Exhibit 8.6 suggests how a concentric circle "grid" might take shape. It identifies factors we would use to compare apartments in our marketplace with those at the more upscale properties we manage; each "level" might include more or different factors for an analysis within a particular market.) In this type of comparison, the analyst is looking at a whole rather than at the individual parts, or their sum. While it may not supersede the traditional approach, this technique provides an alternative methodology that can confirm—or call into question—the conclusions drawn from other analyses.

Brainstorming Intangible Perquisites

The other obvious use of the Levitt paradigm is to brainstorm ways to transform generic units into "expected" or "augmented" apartments. Another look at Clemmer's observations makes the point:

▶ Third-ring enhancements are usually small investments with huge payoffs. The third ring is where the human touch is added. It is those intangible signs of personal care and commitment that say, "We're pleased to serve you. We want to do whatever we can to make your relationship with us as delightful as possible." . . . [The augmented product] is a series of tiny gestures and insignificant signals that make dealing with an organization a rare delight. It is a sense of warmth and attention that makes for true user-friendliness.

Exhibit 8.6 represents the Levitt paradigm as it might be applied to apartment evaluations. There is still something more, as the diagram shows; but how does one describe an apartment that might exist beyond the augmented level? This is where market research has classical applications. With it, you can find out what renters in your market want—and, in particular, what they want that is *not* available in your market. Then you can decide what additional improvements or enhancements can be made to your property and to individual apartments to attract those renters, achieve higher rents, and retain your residents year after year after year, even when alternative housing possibilities—such as single-family homeownership at low mortgage rates—are available.

Moments of Truth Drive the Third Ring.   It should be obvious from this discussion (and exhibit 8.6) that the third ring—the augmented product—is the key. While the potential product is the apartment that will be forever on the horizon—the ultimate goal of your continued striving to make

Exhibit 8.6

The Paradigm of the Rings as an Apartment Marketing Grid

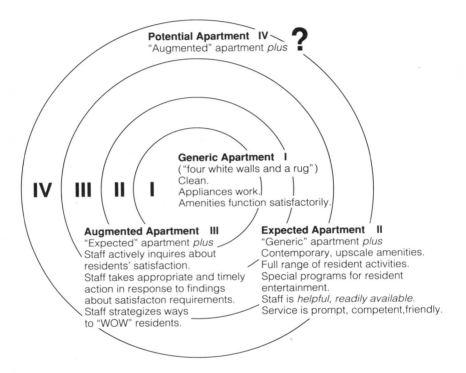

Potential Apartment IV
"Augmented" apartment *plus* **?**

Generic Apartment I
("four white walls and a rug")
Clean.
Appliances work.
Amenities function satisfactorily.

IV   III   II   I

Augmented Apartment III
"Expected" apartment *plus*
Staff actively inquires about
residents' satisfaction.
Staff takes appropriate and timely
action in response to findings
about satisfacton requirements.
Staff strategizes ways
to "WOW" residents.

Expected Apartment II
"Generic" apartment *plus*
Contemporary, upscale amenities.
Full range of resident activities.
Special programs for resident
entertainment.
Staff is *helpful, readily available.*
Service is prompt, competent, friendly.

As noted in exhibit 2.2, in the marketplace, the *generic product* (I) is what it is; in general, it is sold on the basis of price. The *expected product* (II) includes features and amenities equivalent to comparable properties; it is sold on the basis of quality. The *augmented product* (III), on the other hand, encompasses features and amenities that exceed the competition; because a major component is personal service, its selling point is a relationship. This is what can make your apartment the market leader.

Note, too, that while Levitt includes a fourth ring, as shown here, his *potential product* (IV) represents an ultimate theoretical entity as it might exist *if every conceivable enhancement could be added to it.* We contend that efforts to sustain the leadership positioning of your augmented apartment over time will, in fact, comprise the evolutionary component that makes it the ultimate potential apartment product.

the augmented product even better—it is the third ring that will be constantly evolving. As Clemmer described it, this is where it all pays off:

▶ What about your moments of truth? Who decides whether to bend a rule to help out a customer? Who decides whether to answer that phone on the second ring? Who spots the error in the invoice and pulls it out for correction? The answer, 9 out of 10 times, is that employees make those third-ring decisions. *If you studied a thousand moments of truth in a given day, you probably would find that 900 of them were managed by an employee with no supervisor or manager in sight. Employees live in, control, and get their job satisfaction (or hatred) from the third ring. This is their territory. They own it.*

As we noted earlier in this book, hiring nice people is important—even critical—to serving your customers properly. It is your frontline employees who create the "augmented" aspect of your apartment product, and they are the source of any perceptions of further enhancements—i.e., the notion of the "potential" apartment product.

The Benefits of Benchmarking

In this chapter, we have suggested several applications for benchmarking in the apartment industry. Here, in conclusion, is what Robert C. Camp, one of its inventors, has suggested as its utility:

▶ Benchmarking can benefit a company in several ways:

- It enables the best practices from any industry to be creatively incorporated into the processes of the benchmarked function.

- It can provide stimulation and motivation to the professionals whose creativity is required to perform and implement benchmark findings.

- Benchmarking breaks down ingrained reluctance of operations to change. It has been found that people are more receptive to new ideas and their creative adoption when those ideas did not necessarily originate in their own industry.

- Benchmarking may also identify a technological breakthrough that would not have been recognized, and thus not applied, in one's own industry for some time to come, such as bar coding, originally adopted and proven in the grocery industry. In these instances it is more important to uncover the industry best practices than to concentrate on obtaining comparative cost data. The business unit can determine for itself what cost levels could be achieved if it incorporated the benchmark practices in its own operations.

• Finally, those involved in the benchmarking process often find their professional contacts and interactions from benchmarking are invaluable for future professional growth. It permits the individuals to broaden their background and experience. It makes them more useful to the organization in future assignments.

9

Strategizing the Resident Retention Revolution

The key success factor, where the service system is concerned, is the "customer-friendly" system. Service systems that are low on the friendliness scale tend, by their very design, to subordinate convenience and ease of access *for the customer* in favor of the convenience of the people who work within the system. A customer-friendly system, on the other hand, is one whose basic design makes things easy for the customer.

—KARL ALBRECHT and RON ZEMKE

Benchmarking processes bring about an awareness of the external world. Its greatest value is in learning about practices used by others that are better than those currently in place internally. The outside findings are used directly or used to modify, improve, or adapt external practices to provide useful internal change and improve efficiency and effectiveness. It is a process to find a better way, rather than an attempt to reinvent the proverbial wheel.

—ROBERT C. CAMP

How many times would service have been improved if the salespeople or front-line employees had the responsibility and authority to make decisions on the spot? Instead we often have red tape, rules and regulations, and a detached, "You'll have to see the manager" attitude. Instead of flexibility and accountability we often have a bureaucratic approach to service. Is it any wonder we cannot get good service?

—D. KEITH DENTON

It's not enough for senior executive team members to be "committed" to service/quality improvement; they must be *visibly seen* to be *obsessed* with this as their top priority. Since we all know that actions speak much louder than words, senior managers need to work hard on *visibly signaling their commitment* so strongly and *consistently* that there can be no room for doubt about how critical service/quality is to the organization's future.

—JIM CLEMMER

Americans expect—indeed, demand—immediate gratification. They assume there will be instantaneous and dramatic results whenever energy is expended—and the greater the expenditure of energy, they reason, the more spectacular the results. Pursuing the goal of a customer-driven company culture—a process, rather than an event—runs counter to this belief system. The work is arduous, the results are not necessarily immediate, and the required commitment is life-long. Because the evolution is also potentially both expensive and revolutionary, many organizations may undertake it, but few have the staying power to succeed. Jeffrey Disend has forewarned those about to begin to transform their companies:

▶ It means changing the way all the employees in your organization think about themselves and their customers. It must be an organization-wide process from the top down and from the bottom up. It must be ongoing. And it takes time. Anything else is a waste of your people's time and your organization's money.

Measure the Intensity of Your Commitment to Change

A successful metamorphosis demands focused, daily commitment on the part of every member of the organization. It is useful to remember that the entity involved need not be an entire company, although the task is significantly easier when it is. There are instances when an apartment community management office or housekeeping or maintenance team provides extraordinary resident service, while the rest of the firm lags slightly behind, perhaps concentrating on internal processes.

The apartment industry typically operates in what might be termed "self-directed work groups," functioning in a behaviorally autonomous fashion. Because service, in its essence, is a marketing strategy implemented by one frontline server for the benefit of one customer at a time, a particular organizational atom may develop a service culture different from, larger than, and independent of, any other in the company. In such circumstances, the owner or the apartment manager might be a tyrant—even customer-toxic— nonetheless the site staff manages to deliver superlative customer service.

A logical first step in developing a customer-focused culture is to dissect and study operating systems piecemeal. The apartment business is one in which various outmoded ideas have unfortunately endured well beyond their useful lives. We have, for example, copied forms and manuals for decades without ever asking whether what we were doing was desirable. We tend to add reporting requirements without pausing to consider whether existing, duplicative, inferior ones might be scuttled. Similar examples abound.

Champion Your Residents, *Not* the Status Quo

It's time to investigate the way you do business to see how you can help your residents win. All employees should ask this question as they proceed through each workday: "Is the system (task, form, etc.) that I'm involved with right now in the best interest of our customers?" Or more broadly, "Are our customer service policies, procedures, protocols, and principles designed to serve the customer—or were they really constructed to make things more convenient for the company?" A scrupulously honest answer to this question can serve as a fruitful first step in launching your firm's resident retention revolution.

The undertaking is further complicated by the fact that real estate management operations suffer an ever-increasing administrative burden. They are paper-driven rather than customer-driven—Monday-morning reports tend to be ranked ahead of happy customers. To have a successful resident retention revolution, these priorities will have to be forcefully reordered to put your customers first in line.

The late Sam Walton, founder of Wal-Mart and one of the great champions of the customer-driven company, put it this way:

▶ There is only one boss, and whether a person shines shoes for a living or heads up the biggest corporation in the world, the boss remains the same. It's the customer! The customer is the person who pays everyone's salary and who decides whether a business is going to succeed or fail. In fact, the customer can fire everybody in the company from the chairman on down, and he can do it simply by spending his money somewhere else.

Henry Ford made the same observation: "It is not the employer who pays the wages. Employers only handle the money. It is the customers who pay the wages."

As you review your business practices, remember that nothing about your present way of operating should be considered sacred—or even appropriate. How resident-friendly is your lease agreement, for instance? Are your rules "red" rules—that is, are they essential to the health and safety of the residents or for the protection of the property? Or have you created so many "blue" rules—those designed for the convenience of the site staff—that your residents will be insulted? When you examine your procedures from a wide-angle, customer-sensitive perspective, you may discover to your chagrin that they were either designed or have evolved in such a way that company interests come first and customer interests a distant second. Or as Albrecht and Zemke have cautioned:

▶ There is, in most organizations, a conspiracy of accolades and incentives that tie people to the rules of the system first and the needs of the customer second.

Richard C. Whiteley has prescribed an aggressive pruning of the company rulebook as one of the first steps in the transformation effort:

▶ Review the policies of your company, department, or business unit. The first goal is to eliminate all policies that are "unnecessary" and "not customer friendly." Often old, out-moded, customer-irritating policies remain in force for no other reason than "It's the way we've always done it." Get rid of them. . . . Second, examine the "unfriendly" but "necessary" policies. Challenge them. Are they really necessary? Ask yourself: What would be the consequences of eliminating this policy? Would the resulting problems outweigh the aggravation we're causing our customers by retaining the policies?

Are the stock responses of company employees to residents—for example, "Sorry, that's our policy," or "I understand what you're saying, but we've always done it this way,"—the messages you truly want to convey to your customers? As a matter of fact, do you really *know* what's going on out there at the front line? Do you personally and regularly watch and listen to the interactions that take place between your internal and external customers? "Management by Walking Around," Tom Peters' shorthand description of the optimum way for company leadership to get close to their customers (and stay there), means that managers need to devise ways to leave their plush corner offices and check out what is happening on the front line. The quality of those server-to-customer "moments of truth" will determine your residents' satisfaction—and decide your company's fate.

Adopt Your Customers' Perspective on Your Company's Frontline Servers

Look at your staff from the vantage point of your residents. How amiable are your frontline servers? Are they people *you* would be eager to do business with? Most important, are they the kinds of folks you feel comfortable entrusting with the future of your business?

You can provide technical training that can make virtually any competent candidate a productive employee, but you cannot retrofit people with the congenial attitude that you want your company to display to your customers.

That is a matter of genes or upbringing or a combination of the two; in any event, the socialization process was completed long before a candidate approached you for a job.

Here's the truth of the matter: Service is an affair of the heart; for service to touch the mind of the consumer, it must come from the heart of the server. People are the epicenter of the customer-driven company. Goods and services are generally brought to the market by people, and customers are happiest when they are being attended to by nice people. The great customer service companies overflow with friendly employees. Your job as a revolutionary is to find, hire, train and retain the nicest people available. Too often in the past, the people hired for real estate management positions have been efficient, bottom-line driven, and skilled at enforcing rules. However, with few exceptions, they tend not to be genuinely congenial people. Too often, they sell apathetically, they smile reflexively, and they manage primarily by fear. These kinds of people do not belong in a customer-passionate business. Laura Liswood has underscored this problem:

▶ Many employees in customer-contact jobs are ill-suited by nature to deal with people. They may be trained to work the cash register, know the merchandise, and parrot the words, "May I help you, please?" and "Thank you." But they lack the outgoing personality, enthusiasm, and honest desire to serve.

Folks like these are so entrenched in their outmoded marketing and management styles that they probably are not capable of embracing the notion of *delighting* customers. They are easy to recognize. Their litany goes something like this: "If you give the resident an inch he will take a mile," and "If we offer something to one of them they'll all want it."

Such beliefs are ruinous to a customer service culture. Each of your residents is unique, precious, and irreplaceable—and deserves to be treated as such. Because the happiness of residents is the indispensable foundation of the apartment business, everyone in your company needs to renew their pledge to resident satisfaction every day. Apartment managers might choose to benchmark Donald Libey by adopting this *mantra* as their daily devotion:

▶ [Customer focus] has no vacation, no time off, no afternoon away. It takes no break during the morning or the afternoon, has no lunch hour, and is incapable of leaving its place of duty. It is forever and always, eternal, and ever-vigilant.

Your Goal: Let the Resident Win!   Apartment managers regularly hear owners say, "I know what I should be doing, but I have a manager who has been with me 20 years. He's doing what he was taught to do back then, but he refuses to do this (resident retention) stuff. I can't fire him."

Unfortunately, managers such as these are ubiquitous. We recommend that owners give them a chance to change. Make it clear to them that a revolution is underway. Challenge them to become excited about—and involved in—this new approach to customers. Make them a central part of the transformation. Invite them to take the lead. Meanwhile, you may have to redefine the reward system and clearly explain the change and mean it. Managers need to be confident that your perspective has changed and that they will not be judged by both standards. However, if they cannot genuinely play an active role, you will have no choice but to hire someone else who will: Heeding the call to "Let the Customer Win!" means that those who cannot do so will lose.

As you assess how resident-passionate each of your employees is, you may find yourself having to fill some vacated positions. When that happens, ensure that in your revamped hiring procedure, just as in every other company function, you put your customers' best interests first. This is the message once again: Do everything you can to *hire the nicest people you can find.* If you are forced to choose between a candidate with a great attitude and one with great technical skills, pick the nice one. Skills can be taught; attitude is inbred. Here's what William A. Band had to say about the importance of demeanor at the frontline:

▶ When respondents [in a 1988 Gallup survey of American consumers] were asked what they considered to represent high quality in services, the characteristics most frequently mentioned were: "courtesy, promptness, a basic sense that one's needs [were] being satisfied, and the attitude of the service provider." In other words, American consumers are not expecting accuracy and convenience so much as they are saying, "treat us nicely."

In chapter 8, we suggested revising the traditional apartment marketing grid, proposing one that will allow marketers to arrive at appropriate pricing levels by including for consideration such intangible factors as the quality of security, building construction, and staffing. (See exhibits 8.2, 8.3, and especially 8.6 and the related discussions.) We believe that renting decisions are based at least as much on these elements as the amenities-totalling exercise that has characterized grid analysis previously. When vacancy rates are high, prospective residents have a choice among the objective "buy factors," and it is the subjective issues that will make or break the sale. In other words, there are business and economic reasons for exploring the intangible perquisites. That is why we believe it is equally important for "mystery shoppers" who are hired to evaluate the quality of on-site marketing presentations to concentrate their attention on the cheerfulness, helpfulness, and overall friendliness of *all* of the site personnel—not just the leasing agents. The "likability quotient" derived from these shopping exercises can become a significant element in evaluations of the staff's performance and bonuses, even their continued employment.

Customer Ergonomics:
Make Your Company Resident-Friendly

Companies that decide to improve the quality of the service they offer their customers need to appraise early on what we call "customer ergonomics"—that is, how friendly their customers perceive them to be. One example of ergonomics, of course, is the "red" rule/"blue" rule distinction. Another is the company's dedication to "hiring nice." Those companies that are *customer-driven* routinely and rigorously assess how easy and how pleasant it is for their customers to do business with them, and relentlessly tear down any barriers they encounter that complicate things for their clients.

The measure of the customer-friendly firm is its attitude toward complaints. Ergonomically designed companies recognize two essential truths:

1. The absence of complaints means that underlying company-customer relationships are actually unhealthy, and

2. Complaining customers are either a gold mine of future business or a blueprint for disaster.

The first step in creating a complaint-friendly environment is to seek out and welcome customer input, be it positive or negative. As Michael LeBoeuf has remarked:

▶ [Complaints] aren't annoyances but opportunities to get better and build customer loyalty. Be wary of long-term customers who never complain. Nobody is ever totally satisfied for an extended period of time. Either they aren't being candid or they aren't being asked the platinum questions.

We recognize that it is counter-intuitive to welcome complaints. Human nature perceives an unhappy customer as a troublemaker at best or, more likely, as a lost customer. Many businesses adopt the attitude that unhappy customers are annoying squawkers, nitpickers, or outright thieves. Such labels get stuck on practically everyone who complains, which means that disaffected customers become more vulnerable to poor treatment, without regard for the real merits of their problems.

This attitude is entirely misguided: Complaining customers are, in effect, inviting the company to earn their continued business; their complaints are actually camouflaged requests for service. As Heskett and his colleagues have noted:

▶ Managers either purposely or unwittingly suppress complaints, viewing them as negative marks on short-term performance rather than what one breakthrough service manager has called the "golden nuggets of information" that provide the basis for recovery. As a result, some of the most important information available to a service company is lost.

The management company and the property owner must establish an atmosphere that is conducive to surfacing and resolving complaints. There is no point in punishing someone who receives twenty complaints; what should be punished is having complaints that are unresolved.

The absence of complaints means that the company has gotten out of touch with its customers. The consequences are dire: The firm almost certainly will continue to lose more of its current clientele—without knowing why—and will likely forfeit additional business with potential customers because of negative word-of-mouth advertising. As Milind Lele remarked:

▶ Customer dissatisfaction presents a serious threat because many unhappy customers don't complain—at least, not to the company. Instead they tell family and friends about their dissatisfaction. A good number of them switch to other suppliers.

How many noncomplainers will actually defect? D. Keith Denton, citing a study conducted by the White House Office of Consumer Affairs, quantified the magnitude this way:

▶ [The study] found that for every complaint at company headquarters the average business has another 26 customers with problems, at least six of which are serious. The cold facts are that anywhere from 65 to 90% of those noncomplainers will not buy from that business again.

On the other hand, soliciting customer complaints can provide abundant benefits. First, if company leadership becomes involved in actually fielding the complaints, invaluable information will be made available to the top of the organization. Michael LeBoeuf made this recommendation:

▶ *Get people at the top actively involved in both listening to and helping resolve customer complaints.* This is an excellent way for top management to learn customer wants and then respond with action to meet those wants. Too many managers make decisions in a vacuum without understanding the needs and wants of the customers who make the business possible.

Second, the complaint procedure can stimulate company leadership to *empower* its frontline employees to respond effectively to the concerns of its clientele. According to Linda Lash:

▶ Most companies have found that empowering the front-line saves money in the centralized customer service department because it reduces the number of complaints received. [Conversely,] disgruntled customers who harbor their complaints until they get time to write or call the company's headquarters office intensify and embellish the complaint, making it more costly to handle and allowing time for dangerous word-of-mouth advertising.

Complaints Document Your Failpoints and Provide Profit Centers. The third impetus for a company to surface customer complaints is that the outcome of the process is essentially a report card of service failpoints: A system that documents and classifies complaints pinpoints the areas of greatest customer irritation that need immediate attention. When faithfully recorded and carefully catalogued, customer complaints can provide worthwhile guidance for company management in areas ranging from personnel selection and staffing needs to preventive maintenance. As Zeithaml and coworkers have noted:

▶ Complaints can become part of a larger process of staying in touch with customers. In particular, they can provide important information about the failures or breakdowns in the service system. If compiled, analyzed, and fed back to employees who can correct the problems, complaints can become an inexpensive and continuous source of adjustment for the service process.

The real incentive for companies to become complaint-friendly, however, is that it is financially sensible to do so. As Linda Lash spelled it out:

▶ The paramount reason for a company or organization to spend money on resources to handle complaints and inquiries is to get repeat business. Repeat business generates revenue and profit and turns what is typically viewed as a cost center into a revenue-generating and profit-generating business activity.

Remedying service failpoints lessens the "hassle factor" of customers' dealings with the company. Reducing customer hassles is another way to make the firm ergonomically sound. Berry and Parasuraman had this to say about the subject:

▶ Whenever customers experience a service problem, they are forced to sacrifice something they would not have to if the service had been performed right the first time. . . . An excellent service recovery effort must make amends for the hassle factor. Companies must do more for the customer than merely reperforming the service.

Put Your Frontline Servers *In Charge*

Even the friendliest, most highly trained employees will fail unless they are empowered to solve their residents' problems on the spot. Because the apartment industry is rule and policy driven, enforcing rules and regulations is a necessary part of the job description of site personnel. Unfortunately, employees are usually required to get permission from one or more of their supervisors each time they believe that a rule should be bent or a policy broken. Because residents often have pressing needs that demand a quick response, they feel frustrated and angry when they have to wait while superiors are consulted about what should be done.

Most solutions are pretty simple, inexpensive, and based on common sense. Let your residents *win* by empowering your employees to fix what is broken on the spot. As Zemke and Bell have pointed out:

▶ [The internal clout of empowerment] results in the service deliverer acting with responsible competence and assertive confidence to take actions not covered by the firm's rules, regulations or procedures. Empowerment is the self-generated exercising of judgments. It's doing what needs to be done rather than doing what one is told.

Indeed, if your hiring and training procedures are sound, you should have confidence in the capability of your employees to take action for your customers on behalf of the company without the need for close supervision.

Empowered employees understand their company's commitment to customer satisfaction and display this positive message to their clients. This has beneficial consequences for both employee morale and repeat business. According to Heskett and coworkers:

▶ The effective response to service failures and complaints not only has a high payoff in terms of long-term business, it sends positive signals to both customers and employees that the service company's policy is to encourage corrective action and achieve customer satisfaction, enhancing the company as a place to work in the minds of its employees.

Linda Goldzimer has explained how complaint-solicitation improves customer relations:

▶ By encouraging your customers to provide feedback, particularly complaints, you are showing concern, interest, *and the desire to satisfy* your customers. The very act of soliciting feedback is a positive signal to your clients.

Customer Ergonomics in the Apartment Business.   A common complaint at apartment properties is that residents lose fistfuls of money in laundry machines. Doing laundry is a miserable job; it becomes even more disagreeable when (as often happens) the equipment malfunctions. Under these circumstances, fuming residents have to track down a member of the site staff and recount their problem in the hope of receiving a refund so they can return to the unpleasant task of doing laundry. (Installing a phone that rings directly in the management office would eliminate this hassle.) In addition to their financial losses (often minimal), residents have, in the process, lost time and patience (almost always substantial)—yet typically, no one bothers to compensate them for any of the damage. There are alternatives to this:

> One of our managers refunds double or triple the amount of their losses to disgruntled residents. She says, "I'm so sorry you had trouble. Here, do a couple of loads on me." She also encourages residents to call her from their apartments if breakdowns occur, and she refunds the money to them personally. Because this response is both instantaneous and out of proportion to the injury suffered, residents view the manager as a sympathetic friend who values their time and truly wants to minimize their inconvenience.
>
> Another of our managers routinely collects laundry money from the machines in his building. Whenever he is emptying the machines and he encounters a resident doing laundry, he reaches in the bag and pays for the washer and dryer. He says this little touch changed his whole attitude about his work. He used to dislike emptying the machines, but the opportunity to be a Good Samaritan gave the job a delightful new dimension. He now looks forward to the trip around the community almost as much as his customers enjoy seeing him.

These examples illustrate a simple truth about resident retention and customer service in the apartment business: A successful approach requires a combination of the Golden Rule ("Do unto others . . . . ") and the Boy Scout Oath ("Do a Good Turn Daily"). This attitude has the dual benefit of delighting residents, which increases the chances of attracting their continued patronage and creating positive word-of-mouth, which increases the chances of attracting the patronage of others.

Encourage Your Residents' Positive Word-of-Mouth

Beneficial word-of-mouth is essential to the success of an apartment community, just as it is to anyone in the business of selling services. James Heskett and his colleagues have explained why:

▶ [Products possess] search qualities and experience qualities. Search qualities are qualities that a consumer can determine prior to purchasing a product; experience qualities are those that can be determined [only] after the purchase.

Renters are able to judge the satisfactoriness of apartment living only after they have actually experienced it—that is, after they have undergone the hassle of apartment hunting, packing and moving, settling in, and the rest of the discomfort that is inherent in a new housing situation. Thus, the "experience qualities" of apartments overwhelm "search qualities" as a way of evaluating apartment living. Consequently, prospective renters are much more likely to seek out and rely on information from personal sources (relatives and friends) than from impersonal sources (e.g., advertising) before making the decision to rent a particular apartment. Word-of-mouth recommendations, therefore, are an invaluable underpinning of a property's marketing program.

Because word-of-mouth advertising is so vital to success, apartment marketers ought to strategize techniques to encourage it. WilsonSchanzer Real Estate Services in San Antonio, Texas, has devised an unusual way to reward residents for prospect referrals. Because Texas (and many other states) prohibits remuneration for unlicensed referrals, they had to craft a bonus program that would be consistent with Texas law.

> The WilsonSchanzer "Home Improvements Program" is an imaginative plan that awards points for resident referrals (in 25-unit increments). Residents can either collect apartment upgrades immediately after making a successful referral or stockpile them and receive a higher-value bonus. The choice of improvements includes redecorating, new carpeting or wallpaper, ceiling fans, alarm systems and the like. (The roster may be customized for the particular property.) Perhaps the best feature of the Home Improvements Program, however, is that the reward is essentially a capital upgrade that remains with the apartment on a long-term basis.

By contrast, Cantrell, Harris & Associates, a San Francisco-based management company, has instituted "Champagne Taste," a program to reward resident referrals at an upscale property in Raleigh, North Carolina.

> The firm devised a die-cut door hanger in the form of a champagne bottle (describing the program) that can be hung on each apartment door. When residents refer a prospect who signs a lease, the company treats them to a champagne brunch at a top restaurant in the city. In addition, the *new* resident receives a bottle of pink champagne, two glasses, and a "Welcome Home!" card signed by the manager.

Root Out Your Residents' Hassles

A very powerful marketing message to potential residents is that apartment living is "worry-free." People who cannot maintain single-family homes and grounds for physical reasons or who consider this work to be a burden—businesspeople, students, the infirm and elderly, to name just a few categories—are natural renters. Residents who select apartment living because it is hassle-free are potentially life-long renters. The competition for *their* business is not single-family homeownership (as is so often the case for others); instead, it is another apartment property that can deliver worry-free living.

Exhibit 9.1
Reasons Why Renting Is Smart

RENTING IS SMART

FOR PEOPLE WHO . . .

- Wheel around in Winnebagos half the year
- Love the crunch and color of autumn leaves that they don't have to rake
- Don't want to stock a pegboard full of tools
- Want to smell the roses, not plant, prune and pamper them
- Think that personally operating a lawnmower is an unacceptable dent in their schedule
- Don't know what to do with a leaky roof
- Want to enjoy the snowfall without hauling out a shovel

Source: Minnesota MultiHousing Association.

Recognizing the potency of convenience as a marketing message, the Minnesota MultiHousing Association (MHA) has adopted the slogan "Renting Is Smart" for its entire multimedia campaign, which includes newspaper and magazine advertising, brochures, and billboards. In addition, MHA members are encouraged to use the slogan in their individual advertising campaigns. Periodically, various MHA publications catalog reasons why renting is smart; a number of these reasons are indicated in exhibit 9.1.

Alleviating the "hassle factor" that is inherent in homeownership is a tool that apartment managers can employ not only as an advertising message, but also as a resident retention technique. Dominion Management, an Atlanta-based company, uses a flyer titled "Renting Tips the Scales in Your Favor" as a renewal piece. Summarizing the time and expense—i.e., the *hassle*—that residents would experience if they moved from their Dominium community when their leases expire, the brochure is sent twice during the lease term—once just before renewal.

The front of the brochure depicts a scale, with the word BUY outweighed by the word RENT. The back points out several reasons why "renting is the wisest choice." Finally, the interior of the piece illustrates the costs of purchasing an $85,000 house or condo, financing 90 percent of the price with a $9\frac{1}{2}$-percent conventional mortgage. Amounts are listed for the downpayment and closing costs; out-of-pocket expenses incurred in moving, purchasing appliances and the like; monthly bills to maintain a house (mortgage, utilities, etc.), and annualized costs for major improvements (carpeting, exterior painting, roof replacement, etc.). The "recap" shows a first-year expense of homeownership as $31,525.00 and concludes with the question, "Doesn't this figure tip the scales in favor of renting?"

Partner With Your Customers to Reduce Their Hassles and Build Your Business

The "hassle factor" crops up in other situations as well. Establishing and nurturing creative partnering arrangements between sellers and buyers—i.e., between apartment communities and renters and suppliers—is primarily an attempt to cut down on the hassle that is inherent in continually developing new relationships. Partnering is the optimal economic arrangement because it establishes long-term "win-win" professional interdependencies. Here's what Donald Libey has written about the subject:

▶ Your customers don't want to go somewhere else. They have a desire to be loyal. . . . Bio-psychologically, The Customer's drive to survive is directly transferred to the supplier when the decision to trade is made. The Customer wants you to guarantee survival. The Customer is literally trusting you with a portion of personal survival.

Zemke and Bell echoed this sentiment:

▶ More and more of the world's economic work gets done through long-term relationships between sellers and buyers. It is not a matter of just getting and then holding on to customers. It is more a matter of giving the buyers what they want. Buyers want vendors who keep promises, who'll keep supplying and standing behind what they promised. The era of the one-night stand is gone. Marriage is both necessary and more convenient. Products are too complicated, repeat negotiations too much of a hassle and too costly. Under these conditions, success in marketing is transformed into the inescapability of a relationship. Interface becomes interdependence.

Regardless whether the mutual attachments advocated by Zemke and Bell will develop between apartment properties and vendors, the "bio-psychological" partnering relationship that Libey describes is unquestionably present in the multifamily environment. While it might seem surprising to some to describe landlords and residents as "partners," consider this: When landlords are financially successful, they are more likely to staff their properties with top-quality personnel, provide superior maintenance and housekeeping services, and implement desirable capital upgrades, all of which benefit their residents and make apartment living exceptional. Because the landlord-renter relationship is continuous—unlike the typical seller-buyer association in the retail milieu, which is generally intermittent—residents are "invested" in the success of the suppliers of their housing. Conversely, if prospective renters were shrewd enough to know the detrimental consequences of receivership or bankruptcy to a multifamily property, it is exceedingly unlikely that they would choose to rent at one—they would rightly suspect that their renting experience would be unfavorably affected by the negative financial and legal status of the property. Indeed, they would probably prefer to rent at an apartment community that is economically healthy.

Housing, whether owned or rented, is an essential, *primal* need for humans; landlords and tenants are necessarily affected similarly by the fiscal performance of apartments. Because this is so, landlords and tenants are *inevitably* partners. This perspective of the landlord-tenant relationship is radically different from the traditional view of the parties as adversaries, but viewing them in this light is helpful in designing retention strategies that can be beneficial to all.

Laura Liswood has summarized the importance of the partnering relationship, emphasizing that companies need to be accommodating to the personal needs of their customer "partners":

▶ A good and long-standing customer expects a reciprocal relationship with the company. The customer demonstrates good will through repeat buying and on-time payments, and the company is expected to reciprocate with some good will of its own. It might be an overstatement to call this arrangement a "friendship," but most of us *do* feel more kindly toward a company that treats us like a friend. We like to think that our business is appreciated and that we represent something more than a speck on a computer chip or a name on a mailing list. That's why it's important that a company's delivery chain or customer-interaction process—no matter how much it is automated and computerized—be designed to allow for the personal touch, to accommodate exceptions, and to show real responsiveness to the unique needs of individual customers.

Benchmark Ideas of Others that You Can Put to Work for You

Benchmark other organizations both inside and outside your industry. Appropriate as many great ideas as you can find, and put them to work in your own company. For example, the availability of certain kinds of toys for diners' children at the local "burger palace" may give you ideas for inexpensive additions to your leasing offices. Just as important, one or more of the personnel working at the restaurant may be so dazzling you will want to interview them for frontline positions in your company. The "Not Invented Here" syndrome is destructive of excellence and detrimental to innovation. The wisdom of benchmarking is that it helps to avoid reinventing the wheel in a surprising variety of different ways. Indeed, Robert Camp, one of the experts on the subject, summarized its purpose this way:

▶ *Incorporate the best.* Learn from industry leaders and competition. If they are strong in given areas, uncover why they are and how they got that way. Find those best practices wherever they exist and do not hesitate to copy or modify and incorporate them in your own operation. Emulate their strengths.

Zeithaml and her colleagues illustrated the use of benchmarking to motivate customers to complain, commending inventive use of technology as a way to stimulate customer feedback:

▶ British Airways . . . installed customer-complaint booths at Heathrow Airport where disgruntled passengers could air their grievances on videotape. Besides giving customers immediate relief from their annoyances, British Air found that the complaint videotapes gave vivid information to management about customers' problems and expectations.

The British Airways example is illustrative for the apartment industry: It is entirely appropriate to borrow an idea from another enterprise—for example, the hospitality industry—to help you become complaint-friendly. Compass Alliance Real Estate Services in San Antonio, Texas, provides its residents with a rectangular card that has been pre-cut so it can be hung on an apartment doorknob. The card, titled "At Your Service" reads as shown in exhibit 9.2.

Compass employs another device modeled after the hospitality industry to encourage new residents to complain if the condition of their apartment at the time of move-in does not meet their expectations. The contents of that card are shown in exhibit 9.3. In this instance, although unwittingly, Compass Alliance benchmarked another business when it instituted the satisfaction card, which is personally signed by the maintenance person in charge, indicating that the apartment has been inspected and determined to be ready for move-in. In *Delivering Knock Your Socks Off Service,* Kristin Anderson and Ron Zemke included an admonition from a poster they had seen hanging in an automobile repair shop: "Every job is a self-portrait of the person who did it. Autograph your work with excellence." In effect, an employee's signature becomes a guarantee that the work is satisfactory. It not only verifies that the

Exhibit 9.2

Doorknob Hanger Inviting "Complaints"

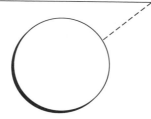

AT YOUR SERVICE

As you know, we constantly strive to offer the best service in town. So today we come to you to ask if you have any maintenance needs we may meet. Simply fill out this form and hang it on your door in the morning. We will come by to pick it up and schedule repairs. Thank you for your time and input.

Please check problem areas:

Kitchen sink _____   Heater _____
Bath sink _____   Air Conditioner _____
Bath tub _____   Lights _____
Range _____   Switches _____
Refrigerator _____   Electrical outlets _____
Disposal _____   Doors _____
Other _____   Locks _____
　　　　　　　　　　　　　　　　Other _____

Nothing needed but thanks _____

Please describe: _____
_____

Courtesy of Compass Alliance Real Estate Services, San Antonio, Texas.

Exhibit 9.3
Signed "Guarantee" of Service Quality

YOUR NEW HOME
Was Personally
Serviced and Inspected
By: _____

Compass Alliance requires

Excellence In Service

Please let us know if we have
met that requirement.

Courtesy of Compass Alliance Real Estate Services, San Antonio, Texas.

condition has been inspected and determined to be adequate, but invites the customer to complain if the work is at all deficient.

Leverage *KAIZEN* Regeneration of Your Company for the Long Term

As you transform your firm, recognize that this activity is not a static enterprise, nor is it a one-time thing with a particular endpoint. If the work is to be lasting, it must be continuous. Ask yourself, "Why do we do this? Is it still a good idea?"—daily, weekly, monthly, and in formalized annual review processes. Always be in the business of pruning and sharpening your operations with your residents' delight uppermost in your mind.

Remember, too, that not all of the customer service deficiencies you may unearth in your firm need to be remedied the instant you discover them: The *evolution* to service excellence should be a KAIZEN process, an operation that occurs day-by-day, a little bit at a time. As Professor Theodore Levitt has pointed out:

► Trying routinely to get better one step at a time is a far better way to get better than shooting constantly for the moon . . . . Sustained success is largely a matter of focusing regularly on the right things and making a lot of uncelebrated little improvements every day. Getting better and better one step at a time adds up.

The KAIZEN approach, besides being gradual, can also involve rather insignificant improvements that prompt more pivotal ones. For example, during the metamorphosis to the resident-passionate company, you might choose to benchmark T. Scott Gross:

▶ There is no greater way for a business to demonstrate status to customers than to know them by name. . . . Make it a habit to learn the name of at least one new customer every day. Just walk right up and introduce yourself. This may be more difficult than you expect, but only with regular customers that you should already know.

Donald Libey, one of the most thoughtful and provocative of the service commentators, underlined the importance of knowing customers' names:

▶ Every customer you will meet has a name. . . . [T]he person's name is intensely personal and distinguishing.

In every regard, according a person's name the proper dignity brings proper dignity to the process of commerce. People want to be treated with dignity. People want to feel as if they are respected for who they are. And who they are is, first and forever, the unique name they possess within the family structure.

Differentiation of customer treatment begins with a policy of names. If a company will adopt a policy of referring to every customer as Mr., Mrs., or Ms., in *every* instance, *always,* that company will immediately and permanently improve its image with the entire customer base.

The exhortation to learn customers' names gradually is an example of leverage—that is, initiating an improvement in one area that is likely to stimulate more substantial benefits elsewhere—in this instance, the hope that useful personal interchange will develop from personal greetings. Peter Senge linked leverage with KAIZEN more directly:

▶ The bottom line of systems thinking is leverage—seeing where actions and changes in structures can lead to significant, enduring improvements. Often, leverage follows the principle of economy of means: where the best results come not from large-scale efforts but from small well-focused actions.

Indeed, small changes tend to build on themselves, to become self-reinforcing. Positive movement is amplified, producing more—and more substantial—movement in the same direction. Action snowballs, with more and more and still more of the same. Some service observers have compared this to the Pygmalion effect, describing it as a "virtuous cycle."

Sometimes, the way *things* are named connotes the warm feelings people have toward them. In the apartment business, for example, the term "apartment community" is often substituted for "project" or "complex"; "resident" or "neighbor" is used for "tenant" and "home" for "unit." After all, anyone who says, "I'm going to my unit," is undoubtedly indifferent about the experience; but a person who says, "I'm going *home,*" is probably looking forward to the special feelings that only home can elicit. Thus, by leveraging language—by updating the terminology you employ when referring to your customers and your product—you may also be enhancing the lifestyle provided in your apartment properties.

Karl Albrecht has commented about the leverage gained by correcting the way servers refer to their customers:

▶   Centering on the customer is easier said than done. In an organization, the language that people use when referring to customers, or when describing service-quality programs, signals very clearly how they view their customers and how they see themselves as relating to them. Many organizations have evolved a special terminology that enables them to *avoid* referring to people as customers.

The piecemeal strategy to improvement is especially appropriate in an environment in which the goal is innately a shifting target. As David Freemantle has observed, "Customer service is a moving horizon, the high standards of today can be the low standards of a few years time. Constant improvement is a necessity."

One way to invigorate your company's customer focus is to streamline operations so as to meet your residents' expectations of punctual performance. Savvy retailers are increasingly aware of their customers' need for *immediacy.* According to Libey:

▶   The expectation for immediacy is so high that the merchant is measured less on value and quality and more on convenience and the ability to satisfy the immediate whim. . . . The increased level of disposable income contributes to immediacy. Coupled with the rise of quantitative values and the acceptance of credit financing, the capacity exists to afford immediacy. Customers will pay more to get what they want immediately, and they have the resources to spend. If you want a new car tonight, you can have a new car tonight. . . . We can afford to be instantly gratified.

Lead the Revolution and Reward Your Revolutionaries

Once you are satisfied that your firm blooms with nice people, both old employees and new, you need to coach them to deliver spectacular customer service. Recall that people learn in different ways. Some adults learn new skills best when they read about them; these employees should have access to the extraordinary variety of cutting-edge service literature (such as the books cited in the Bibliography). Others master techniques by listening to people talk about approaches; for these employees, a number of the customer service-related texts may be found on audiotapes. Still others comprehend best by mimicking the behavior of others—most especially, the leaders in their own companies. This latter model—what might be termed "benchmarking leadership"—is an essential inspirational wellspring of the service culture. As Scott Gross observed:

▶ Excellent customer service occurs only when employees have an excellent, visible standard that they can imitate and against which they can compare their own behavior. The good news is that the standard is always visible. The bad news is that the visible standard is not always a *visible standard of excellence*. . . . As the owner, CEO, or manager, you bear the special responsibility of being the most visible standard. If you are in any way unsatisfied with your employee's customer service behavior, there is only one first step to take. Look in the mirror!

Karl Albrecht also commented on the significant role that leadership plays in the regeneration process:

▶ If there is one lesson [I have learned] . . . , it is that leadership is the crucial ingredient in achieving service excellence on the part of organizations. There needs to be an element of executive evangelism in operation; not only the chief executive but the other senior managers must preach, teach, and reinforce the gospel of service quality.

Effective leadership in the customer-driven company requires that these trailblazers completely immerse themselves in the company's transformation. As Richard Whiteley has noted:

▶ Successful managers who carry out these customer-focused principles are creating a new view of leadership. Today, top corporate leaders . . . have shown what real leaders must do. They personally put the customer first. They promote their companies' visions. They become "students for life," constantly seeking new ways to learn. They believe in and invest in their people. They build customer-focused teams, celebrating successes and encouraging collaboration. And, finally, they "lead by example," personifying the organization's purpose.

"Preaching," "teaching," and "reinforcing" the service gospel—three of the activities that the service teachers challenge company leadership to undertake—should be supplemented by one other: "Rewarding." Michael LeBoeuf has outlined the importance of including rewards as a means of challenging internal customers to become involved in the transformation of their companies:

▶ Make it a contest, complete with rewards and recognition for those persons or groups with the best answers. If an idea makes or saves money, consider giving a piece of the profits to the creator. And most important, when you get a good idea, put it to work and let it be known that it's an employee-generated idea. People like to be proud of what they do and will support what they help create. Once employees see that you are serious about putting their ideas to work, you'll get plenty of them.

Poirier and Houser expanded on LeBoeuf's idea, urging that employee bonuses be funded from the company's increased earnings generated by their recommendations:

▶ The process of cultivating workers' input can be called employee involvement, participative management, or employee participation. The labels are unimportant. The idea is to tap the creativity and knowledge of the human resources of an organization. Mutual benefits can include increased profits from lower costs. They should also include making the job of achieving those results less arduous and more satisfying. . . . Since their work ultimately brings the desired results, workers have a right to know how they affect the chosen course of action and to have some measure of control over what they do or, at least, over how they do it. The final, perhaps most crucial, link occurs when management ties worker performance directly to the fortunes of the organization by creating a pool from earnings that can be distributed to those creating the necessary improvements.

Although the subject of designing a reward system for company employees is beyond the scope of this book, it can be helpful to benchmark the models employed by successful companies. One of these, the Ryan Companies, a Minneapolis-based construction and property management firm, has developed a program "based on immediate verbal and written recognition for exemplary performance." As a commitment to their Quality Improvement Process, "this program encourages continuous acknowledgment of quality performances."

The "Ryan Recognition Program" employs shamrock designs as a basis for company awards. All employees are eligible to receive *and* distribute shamrocks, which are certificates of recognition that recognize performance that "goes above and beyond normal expectations." Employees collect shamrock forms, which can be redeemed for merchandise awards selected from a gift catalog.

Employees are encouraged to reward their peers for recommending "value ideas" and performing exemplary customer service. For the customer service category, for example, the "award application" reads as follows:

1. Write the name of the employee deserving the recognition.
2. Briefly describe the commendable performance.
3. Identify when it happened.
4. Sign your name.
5. Date when you issued the Shamrock.
6. Fill in the recipient's supervisor name.
7. Send the original Shamrock to the award recipient!
8. Send the yellow copy to the supervisor listed on the certificate.
9. Submit the pink copy to a member of the Recognition Team for program records.

In addition to rewards for outstanding customer service, the Ryan program recognizes employees on their birthdays and employment anniversary dates, as well as those who either "[exemplify] respect, integrity, community involvement, and other qualities" or proposes "an innovative idea that promotes COST SAVINGS, TIME SAVINGS, OR ADDED VALUE."

"Co-Produce" Service With Your Customers' Help

Shrewd companies involve their customers in delivering the service they receive. This concept, known as service "co-production" or "self-service," has been employed for several years in many retail fields. As Heskett and coworkers have observed:

▶ Self-service concepts employ customers as part of the service delivery system. The most effective insure that customers are trained, through clear instructions, in how to be good "helpers." The range of activities in which customers are willing to engage is rather remarkable. Whether they pump their own gas, as a majority of U.S. consumers do; bus their own dishes; or haul their own furniture purchases, customers enable service providers to reduce demand on the delivery system during peak periods, thereby providing incentives in the form of lower prices to encourage customers to increase their participation further.

The commentators applaud self-service as a means of making service-delivery less expensive for the service purchaser, and easier and more convenient for the service provider. Davidow and Uttal, for example, had this to say:

▶ To more market-oriented managers, involving the customer is the key to increasing service productivity. While admitting that the more high touch a service is, the less efficient and controllable it tends to be, members of this school point out that self-service is often better service. Designing self-service operations that encourage and support customer participation, they contend, is the only way to achieve big leaps in service productivity without sacrificing quality and effectiveness. Striving to isolate customers from the production system is woefully misguided.

The notion of encouraging purchasers to become involved in producing their own service—e.g., by recycling certain materials that supply raw materials for other products while simultaneously providing environmental benefits—is an essential aspect of what we have described as "partnering," that is, the process of developing relationships between buyers and sellers. As we shall demonstrate later in this chapter, partnering alliances can have positive economic consequences for suppliers and consumers; such affiliations can be beneficial to landlords and residents as well.

In the apartment industry, the concept of self-service may be employed to assist renters in becoming more responsible apartment occupants, which provides direct benefits to themselves and assists their landlords and other residents as well. This is demonstrated in the following examples:

The Columbus (Ohio) Metropolitan Housing Authority (CMHA) has instituted a pre-occupancy class for residents of the public housing it manages. The purpose of the program is to acquaint prospective residents of public housing about their privileges and responsibilities; to foster cooperation among residents and to improve living situations for family/senior housing projects; and to inform residents about essential living skills and available community resources/services.

Prior to January, 1991, when the training procedure was initiated, CMHA was experiencing a high incidence of maintenance problems and legal actions that staff theorized might be remedied by an educational effort. The CMHA program director enlisted the assistance of co-sponsors to teach the courses in their areas of expertise. Pat Hartman, CPM®, Director of Housing Management and Services, characterized the program's purpose this way:

▶ Good tenants are not "found"; they are educated. We had learned in the past that it was difficult to have residents expect to perform in compliance with a lease agreement when the duties and responsibilities had never been explained to them. With the population that we service (the average applicant is a 19-year old female with two or three children) many of the expectations of normal lessees could not be realized, such as home care, health and safety issues.

CMHA requires all prospective tenants of public housing to attend a three-hour class one week prior to move-in. Approximately 25 attend each session; courses are held in a maintenance training center outfitted with appliances and other features of the living units. Staff and course co-sponsors teach six modules:

Orientation: Legal responsibilities of parties, rent collection practices, housekeeping standards, prohibited activities, re-certification requirements/continued occupancy, lease termination.

Maintenance Services: Procedure for maintenance and repairs, scheduling, right of entry.

Tenant Safety: Preventable losses, unsafe practices.

Family Life Skills: Demonstration of basic household cleaning, including practical tips, recommended products.

Health Outreach: Available low-cost health/medical services.

Rights and Duties of Public Housing Tenants: Tenants' rights, grievance procedures, maintenance charges, transfers, annual re-certification.

The program has resulted in a significant decrease in the incidence of maintenance requests and legal proceedings; equally important, CMHA staff report improved tenant housekeeping skills, decreased insurance premiums, and improved relations between CMHA and the co-sponsors, particularly the local legal aid society. According to Pat Hartman:

> ► The success of the program is evidenced by a drive through [one] of our communities. We now have grass in some of the communities where there was none before and communities are much cleaner. We have not had any major incidents of crime or drug-related activity in months. . . . Our problems of the past in dealing with residents who expected us to solve problems for them instead of utilizing their own resources have greatly decreased.

A similar approach has been initiated by the Cantrell firm at a property it manages in Atlanta. After experiencing continued vandalism by residents' children during the spring and summer, the company established "Kid Brigade," organizing the children to pick up the common areas of the property in exchange for money deposited into a party fund. Two supervised summer parties are held for participants in the brigade. The program provides the children with a group activity that benefits the apartment property, as well as allowing them to have fun.

As these examples indicate, informed participation in co-producing service for themselves benefits not only the residents, but also the management staff and the property owner. It also contributes to renters' pride in themselves and where they live.

Brainstorm the Course of Your Revolution

Because the transformation from company-driven to resident-responsive demands the active involvement—indeed, the *passion*—of everyone in the company, it makes sense to involve everyone in the process of designing the renovated firm. Whether you call it "brainstorming," "think tank," "outer-circle thinking," or something else, your team needs to be involved in a formalized group exercise. Band described this as:

▶ An unrestrained and creative process for generating ideas and suggestions by all members of a group for solutions, especially nontraditional ones, to customer satisfaction problems. . . . Effective brainstorming consists of the following steps. First, the session leader defines the scope and direction of the issues to be discussed. Group members are then given time to write down their ideas, after which each person is called upon to contribute one idea. The process is repeated until all ideas have been heard. The group leader simply records the ideas on a flip chart or blackboard; evaluation or criticism is not allowed at this stage. Once the ideas have been listed, the discussion is opened up to generate and record new thoughts.

Band goes on to describe a somewhat more refined brainstorming exercise known as "nominal group technique":

▶ This method begins the same way as brainstorming does, generating and combining ideas. The surviving ideas are numbered for identification, then each member privately ranks the top five ideas. The rankings are compiled from each person's rating to form a collective score for each idea. (The supervisor's vote is taken last to avoid prejudicing of the group.) The winning idea emerges from the voting.

However elegant the technique you employ, your purpose is to cultivate maximum employee participation in the planning process. The goal is to stimulate the imagination and tap the creativity of the human resources of your organization. Participants in the process might include the site manager, leasing staff, maintenance personnel, housekeepers, janitors, porters, painters, gardeners, and security staff. It is imperative that the team who will execute the customer service program participate in designing it. During the initial planning stages, meet as often as weekly, and no less than monthly. Because your brainstorming sessions are valuable learning exercises as well, staff members can teach each other all your company needs to know about WOW! resident service.

Michael LeBoeuf created an interesting parallel between designing a service strategy and scorekeeping at a sports event:

▶ Here's a good rule of thumb: When it comes to service quality, customers know the score but employees know how it got that way. Ask customers to tell you what your level of service quality is and what to work on to improve it. Then ask employees why your level of service quality is what it is and how to go about improving it.

To carry the sports analogy one step further, the customer is the scorekeeper, but the employees are the players and coaches that can tell you why things are going the way they are and how to make them better. While you need to know what the score is, you also need to know why it got that way and how to go about improving it. And employees are your best source for this type of information. The person who does the job every day usually has the best insight about why things do or don't work and the best ideas for making improvements. Simply asking employees for their ideas provides a tremendous, but often overlooked, reservoir of knowledge and creativity. Why not tap it?

Start off by vividly characterizing for the participants your commitment to delivering superior service to residents. Tell the staff that what you are after is not good—or even great—resident service. These aren't enough: You're looking for WOW! service to residents, service that will "knock their socks off," service that will make the company not just the best, but *legendary*.

One way to proceed is to draw three concentric circles on a chalkboard or flip chart. Describe the Levitt Paradigm to the staff and invite them to list the characteristics of competitive apartments in the first two circles.

You will recall that the so-called "generic" product (inner ring) consists of the bare essentials required of an apartment—what we have termed the "four white walls and a rug" together with certain working appliances and fixtures. (See exhibit 2.2 in chapter 2.) Moving outward to the second ring, the "expected" product, in addition to the attributes of the "generic" apartment, might offer contemporary, upscale amenities that are characteristic of other properties in its market, together with a friendly, competent, helpful on-site staff.

By contrast, the third-ring "augmented" product exceeds customer expectations. In the apartment business, these goods, in addition to offering the qualities and characteristics of "expected" apartments, might be similar to the finest hotels and resorts. They would be absolutely unique in their markets, with site personnel who are without peer. Visualizing, describing, and documenting the "augmented" product is the goal of your group exercise. It may take a few minutes for everyone to feel completely comfortable with participating; but once the ideas begin to flow, the results can be superb.

If you get off to a slow start, you might invite the participants to respond to two questions. These come from LeBoeuf:

▶   What's the biggest, most frequently occurring problem that you face in trying to serve the customer?

If you were the president and could make only one change to improve the quality of customer service, what would you do?

As you conceptualize the augmented apartment, brainstorm what you could do for your residents that would be so unique, so wonderful, and so surprising that they would dash to a phone, call a friend and say, "You won't *believe* what my landlord did for me today!" Experiencing the augmented apartment is, in Scott Gross's characterization, "the story you can't wait to tell."

Because the group may need a jumpstart, here are some of the ideas that have come from our company's brainstorming:

Because many of our residents are families with small children, we could have crayons and loose coloring book pages in our offices, so that when children come into the building with their parents they can be entertained with a fun activity. And maybe you could have a display wall where these pieces of artwork and any other donated works could be prominently hung.

Many of our properties have large populations of young people. Most parents work and children have a great deal of leisure time, which poses a problem. We might organize the families to co-produce programmed activities for our young customers. This is how it might work: Parents would sign up for two hours once a month to chaperone, coach, or supervise the activities. We could divide the youngsters into groups: ages 3 to 5, 6 to 9, 10 to 12, 13 to 15, and 16 to 18. We could plan activities for each group on Fridays, Saturdays, and Sundays. Common areas of the property that are normally off-limits to the youngsters could be opened. Maybe we could sponsor a pool night each week, and an entire day when children could use the party and game tables without having to have a parent with them—supervision would be provided by parent-volunteers. (The site could pay for some pizza occasionally, and we could purchase T-shirts for a couple of the sports teams.) The way I figure it, the parents can get about 16 hours of free babysitting every week in exchange for two hours of supervision a month.

Children in an apartment community sometimes pose safety issues, especially during holidays. Halloween is too dangerous for the kids in some of these neighborhoods. Our site personnel could solicit candy contributions from the residents, and we might get donated bags from local grocers to hold the goodies. Then we could invite the children in the community to an old-fashioned Halloween party, with a magician and staff-sponsored bobbing for apples.

It is possible to strategize ways to provide WOW! service that will also constitute planning for service recovery. Here is an example taken from our own company.

> We manage apartments in a climate that is extremely cold and snowy. Despite our best efforts, residents at our properties are likely to be snowbound overnight once or twice each winter. Because inclement weather is predictable, we invited each of our management teams to do some advance planning for the next heavy snowstorm. When it came, they were ready.
>
> One March night snow began to fall at a very rapid rate. By the following night nothing in the city was moving. Residents of a 250-unit highrise were trapped; the electricity failed. The emergency generators kept the heating systems functional, but lights were out and the building was silent. The manager and her team kept torches and flashlights in the management office, illuminating some halls, the party room, and lobby. Just as they had planned, the team then went from door to door and invited all residents to a pajama party. The only requirements were that they attend in robes and slippers, and that they bring flashlights, their best board games, and whatever junk food they could find in their kitchens. While the world outside was digging itself out, the people at this property played the night away. They got to know each other very well—much better than they ever would have if the crisis had not occurred. They bonded with each other and the staff, and that night they became an "extended family."

One creative team came up with an idea that not only served to retain customers but also became part of the local folklore.

> In a downtown midrise historic rehab property populated by young professionals, there had been no way to retrofit the building with a pool during renovation. Residents and prospects often commented that the only feature the building lacked was a pool. In one of the brainstorm sessions, the staff debated about what purpose a pool served. They decided that it simply provided a way to cool off after hours of sunbathing on the deck. The site team concluded that small plastic kiddie pools might serve the same purpose, so they purchased two of them and invited the entire community to a pool party. The residents loved it, and prospects admired the management team's creativity.

One of the characteristics of American society is that food seems to be involved in any and all celebrations. Because eating with someone also symbolizes friendship, it is appropriate to treat residents like friends. That is perhaps why so much of retention planning involves food.

> Most apartment communities sponsor resident parties—summer, winter holiday, pool opening and closing, and a number of others. While some are very elaborate, most are simple. It is possible to commit considerable funds to these events, with food, entertainment, games and prizes. Others are supported by a very thin budget and have mostly "pot luck" events. Our favorites are quite spontaneous and very inexpensive. For example, some staff members greet morning commuters at the door or driveway with juice and rolls or coffee and donuts. Others have periodic dessert get-togethers where homemade desserts and coffee are served. One group gets pies from a local specialty shop for a pie-tasting evening. In one community, the staff sponsors a wine-tasting get-together in the laundry room, so that residents can get to know each other while they're washing clothes.

The truly superlative ideas are those that surprise the customer. Regular events are considered ordinary; they tend to get boring. Because they are recurring, they lose their capacity to WOW! customers. Worse, when truly unique ideas become predictable because they are delivered routinely, they become a part of the expected product. As Scott Gross has cautioned:

▶ "Unexpected" is key to the definition of truly Positively Outrageous Service. It's the element of surprise and novelty that jolts the attention of the customer or patron and creates an experience that's memorable because it is so different from the expectation. Even if you are expecting the unexpected and don't know exactly *what* to expect, I guess you could call that the unexpected!

Go Out and Start a Revolution!

The extraordinary variety of customer service techniques that have been developed, tested, and refined in the retailing and consumer services environment provide a vivid benchmark for the apartment milieu. Activities, however, are merely a reflection of, and not a substitute for, the fundamental attitudinal metamorphosis that has to precede a revolution that would revamp a company's approach to its customers.

Yet, we believe a revolution in the way apartment managers and marketers treat their customers is predestined—and desirable. This is true in part because the owners of multifamily properties will increasingly demand that managers demonstrate responsiveness toward residents as a way not only of maintaining and improving the value of the assets under their care, but also as a means of reducing expenses in an economically unsettled climate. This view is exemplified in the following excerpt from *Managing the Future: Real Estate in the 1990s:*

▶ As the net income from managed properties slips in response to rising taxes and sagging real rents, [property] managers will be pressed to fill vacant space while at the same time cutting expenses and improving their controls. Those who can procure new tenants and retain the old ones without compromising property economics will do better than the rest.

The IREM Foundation study accentuates the need to devise ways to improve the volume and quality of business that apartment owners are doing with their current residents. So-called retention marketing represents an awareness that service industries are actually in the business of *manufacturing satisfied customers.* Michael LeBoeuf, one of the most provocative of the service commentators, made this point:

▶ Stop for a moment and consider just how valuable customers are. They alone make it possible for you to earn your livelihood in the way that you do. Treat them well and satisfied customers will be your best source of advertising and marketing. Give them good value and they will continue to reward you with their dollars year after year. All the slick financial and marketing techniques in the world are no substitute for an army of satisfied customers. Don't ever make the mistake of thinking of buildings, computers, consultants, or even employees as your company's greatest assets. Every company's greatest assets are its customers, because without customers there is no company. It's that simple.

As the apartment industry evolves from resident-tolerant to resident-responsive to resident-driven and beyond, successful apartment managers will be able to differentiate their product primarily by means of the personal touch that the site staff displays to their customers. Albrecht and Zemke summarized the importance of this approach succinctly:

▶ [Service] is the new standard used by customers and consumers to measure organizational performance. Increasingly, the marketplace is opting to do business with those who serve, and declining involvement with those who merely supply.

Yet another reason for the multifamily industry to follow the customer service lead of retailers is that many of those who initiated and implemented the revolution in the retail trades are apartment residents themselves. They understand from their everyday business experiences that customers are entitled to an elevated level of treatment, and they expect similar attention from their landlords.

This unique confluence of external pressures, coming as they do from major owners of investment real estate, the commercial environment in which apartment managers function, and apartment residents themselves, makes it inevitable that managers begin by reexamining the way they deal with residents, with a view to completely revamping their approach. Indeed, these are the hoofbeats of a revolution, and as Donald Libey warned, "When you hear hoofbeats, expect horses."

The customer-retention techniques derived from retailing that are summarized in this book go well beyond the sloganeering that has been characteristic of many of the "self-improvement" cycles that American business has suffered during the past two decades or so. One of the reasons that the customer service revolution has endured is the fact that its progenitor was Jan Carlzon, an especially intelligent, thoughtful, and dynamic individual. Carlzon's genius lay in his ability to recognize certain interconnected realities of management—most prominent among them the fact that SAS customers formed indelible impressions about the quality of his company in 15-second increments, well beyond his—or any manager's—ability to influence (or even supervise) these decisive "Moments of Truth."

The "Moments of Truth" concept, in turn, led Carlzon and others to explore such ancillary concepts as empowerment, benchmarking, internal and external customers, the role of leadership, employee rewards, and much more. Here's an example of one of the implications of *empowerment* from Carlzon's seminal book, *Moments of Truth:*

▶ If we are truly dedicated to orienting our company toward each customer's individual needs, then we cannot rely on rule books and instructions from distant corporate offices. We have to place responsibility for ideas, decisions, and actions with the people who *are* SAS during those 15 seconds: ticket agents, flight attendants, baggage handlers, and all the other frontline employees. If they have to go up the organizational chain of command for a decision on an individual problem, then those 15 golden seconds will elapse without a response, and we will have lost an opportunity to earn a loyal customer.

One offshoot of Carlzon's thinking, in our view, poses intriguing possibilities for the future of service in American business in general and apartment management in particular. This concept, known as "partnering," recognizes that there is a commonality of interest between a company's "internal" and "external" customers—that is, between its owners, managers, line staff, and clients. Because these apparently dissimilar parties are uniformly invested in the success of the company as a going concern, opportunities arise that may benefit all of these seemingly diverse and incompatible participants.

Many management companies are potentially the best customers of their suppliers—most firms are very good customers in terms of the quantity of business they do, year after year, with their vendors. They purchase huge quantities of products, ranging from cleaning supplies and plumbing parts to appliances and carpeting. Despite evident opportunities to make bulk purchases, many managers buy piecemeal, meeting only their immediate needs. In truth, real estate managers often approach these business dealings as if they were merely sporadic, despite the fact that their relationships with their suppliers are ongoing.

The principles of partnering would recommend that purchasers who enjoy a "best customer" status with their suppliers ought to leverage this advantage, while not creating a corresponding disadvantage to the seller. Here is an example.

In reviewing its purchasing history and its current budgetary projections, a management company may determine that it purchases at least $300,000 worth of carpeting annually. Some years, the firm spends more than $500,000 on this commodity. Nonetheless, in accordance with the owners' directives, the company routinely acquires carpeting from the low bidder on small lots. Indeed, low-bid contracting is a hallmark of property management.

Assume that the manager decides to explore the possibility of partnering with the carpet supplier. She might say to them, "You know, we buy a lot of carpeting every year. We've consistently done $300,000 or so of business with your company and others in the city. I'd like to find out whether it would make sense for your firm to become the sole-source supplier for us. I'm thinking that if you knew, in advance, the volume of business we would do, say, by quarter and by location, maybe we could do better on price, and perhaps get better quality than we've gotten previously."

The supplier might respond by saying, "I know that we've done a lot of work with your company, but I had no idea that you bought so much carpeting every year. I'll tell you this: We don't have many customers that do that kind of volume with us. Offhand, it seems to me that if we could do some advance planning, I'll bet we could save us both some money. I think we ought to sit down and sketch out your needs, especially the amount of product you'll need in each general location. If we could plan to store some carpeting at a couple of your sites, the savings would be *enormous*."

As this hypothetical discussion illustrates, some conventional rules (confidentiality of information, multiple-bidding requirements, and the like) need to be modified—or discarded—if partnering is to work. The long-term benefits of such relationships can be expected to be generally lower costs to both partners and an overall heightened awareness of each partner's needs by the other. More important, when business is awarded on a basis other than mere price, and when buyers and sellers are equally invested in one another's long-term profitability, both parties are bound to realize unexpected benefits from the relationship. Alliances constructed on "best-customer" foundations, rather than on price alone, may revolutionize American commerce.

Another aspect of partnering, called "aftermarketing," recognizes that acquisition marketing—deal-making—needs to be subordinated to retention marketing—that is, long-term customer satisfaction. Terry Vavra, an advocate of aftermarketing, has made this distinction and underlined its validity:

▶   Marketing must change its mentality from completing a sale to beginning a relationship; from closing a deal to building loyalty. Yet in the daily planning of marketing effort, more attention is generally directed at conquest—winning new customers to one's brand, product, or service. It is much rarer to find a company also devoting attention to maximizing the satisfaction of current customers. In such a company, the customer would not only be right, but his or her opinions would be actively sought out. This is the spirit of aftermarketing activities.

Whether the resident retention movement in your firm will be a "revolution," albeit one that matures and deepens over time, depends on the transformation of the attitude of your company's leadership toward its internal and external customers. The impact on internal customers of a business approach that looks outward to the satisfaction of its clients rather than inward to its own bureaucratic processes has been described by Davidow and Uttal:

▶   First of all, driving a company to produce outstanding service flies in the face of conventional wisdom. Instead of being told to keep their eyes glued to the bottom line of the income statement, employees are asked to forget purely financial considerations and pursue customer satisfaction at all costs. Few employees will respond unless they see that top managers are irrevocably committed to achieving a service vision.

In this same vein, Karl Albrecht has described the depth and breadth of the transformation that companies must undertake:

▶   There must be a fundamental revision in our way of thinking about customers, about service, about leadership and management, and about the culture of organizations if we are to build and maintain the kind of competitive customer-winning capability that will be able to survive and thrive into the twenty-first century. That change in thinking will take the form of a basic relearning of most of what we know about those subjects, and a reconceptualization of that knowledge.

Company leaders will lead the customer service revolution if there is to be a revolution at all. Their words and deeds are, in Davidow and Uttal's phrase, "the touchstones of [company] culture." Although the transformation is greatly facilitated if internal customers are responsible for planning and monitoring it, "customer service" and "resident retention" will be but dust in the wind unless company leadership is fanatically committed to the revolution. The importance of top-level commitment was pointed out by Richard Whiteley:

▶   The companies making real progress in serving their customers are led by people who themselves put the customer first. More than that, they believe passionately in giving the customer what he or she wants. They spend much of their time with their customers and they become the voice of the customer within their organizations.

However, while company leadership is obligated to launch the revolution, the people responsible for implementing it are found at the front line: The firm's "internal customers." As we have noted earlier, *customer service is a marketing strategy implemented by one frontline server for the benefit of one customer at a time.* Because implementation occurs in a multitude of random ways in a multiplicity of locations, frontline servers must have the necessary authority to act on behalf of the company in order to serve their external customers. In these circumstances, as Laura Liswood has observed:

▶   The best managers try to meddle as little as possible in the jobs their subordinates are doing. They strive to do their own jobs right the first time, while instilling that same ethic in their subordinates and peers. In customer-retention management, this philosophy of "letting go" is especially important. It means letting go enough so that the people closest to the customers can do their jobs right.

After "empowering" its frontline servers, company leadership needs to support and encourage them in a variety of person-to-person ways. As Zeithaml and coworkers have noted:

▶   Service leaders lead in the field, where the action is, rather than from their desks. They are visible to their people, endlessly coaching, praising, correcting, cajoling, sermonizing, observing, questioning, and listening. They emphasize two-way, personal communications because they know this is the best way to give shape, substance, and credibility to the service vision and the best way to learn what is really going on in the field.

This "in-the-field" leadership style pioneered by Jan Carlzon and executives of major American corporations has the potential to reorganize the company, as Carlzon had to do at SAS:

▶ In a customer-driven company, the distribution of roles is radically different. The organization is decentralized, with responsibility delegated to those who until now have comprised the order-obeying bottom of the pyramid. The traditional, hierarchical corporate structure, in other words, is beginning to give way to a flattened, more horizontal, structure. This is particularly true in service businesses that begin not with the product but with the customer.

Effective, energized leadership. Empowered, excited frontline servers. The company is now ready to do business with and for its external customers, its resident-"partners."

The course of the revolution will undoubtedly require the firm at some point to institute a resident-feedback system, assess and implement techniques to reduce hassles that residents encounter in dealing with their apartments, study ways for residents to become involved in their own service-production, and much more. Benchmarking other companies, both inside and outside the apartment environment, may provide useful guidance.

The scope of revolutionary activities seems to be daunting, even overwhelming. Yet it is possible—and certainly desirable—for the company to proceed with its revolution in its own way and at its own pace. At the outset, then, it is useful to keep two Japanese concepts in mind. *Dantotsu,* or "shared fate," means roughly, "We're all in this together." In fact, the companies that have had the most success in transforming their businesses for the benefit of their customers have involved their own internal customers in every aspect of the transformation. *KAIZEN,* on the other hand, is an admonition to "take it slowly." Revolutions need to be made manageable. As Davidow and Uttal have cautioned:

▶ Since the task is so large, you have to decide which elements to stress first, where to place the heaviest bets. And that decision hinges on the evolutionary stage of competition in your industry and on the competitive position your company occupies.

Apartment managers, those are hoofbeats you are hearing; the horses are not far away. Get out and lead *your* own resident retention revolution.

The Roads to a Resident Retention Revolution

Launching the Revolution

Appreciate the primacy of your residents. Do whatever it takes to earn—and deserve—their loyalty. They are the lifeblood of your company.

Hire nice. The most important consideration in selecting new hires is to find the nicest people you can, and put them on the front lines. How helpful and friendly are *your* company's ambassadors?

Hire partners. Your employees, and the quality of their contacts with your customers, will determine whether or not you stay in business. Do you have confidence that your frontline servers are the people you want to entrust with the future of your company?

Know the costs of "conquest" marketing and resident "churn." After you have calculated the cost of gaining signed leases at each of your properties, compute the expenses associated with each piece of lost business. Do you know the economic costs associated with "churning" residents through your properties?

Market for retention. Acquisition marketing is enormously expensive. Set aside dollars to keep current customers. Designate an item in each property's annual budget as "retention marketing." Do some staff brainstorming to plan how to spend the allocation. Make sure you spend every penny of the money you have budgeted for retention marketing.

Seeing the Revolution Through Your Employees' Eyes

Focus on the front line. Because frontline personnel have the most frequent—and often the most unpleasant—interactions with apartment residents, they *are* the property's human "moments of truth." Do you hire the best people you can find for these positions? Do you compensate them attractively? Do you give them all the authority they need to perform? Do you support them without hesitation?

Train your staff to understand your company's ethos BEFORE you teach job skills. "Acculturation" is the process of familiarizing new employees with a company's values and goals. Premier service providers concentrate on acquainting new hires with the company mission before they teach job skills. Do *your* employees understand your company's ethos, its attitudes toward your customers, and its reason for being in business?

Staff for request "rhythms." The accessibility of site personnel to residents, at times that are convenient to them, is a central ingredient of apartment ergonomics. Have you attempted to match your staff's availability—especially the availability of your maintenance personnel—to the needs of your residents?

Empower your staff. Let your employees know that one of their most important responsibilities is to *LET YOUR RESIDENTS WIN!* They need the authority to solve their customers' problems *on the spot;* equally important, they need to know that the organization will uphold their decisions and provide whatever assistance they may need.

Reward the behavior you want to encourage. Do you compensate employees for improvements in a property's overall economic performance or incremental increases in its value? Or is their pay tied, even indirectly, to resident "churn?"

Reward everyone who contributes to improved economic outcomes. Because reduction of resident churn is the business of all personnel of an apartment property, the entire staff should participate in the building's bonus program.

Treat your internal customers like gold. The most successful retailers recognize that their ability to serve and satisfy their external customers—those clients who pay the bills—depends entirely on the dedication of their own employees or "internal" customers. Do *you* pay attention to the job satisfaction of your "internal" customers?

Evaluating the Revolution from Your Residents' Perspective

Remember the value of speed. Retail customers expect expeditious service. They're increasingly willing to pay extra for it; their loyalty to particular retailers increasingly depends on speedy response. Do you know what your residents consider to be "timely" service? And do you consistently meet their expectations?

Be complaint-friendly. At any one time, many—maybe even *most*—of your residents are truly dissatisfied with the quality of apartment living and ready to move elsewhere, perhaps to a competitive apartment property. Have you made it easy for them to let you know what you need to do to keep their business?

Make up for the "hassle factor." When residents experience a problem with their apartments, they expect that the situation will be resolved promptly to their satisfaction. They also deserve some additional benefit, something unexpected, to make amends for the annoyance. What do *you* do to compensate for the "hassle" factor?

Make your service visible. When service is visible to customers, it is likely that they will consider it more valuable; in the absence of visibility, customers are often unaware that service is being provided at all. Have you strategized techniques for making the service you supply to your residents—even routine service, such as common area maintenance and cleaning—*apparent* that you have performed it?

Guarantee your product. Guarantees can convey a powerful marketing message to prospective residents. They illustrate confidence in the product, and they bring to light customer dissatisfaction. Have you brainstormed ways to guarantee your apartments?

Recover from service deficiencies. Service "recovery"—fixing problems once they are uncovered—is an essential component of a property's service image. Is your service recovery program consistent with the quality of your product?

"Co-produce" service. Many retailers involve their customers in producing the service they receive. Self-service reduces expense. Some apartment marketers are beginning to engage residents in generating their own service, which also benefits the apartment community in general.

Improve your customer "ergonomics." How easy is it for your prospective residents and your current residents to do business with you? Streamline your procedures from the perspective of your residents so that your company is ergonomically *friendly.*

Under-promise/over-deliver. A frequent complaint of retail customers is that their suppliers have promised things they either could not deliver or did not intend to deliver. The "over-promise, under-deliver" syndrome is prevalent in the real estate industry. Do *you* manage your residents' expectations by promising something *less* than what you intend to deliver to them, or do you set them up to be disappointed by performance that doesn't meet your promise?

Build a "customer-in" organization. Ultimately, the future of your company depends on the long-term loyalty of your residents. When you pay attention to your residents' needs—when you listen to their *voices*—you are in the process of constructing a "customer-in" organization that merits the loyalty of its clients. Does *your* company react when it hears the voices of its residents?

Thin the rulebook. It is human nature to over-regulate the behavior of others. Decide what rules are *absolutely essential* to protect human safety and the apartment community. Keep them, and get rid of everything else.

"WOW!" your residents. *Dazzle* your residents with an occasional, unexpected, moment of truth that you have scrupulously planned to delight them. Personally wash their cars some Spring Saturday. Serve them coffee, juice, and rolls in the parking lot at 7 A.M. Throw an impromptu Memorial Day opening-the-pool party. Whatever it is, let your residents know that you *love* them!

Looking Outward for Revolutionary Guidance

Benchmark. Analyze how the best companies attract customers, market to them, and keep them coming back, year after year. How do they do it? Take the best ideas you discover, and put them to work for *you!*

Partner. Win-win commercial relationships provide benefits to buyers and sellers that they can find nowhere else. Strategize ways to make your residents—and perhaps your suppliers—your *partners.*

Manage "moments of truth." Little things—the freshness of your signage, the friendliness of your site staff, the appearance of the front lobby— determine whether an apartment property will be successful. These individual "moments of truth" need to be identified, understood, and then managed.

Test failpoints. Apartment systems break down over time, and they do so in very predictable ways. Have you analyzed how apartment units, common areas, and amenities in particular properties fail, and have you taken preventive measures to avert such failures?

Do some "outer-circle" thinking. Designing an apartment that doesn't yet exist—that is, the *ultimate* rental living experience—is challenging work. Set aside some time to meet with your entire staff, and perhaps a supplier and a resident or two, to brainstorm ways that you can use to provide the high-touch, personal value that will *immortalize* your apartment community in the minds of your prospects and customers.

Devise a mission statement. Has your company formulated a statement that describes its distinctive competence? Have your employees tackled the task of describing why you are in business and what is special about your firm? Mission statements contain the graphic depiction of a company's uniqueness as seen from the inside of the firm.

"Flatten" the company's structure. The most customer-responsive firms realize that the typical bureaucratic organization distances customers from the top of the company. Those businesses that cater to their customers are blessed with leaders who get out on the front line to meet and satisfy their clients face to face.

Approach the revolution with a spirit of KAIZEN. Companies that undergo the transformation to a customer focus understand that a successful revolution can be a metamorphosis, rather than a cataclysmic event. One possibility is to approach the task with an attitude of patience, rather than one of immediacy.

Endnotes

The sources of quoted materials are indicated here in the order of their presentation within the text of each respective chapter, beginning with chapter opening quotations and ending with citations within sidebars (boxed text examples), using authors' last names and shortened versions of book titles. Full publication data are presented in the Bibliography. (Sources of select illustrations are indicated within individual exhibits.)

Prologue (pp. 1–3)

Liswood, *Serving Them Right,* p. xxxii.

Chapter 1, The Customer Service Revolution (pages 4–14)

Harvey Lamm quoted in Band, *Creating Value for Customers,* p. 49.

Libey, *Libey on Customers,* p. 104.

Ford Motor Company figures from *Market Share Reporter: An Annual Compilation of Reported Market Share Data on Companies, Products, and Services [1993]* (Detroit: Gale Research, Inc., 1993), pp. 308, 309, and 311.

Flock of geese analogy is from Schonberger, *Building a Chain of Customers,* p. 34.

Elephant analogy is from Albrecht and Zemke, *Service America!* p. 169.

Population and housing statistics are from 1990 census data published by the U.S. Department of Labor, Bureau of the Census.

Thrift downfall figures from *Business Week,* March 8, 1993, p. 80.

RTC sales figures from "The Silver Lining," *RTC Affordable Housing Disposition (AHDP) Newsletter* 2(4):6, Fall 1992/Winter 1993.

IREM Foundation, *Managing the Future,* p. 3.

IREM Foundation, *Managing the Future,* p. 45.

RERC/Equitable, *Emerging Trends (1994),* p. 27.

Carlzon, *Moments of Truth,* p. 3.

Albrecht, *At America's Service,* p. 26.

Carlzon, *Moments of Truth,* p. 5.

Carlzon, *Moments of Truth,* p. 26.

Carlzon, *Moments of Truth,* p. 5.

Carlzon, *Moments of Truth,* p. 43.

Carlzon, *Moments of Truth,* pp. 52–53.

Albrecht, *At America's Service,* p. 134.

Carlzon, *Moments of Truth,* p. 3.

The story of the sultan and the wizard is from "Beware the Study of Turtles," an essay by Charles Krauthammer in *Time* 141(26):76, June 28, 1993 (emphasis added). Copyright 1993 Time Inc. Reproduced with permission of the publisher.

Carlzon, *Moments of Truth,* p. 24.

Chapter 2, The Roads to Revolution (pages 15–36)

"High touch" as related to service means, "lots of flexible, warm, human interactions." Davidow and Uttal, *Total Customer Service,* p. 56.

Disend, *How to Provide Excellent Service,* p. 210.

Rick Johnson quoted in Disend, *How to Provide Excellent Service,* p. 101.

Donald Porter quoted in Albrecht and Zemke, *Service America!* p. 32.

Rosenbluth and Peters, *The Customer Comes Second,* p. 52.

Rosenbluth and Peters, *The Customer Comes Second,* p. 25.

Reference to "lighthouses for change" is from Zeithaml et al., *Delivering Quality Service,* p. 145.

Rosenbluth and Peters, *The Customer Comes Second,* p. 39.

Rosenbluth and Peters, *The Customer Comes Second,* pp. 51–52.

Rosenbluth and Peters, *The Customer Comes Second,* pp. 55–56.

"Mike" Morita quoted in Albrecht, *At America's Service,* pp. 118–119.

William Ouchi quoted in Zemke and Bell, *Service Wisdom,* p. 155.

Gross, *Positively Outrageous Service,* p. 1.

Davidow and Uttal, *Total Customer Service,* p. 1.

Dunckel and Taylor, *The Business Guide,* p. 15.

Discussion of the Levitt paradigm (four levels of attributes of products) is adapted from the characterization in Disend, *How to Provide Excellent Service,* pp. 105–107.

Ted Levitt quoted in Disend, *How to Provide Excellent Service,* p. 107.

Freemantle, *Incredible Customer Service,* p. 48.

Service Visibility and "Getting Your Hands Dirty" (pages 19–21)

Zemke and Schaaf, *The Service Edge,* p. 3.

McCann, *The Joy of Service,* p. 86.

LeBoeuf, *How to Win Customers,* p. 57.

Davidow and Uttal, *Total Customer Service,* p. 98.

Soichiro Honda quoted in Whiteley, *The Customer-Driven Company,* p. 200.

What Is Service? (page 30–31)

Attributes of service adapted from Albrecht and Zemke, *Service America!* pp. 36–37.

Zemke and Schaaf, *The Service Edge,* pp. 13–14.

Heskett et al., *Service Breakthroughs,* pp. 153–154.

Chapter 3, Revolutionary Hiring and Zapping (pages 37–60)

Zeithaml et al., *Delivering Quality Service,* p. 152 (emphasis added).

Vavra, *Aftermarketing,* p. 251.

Whiteley, *The Customer-Driven Company,* p. 11.

Zemke and Bell, *Service Wisdom,* p. 166.

Gross, *Positively Outrageous Service,* p. 159.

Sewell and Brown, *Customers for Life,* p. 68 (emphasis added).

Gross, *Positively Outrageous Service,* p. 161.

Berry and Parasuraman, *Marketing Services,* p. 153.

Clemmer, *Firing on All Cylinders,* p. 128.

Rosenbluth and Peters, *The Customer Comes Second,* pp. 51–52.

Band, *Creating Value for Customers,* p. 196.

Tom Peters quoted in Clemmer, *Firing on All Cylinders,* p. 149.

Freemantle, *Incredible Customer Service,* p. 109.

Gross, *Positively Outrageous Service,* p. 172 (emphasis added).

Shannon Johnston quoted in Zemke and Bell, *Service Wisdom,* pp. 158–159.

Davidow and Uttal, *Total Customer Service,* p. 126.

Albrecht, *At America's Service,* p. 54.

Disend, *How to Provide Excellent Service,* pp. 170–171.

Libey, *Libey on Customers,* p. 218.

Zeithaml et al., *Delivering Quality Service,* p. 152 (emphasis added).

Disend, *How to Provide Excellent Service,* pp. 92–93.

Carlzon, *Moments of Truth,* p. 5.

Byham, *Zapp! The Lightning of Empowerment,* pp. 9–10.

Zeithaml et al., *Delivering Quality Service,* p. 94.

Disend, *How to Provide Excellent Service,,* p. 20.

Hervey Feldman quoted in Davidow and Uttal, *Total Customer Service,* p. 114.

Heskett et al. quoted in Clemmer, *Firing on All Cylinders,* p. 45.

Albrecht, *At America's Service,* p. 224.

Jan Carlzon quoted in Heskett et al., *Service Breakthroughs*, pp. 110–111.

Beer et al. quoted in Clemmer, *Firing on All Cylinders*, p. 54.

Glen, *It's Not My Department*, p. 53.

Anderson and Zemke, *Delivering Knock Your Socks Off Service*, p. 106.

A. S. Neill quoted in Zeithaml et al., *Delivering Quality Service*, p. 153.

Pre-Employment Psychological Testing (page 43)

For implications of the Americans with Disabilities Act of 1990 (ADA) regarding psychological testing in pre-employment screening, see 42 U.S.C. Sec. 12101–12213 (1992).

The decision in *Soroka v. Dayton Hudson Corporation* can be found at 1 Cal. Rptr. 2d 77 (Cal. Ct. App. 1991).

"Firing" Customers: The Pareto Principle (pages 52–54)

Berry and Parasuraman, *Marketing Services*, p. 19.

Albrecht, *At America's Service*, p. 114.

Berry and Parasuraman, *Marketing Services*, p. 50.

Albrecht, *At America's Service*, p. 113.

Chapter 4, The Retention Revolution (pages 61–74)

The "Death Wish Paradox" is from Clancy and Shulman, *The Marketing Revolution*, p. 238.

Advertising expenditures reported in Vavra, *Aftermarketing*, pp. 11–12.

Clancy and Shulman, *The Marketing Revolution*, p. 237.

Statistics from a survey on "Why Customers Quit" quoted in Leboeuf, *How to Win Customers*, p. 13. The same data were reported in Morgan, *Calming Upset Customers*, p. 6.

Anderson and Zemke, *Delivering Knock Your Socks Off Service*, p. 8.

TARP statistics cited in Albrecht and Bradford, *The Service Advantage*, p. 199; also in Zemke and Schaaf, *The Service Edge*, p. 4.

IREM Foundation, *Managing the Future*, p. 3.

Interviewee results from IREM Foundation, *Managing the Future*, p. 45.

Survey respondent results from IREM Foundation, *Managing the Future*, p. 45.

Liswood, *Serving Them Right*, p. 115.

Average acquisition and retention costs are from Morgan, *Calming Upset Customers*, p. 6.

Poirier and Houser, *Business Partnering*, pp. 57.

Poirier and Houser, *Business Partnering*, pp. 58.

Barbara Bund Jackson quoted in Band, *Creating Value for Customers*, p. 38.

Band, *Creating Value for Customers,* p. 38.

Libey, *Libey on Customers,* p. 38.

Chapter 5, The Complaint Revolution (pages 75–84)

Sewell and Brown, *Customers for Life,* p. 40.

Liswood, *Serving Them Right,* pp. 6–7.

Whiteley, *The Customer-Driven Company,* p. 64.

Albrecht, *The Only Thing That Matters,* p. 109.

USOCA figures from Disend, *How to Provide Excellent Service,* p. 199.

USOCA research, as reported in the *New York Times* (March 26, 1988), quoted in Goldzimer, *I'm First,* p. 69.

Davidow and Uttal, *Total Customer Service,* p. xviii.

Lele, *The Customer is Key,* pp. 209–210.

Clemmer, *Firing on All Cylinders,* p. 16.

Research data from the USOCA reported in Disend, *How to Provide Excellent Service,* pp. 72–73.

John Goodman quoted in Davidow and Uttal, *Total Customer Service,* p. 15.

Stanley Marcus quoted in Liswood, *Serving Them Right,* p. 1.

John Goodman quoted in Zemke and Schaaf, *The Service Edge,* p. 8.

TARP data on customer behaviors reported in Albrecht and Bradford, *The Service Advantage,* p. 199.

Vavra, *Aftermarketing,* p. 127.

Lele, *The Customer is Key,* p. 55.

Libey, *Libey on Customers,* p. 237.

Lele, *The Customer is Key,* p. 209.

Disend, *How to Provide Excellent Service,* p. 73.

Sewell and Brown, *Customers for Life,* p. 28.

Goldzimer, *I'm First,* p. 72.

Patricia Sellers' article in *Fortune* magazine cited in Gross, *Positively Outrageous Service,* p. 37.

Zeithaml et al., *Delivering Quality Service,* p. 54.

Disend, *How to Provide Excellent Service,* p. 20

Guarantees (pages 82–84)

Christopher Hart ("The Power of Unconditional Service Guarantees," *Harvard Business Review,* July-August 1988) quoted by Zemke and Bell in *Service Wisdom,* pp. 280 and 282.

Berry and Parasuraman, *Marketing Services,* p. 7.

Whirlpool quotation from Hanan and Karp, *Customer Satisfaction,* p. 36 (emphasis added).

Glen, *It's Not My Department,* pp. 70–71.

Chapter 6, The Recovery Revolution (pages 85–95)

Donald Porter quoted in Anderson and Zemke, *Delivering Knock Your Socks Off Service,* p. 87.

Sewell and Brown, *Customers for Life,* p. 164.

From "Service Breakdown—The Road to Recovery," (*Management Review,* October 1987), quoted in Zemke and Bell, *Service Wisdom,* p. 269.

Lele, *The Customer Is Key,* p. 142.

Hanan and Karp, *Customer Satisfaction,* p. 101.

Lele, *The Customer Is Key,* p. 139.

The Perception and Performance Principle is an adaptation of a formula in Nykiel, *You Can't Lose if the Customer Wins,* p. 99.

Freemantle, *Incredible Customer Service,* p. 36.

Libey, *Libey on Customers,* p. 102.

Berry and Parasuraman, *Marketing Services,* p. 40.

Gross, *Positively Outrageous Service,* p. 95.

Anderson and Zemke, *Delivering Knock Your Socks Off Service,* p. 25.

Anderson and Zemke, *Delivering Knock Your Socks Off Service,* pp. 25–26.

Berry and Parasuraman, *Marketing Services,* p. 47.

Heskett et al., *Service Breakthroughs,* p. 108.

Clemmer, *Firing on All Cylinders,* p. 46.

Gross, *Positively Outrageous Service,* pp. 97–98.

Gross, *Positively Outrageous Service,* p. 133.

Berry and Parasuraman, *Marketing Services,* p. 52.

Lash, *The Complete Guide,* pp. 136–137.

Anderson and Zemke, *Delivering Knock Your Socks Off Service,* p. 89.

Chapter 7, The Leadership Revolution (pages 96–116)

Mimi Lieber quoted in Zeithaml et al., *Delivering Quality Service,* p. 138.

Band, *Creating Value for Customers,* p. 180.

Robert Crandall quoted in Zeithaml et al., *Delivering Quality Service,* p. 62.

Libey, *Libey on Customers,* p. 113.

Liswood, *Serving Them Right,* pp. 14–15.

Rosenbluth and Peters, *The Customer Comes Second,* p. 35.

Rosenbluth and Peters, *The Customer Comes Second,* p. 121.

Paul Goodstadt quoted in Albrecht, *The Only Thing That Matters,* p. 91.

Rosenbluth and Peters, *The Customer Comes Second,* pp. 227–228.

Disend, *How to Provide Excellent Service,* p. 19.

Band, *Creating Value for Customers,* p. 173.

Albrecht, *The Only Thing That Matters,* p. 11.

Poirier and Houser, *Business Partnering,* p. 7.

Carlzon, *Moments of Truth,* p. 5.

Carlzon, *Moments of Truth,* p. 60.

Disend, *How to Provide Excellent Service,* p. 158.

Band, *Creating Value for Customers,* p. 187.

Senge, *The Fifth Discipline,* pp. 287–288.

Albrecht, *At America's Service,* p. 134.

Libey, *Libey on Customers,* p. 5.

Libey, *Libey on Customers,* p. 94.

Hammer and Champy, *Reengineering the Corporation,* p. 75.

Zeithaml et al., *Delivering Quality Service,* p. 2.

Davidow and Uttal, *Total Customer Service,* p. 41.

Davidow and Uttal, *Total Customer Service,* p. 1.

Disend, *How to Provide Excellent Service,* p. 244.

Senge, *The Fifth Discipline,* pp. 223–224.

Senge, *The Fifth Discipline,* p. 213.

Senge, *The Fifth Discipline,* p. 206.

Disend, *How to Provide Excellent Service,* p. 126.

The distinction between search and experience qualities, as made by Philip Nelson, is described in Heskett et al., *Service Breakthroughs,* p. 37.

Berry and Parasuraman, *Marketing Services,* p. 7.

Libey, *Libey on Customers,* p. 60.

Davidow and Uttal, *Total Customer Service,* p. 41.

Hanan and Karp, *Customer Satisfaction,* p. 83.

Gross, quoting from *Fortune* magazine (June 1990 issue), in *Positively Outrageous Service,* p. 98.

Customer-Focused Marketing (p. 107)

A succinct summary of the attributes described by Libey in *Libey on Customers,* pp. 94–107.

Chapter 8, The Benchmarking Revolution (pages 117–136)

Ralph Waldo Emerson quoted in LeBoeuf, *How to Win Customers and Keep Them for Life,* p. 23.

David T. Kearns quoted in Camp, *Benchmarking (Search)*, p. 10.

Albrecht, *The Only Thing That Matters*, pp. 63–64.

Leibfried and McNair, *Benchmarking (Tool)*, p. 330.

The admonition to "go to school on the winners" is from Whiteley, *The Customer-Driven Company*, p. 16.

Camp, *Benchmarking (Search)*, p. xi.

Albrecht, *The Only Thing That Matters*, p. 64.

Camp, *Benchmarking (Search)*, p. 3.

Camp, *Benchmarking (Search)*, pp. 11 and 15 (emphasis added).

John Sharpe quoted in Clemmer, *Firing on All Cylinders*, p. 27.

Clemmer, *Firing on All Cylinders*, p. 27.

De Rose, *Value Selling*, pp. 1, 2, and 3.

De Rose, *Value Selling*, pp. 73, 76, 81, and 86–87.

Sam Walton quoted in Zeithaml et al., *Delivering Quality Service*, p. 63.

Clemmer, *Firing on All Cylinders*, pp. 36–37.

Clemmer, *Firing on All Cylinders*, p. 36.

Clemmer, *Firing on All Cylinders*, p. 38 (emphasis added).

Camp, *Benchmarking (Search)*, pp. 9–10.

Chapter 9, Strategizing the Resident Retention Revolution
(pages 137–176)

Albrecht and Zemke, *Service America!* p. 77.

Camp, *Benchmarking*, p. 34.

Denton, *Quality Service*, p. 5.

Clemmer, *Firing on All Cylinders*, p. 105.

Disend, *How to Provide Excellent Service*, p. 1.

Sam Walton quoted in Glen, *It's Not My Department*, p. 137.

Albrecht and Zemke, *Service America!* p. 84.

Whiteley, *The Customer-Driven Company*, p. 135.

Liswood, *Serving Them Right*, p. 50.

Libey, *Libey on Customers*, p. 96.

Band, *Creating Value for Customers*, p. 8.

LeBoeuf, *How to Win Customers*, p. 135.

Heskett et al., *Service Breakthroughs*, p. 105.

Lele, *The Customer is Key*, p. 209.

Denton, *Quality Service*, p. 1.

LeBoeuf, *How to Win Customers*, p. 135.

Lash, *The Complete Guide*, p. 123.

Zeithaml et al., *Delivering Quality Service,* p. 54.

Lash, *The Complete Guide,* p. 152.

Berry and Parasuraman, *Marketing Services,* p. 51.

Zemke and Bell, *Service Wisdom,* p. 175.

Heskett et al., *Service Breakthroughs,* p. 104.

Goldzimer, *I'm First,* p. 72.

Heskett et al., *Service Breakthroughs,* p. 37.

Libey, *Libey on Customers,* p. 38.

Zemke and Bell, *Service Wisdom,* pp. 7–8.

Liswood, *Serving Them Right,* pp. 112–113.

Camp, *Benchmarking (Search),* p. 4.

Zeithaml et al., *Delivering Quality Service,* p. 55.

Anderson and Zemke, *Delivering Knock Your Socks Off Service,* p. 128.

Theodore Levitt quoted in Clemmer, *Firing on All Cylinders,* p. 54.

Gross, *Positively Outrageous Service,* p. 99.

Libey, *Libey on Customers,* pp. 24–25.

Senge, *The Fifth Discipline,* p. 114.

Albrecht, *The Only Thing That Matters,* p. 9.

Freemantle, *Incredible Customer Service,* p. 123.

Libey, *Libey on Customers,* pp. 28 and 29–30.

Gross, *Positively Outrageous Service,* p. 202.

Albrecht, *At America's Service,* p. 224.

Whiteley, *The Customer-Driven Company,* p. 17.

LeBoeuf, *How to Win Customers,* p. 170.

Poirier and Houser, *Business Partnering,* p. 164.

Heskett et al., *Service Breakthroughs,* pp. 153–154.

Davidow and Uttal, *Total Customer Service,* pp. 147–148.

Band, *Creating Value for Customers,* p. 161.

Band, *Creating Value for Customers,* pp. 161–162.

LeBoeuf, *How to Win Customers,* p. 169.

LeBoeuf, *How to Win Customers,* pp. 169–170.

Gross, *Positively Outrageous Service,* p. 1.

Gross, *Positively Outrageous Service,* p. 3.

IREM Foundation, *Managing the Future,* p. 9.

LeBoeuf, *How to Win Customers,* p. 23.

Albrecht and Zemke, *Service America!* p. 18.

Libey, *Libey on Customers,* p. 104.

Carlzon, *Moments of Truth,* p. 3.

Vavra, *Aftermarketing,* p. 14.

Davidow and Uttal, *Total Customer Service,* p. 95.

Albrecht, *The Only Thing That Matters,* p. 2.

Touchstones of culture reference is from Davidow and Uttal, *Total Customer Service,* p. 96.

Whiteley, *The Customer-Driven Company,* p. 182.

Liswood, *Serving Them Right,* p. 123.

Zeithaml et al., *Delivering Quality Service,* p. 7.

Carlzon, *Moments of Truth,* p. 5.

Davidow and Uttal, *Total Customer Service,* p. 211.

Bibliography

The following service books were used as resources in the writing of this book. Citations of data and direct quotations are identified in the Endnotes.

Karl Albrecht, *At America's Service: How Corporations Can Revolutionize the Way They Treat Their Customers* (Homewood, Illinois: Dow Jones-Irwin, 1988). Quoted material reproduced by permission of Irwin Professional Publishing.

Karl Albrecht, *The Only Thing That Matters: Bringing the Power of the Customer into the Center of Your Business* (New York: HarperBusiness, 1992). Copyright 1992 by Karl Albrecht. Excerpts reprinted by permission of HarperCollins Publishers, Inc.

Karl Albrecht and Lawrence J. Bradford, *The Service Advantage: How to Identify and Fulfill Customer Needs* (Homewood, Illinois: Dow Jones-Irwin, 1990).

Karl Albrecht and Ron Zemke, *Service America! Doing Business in the New Economy* (New York: Warner, 1985). Quoted material reprinted by permission of Irwin Professional Publishing.

Kristin Anderson and Ron Zemke, *Delivering Knock Your Socks Off Service* (New York: AMACOM, 1991). Copyright 1991 Performance Research Associates, Inc. Quoted material reprinted with permission of AMACOM, a division of the American Management Association. All rights reserved.

William A. Band, *Creating Value for Customers: Designing and Implementing a Total Corporate Strategy* (New York: John Wiley & Sons, Inc., 1991). Copyright 1991 by Coopers & Lybrand (Canada). Quoted material reprinted by permission of John Wiley & Sons, Inc.

Leonard L. Berry and A. Parasuraman, *Marketing Services: Competing Through Quality* (New York: The Free Press, 1991). Copyright 1991 by The Free Press. Quoted material reprinted with the permission of The Free Press, a Division of Macmillan, Inc.

William C. Byham, Ph.D. (with Jeff Cox), *Zapp! The Lightning of Empowerment: How to Improve Productivity, Quality, and Employee Satisfaction* (New York: Fawcett Columbine, 1988). Parts of Joe Mode's Notebook reprinted courtesy of Development Dimensions International, Inc.

Robert C. Camp, *Benchmarking: The Search for Industry Best Practices That Lead to Superior Performance* (Milwaukee: ASQC Quality Press, 1989). Quoted materials used with permission of the publisher.

Jan Carlzon, *Moments of Truth* (Cambridge, Massachusetts: Ballinger Publishing Company, 1987). Copyright 1987 by Ballinger Publishing Company. Excerpts reprinted by permission of HarperCollins Publishers, Inc.

Kevin J. Clancy and Robert S. Shulman, *The Marketing Revolution: A Radical Manifesto for Dominating the Marketplace* (New York: HarperBusiness, 1991). Copyright 1991 by Kevin J. Clancy and Robert Shulman. Excerpts reprinted by permission of HarperCollins Publishers, Inc.

Jim Clemmer, *Firing on All Cylinders: The Service/Quality System for High-Powered Corporate Performance* (Homewood, Illinois: Business One Irwin, 1992). Quoted material reproduced by permission of Irwin Professional Publishing.

William H. Davidow and Bro Uttal, *Total Customer Service: The Ultimate Weapon* (New York: HarperPerennial, 1989). Copyright 1989 by William H. Davidow and Bro Uttal. Excerpts reprinted by permission of HarperCollins Publishers, Inc.

D. Keith Denton, *Quality Service* (Houston: Gulf Publishing Company, 1989). Quoted material used with permission of the publisher. All rights reserved.

Louis De Rose, *Value Selling* (New York: AMACOM, 1989). Copyright 1989 by AMACOM, a division of the American Management Association. Quoted material reprinted with permission of the publisher. All rights reserved.

Jeffrey E. Disend, *How to Provide Excellent Service in Any Organization: A Blueprint for Making All the Theories Work* (Radnor, Pennsylvania: Chilton Book Company, 1991). Copyright 1991 by the author. Quoted material reprinted with the permission of the publisher.

Jacqueline Dunckel and Brian Taylor, *The Business Guide To Profitable Customer Relations* (Vancouver: Self-Counsel Press, 1988). Quoted material reprinted with permission of the publisher.

David Freemantle, *Incredible Customer Service: The Final Test* (London: McGraw-Hill Book Company, 1993). Quoted material reprinted with permission of the author.

Peter Glen, *It's Not My Department! How to Get the Service You Want, Exactly the Way You Want It!* (New York: William Morrow and Company, Inc., 1990). Copyright 1990 by Peter Glen. Quoted material used by permission of William Morrow & Company, Inc.

Linda Silverman Goldzimer, *"I'm First:" Your Customer's Message to You* (New York: Rawson Associates, 1989).

T. Scott Gross, *Positively Outrageous Service: New and Easy Ways to Win Customers for Life* (New York: Mastermedia, Inc., 1991). Quoted material reprinted with permission of Mastermedia, Inc. 16 West 72nd Street, Suite 200, New York, NY 10021. (Copies available for $12.95 by calling 1-800-334-8232.)

Michael Hammer and James Champy, *Reengineering the Corporation: A Manifesto for Business Revolution* (New York: HarperBusiness, 1993). Copyright 1993 by Michael Hammer and James Champy. Excerpts reprinted by permission of Harper-Collins Publishers, Inc.

Mack Hanan and Peter Karp, *Customer Satisfaction: How to Maximize, Measure, and Market Your Company's "Ultimate Product"* (New York, AMACOM, 1989). Copyright 1989 by Mack Hanan and Peter Karp. Quoted material reprinted with permission of AMACOM, a division of the American Management Association. All rights reserved.

James L. Heskett, W. Earl Sasser, Jr., and Christopher W. L. Hart, *Service Breakthroughs: Changing the Rules of the Game* (New York: The Free Press, 1990). Copyright 1990 by James L. Heskett, W. Earl Sasser, Jr., and Christopher W. L. Hart. Quoted material reprinted with the permission of The Free Press, a Division of Macmillan, Inc.

Linda M. Lash, *The Complete Guide to Customer Service* (New York: John Wiley & Sons, 1989). Copyright 1989 by John Wiley & Sons, Inc. Quoted material reprinted by permission of John Wiley & Sons, Inc.

Michael LeBoeuf, Ph.D., *How to Win Customers and Keep Them for Life* (New York: Berkley Books, 1987). Copyright 1988 by Michael LeBoeuf, Ph.D. Quoted material reprinted by permission of the Putnam Publishing Group.

Kathleen H. J. Leibfried and C. J. McNair, *Benchmarking: A Tool for Continuous Improvement* (New York: HarperBusiness, 1992). Copyright 1992 by Kathleen H. J. Leibfried and C. J. McNair.

Milind M. Lele (with Jagdish N. Sheth), *The Customer is Key: Gaining an Unbeatable Advantage Through Customer Satisfaction* (New York: John Wiley & Sons, 1987). Copyright 1987 by Milind M. Lele and Jagdish N. Sheth. Quoted material reprinted by permission of John Wiley & Sons, Inc.

Donald R. Libey, *Libey on Customers* (Washington, D.C.: Libey Publishing Incorporated, 1992). Quoted material reprinted with permission of the publisher.

Laura A. Liswood, *Serving Them Right: Innovative & Powerful Customer Retention Strategies* (New York: HarperBusiness, 1990). Copyright 1990 by Harper & Row Publishers, Inc. Excerpts reprinted by permission of HarperCollins Publishers, Inc.

Ron McCann (as told to Joe Vitale), *The Joy of Service!* (Stafford, Texas: Service Information Source Publication, 1989). Quoted material reprinted with permission of the publisher.

Rebecca L. Morgan, *Calming Upset Customers: Staying Effective During Unpleasant Situations* (San Francisco: Crisp Publications, Inc., 1989).

Ronald A. Nykiel, *You Can't Lose if the Customer Wins: Ten Steps to Service Success* (Stamford, Connecticut: Longmeadow Press, 1990).

Charles C. Poirier and William F. Houser, *Business Partnering for Continuous Improvement: How to Forge Enduring Alliances Among Employees, Suppliers & Customers* (San Francisco: Berrett-Koehler Publishers, 1993).

Hal F. Rosenbluth and Diane McFerrin Peters, *The Customer Comes Second, and Other Secrets of Exceptional Service* (New York: William Morrow and Company, Inc.,

1992). Copyright 1992 by Hal F. Rosenbluth and Diane McFerrin. Quoted material used by permission of William Morrow & Company, Inc.

Richard J. Schonberger, *Building a Chain of Customers: Linking Business Functions to Create the World Class Company* (New York: The Free Press, 1990).

Peter M. Senge, *The Fifth Discipline: The Art & Practice of The Learning Organization* (New York: Doubleday, 1990). Quoted material reprinted with permission of the publisher.

Carl Sewell and Paul B. Brown, *Customers for Life: How to Turn that One-Time Buyer into a Lifetime Customer* (New York: Doubleday, 1990). Quoted material reprinted with permission of the publisher.

Terry G. Vavra, *Aftermarketing: How to Keep Customers for Life Through Relationship Marketing* (Homewood, Illinois: Business One Irwin, 1992). Quoted material reproduced by permission of Irwin Professional Publishing.

Richard C. Whiteley, *The Customer-Driven Company: Moving from Talk to Action* (Reading, Massachusetts: Addison-Wesley Publishing, Inc., 1991). Copyright 1993 by The Forum Corporation. Quoted material reprinted by permission of Addison-Wesley Publishing Company, Inc.

Valarie A. Zeithaml, A. Parasuraman, and Leonard L. Berry, *Delivering Quality Service: Balancing Customer Perceptions and Expectations* (New York: The Free Press, 1990). Copyright 1990 by The Free Press. Quoted material reprinted with the permission of The Free Press, a Division of Macmillan, Inc.

Ron Zemke and Chip R. Bell, *Service Wisdom: Creating and Maintaining the Customer Service Edge* (Minneapolis: Lakewood Books, 1989). Quoted material used with permission of Lakewood Publications, 50 South Ninth Street, Minneapolis, MN 55402. All rights reserved.

Ron Zemke (with Dick Schaaf), *The Service Edge: 101 Companies That Profit from Customer Care* (New York: PLUME, 1989). Copyright 1989 by Ron Zemke and Dick Schaaf. Quoted material used by permission of Dutton Signet, a division of Penguin Books USA Inc.

Other Service Books

The following books provided valuable background information for our understanding of the concept of customer service.

Joan Koob Cannie, *Keeping Customers for Life* (New York: AMACOM, 1991).

Clay Carr, *Front-Line Customer Service: 15 Keys to Customer Satisfaction* (New York: John Wiley & Sons, 1990).

Stephen R. Covey, *The 7 Habits of Highly Effective People: Restoring the Character Ethic* (New York: Simon & Schuster, Inc., 1989).

John A. Czepiel, Michael R. Solomon, and Carol F. Surprenant, *The Service Encounter: Managing Employee/Customer Interaction in Service Businesses* (Lexington, Massachusetts: Lexington Books, 1985).

Robert L. Desatnick, *Keep the Customer! Making Customer Service Your Competitive Edge* (Boston: Houghton Mifflin Company, 1987).

Masaaki Imai, *KAIZEN: The Key to Japan's Competitive Success* (New York: McGraw-Hill Publishing Company, 1986).

Robert C. Kausen, *Customer Satisfaction Guaranteed: A New Approach to Customer Service, Bedside Manner, and Relationship Ease* (Trinity Center, California: Life Education, Inc., 1988).

John Tschohl (with Steve Franzmeier), *Achieving Excellence Through Customer Service* (Englewood Cliffs, New Jersey: Prentice Hall, 1991).

Books on Real Estate Management

The following books were used as resources on real estate trends and apartment marketing.

Emerging Trends in Real Estate: 1994 (Chicago: Real Estate Research Corporation; and New York: Equitable Real Estate Investment Management, Inc., 1993).

IREM Foundation (prepared by Arthur Andersen Real Estate Services Group), *Managing the Future: Real Estate in the 1990s* (Chicago: Institute of Real Estate Management Foundation, 1991). Quoted material reprinted with permission of the publisher.

Kathleen M. McKenna-Harmon and Laurence C. Harmon, *Contemporary Apartment Marketing: Strategies and Applications* (Chicago: Institute of Real Estate Management, 1993).

Index